SANCTIONING PREGNANCY

Pregnancy provides a very public, visual confirmation of femininity. It is a time of rapid physical and psychological adjustment for women and is surrounded by stereotyping, taboos and social expectations. This book seeks to examine these popular attitudes towards pregnancy and to consider how they influence women's experiences of being pregnant.

Sanctioning Pregnancy offers a unique critique of sociocultural constructions of pregnancy and the ways in which it is represented in contemporary culture, and examines the common myths which exist about diet, exercise and work in pregnancy, alongside notions of risk and media portrayals of pregnant women. Topics covered include:

- Do pregnant women change their diet and why?
- Is memory really impaired in pregnancy?
- How risky behaviour is defined from exercise to employment
- The biomedical domination of pregnancy research

Different theoretical standpoints are critically examined, including a medico-scientific model, feminist perspectives and bio-psychosocial and psychodynamic approaches.

Harriet Gross is a Senior Lecturer in Psychology at Loughborough University. After working in the book trade, she took a degree in psychology and subsequently became an academic. She is a developmental psychologist, and researches and publishes in the area of the psychology of pregnancy and women's health.

Helen Pattison is a Health Psychologist, and Associate Director of Research in the School of Life and Health Sciences at Aston University. She researches and publishes in the areas of reproductive health, parental health behaviour, self-management of health, risk perception and communication.

WOMEN AND PSYCHOLOGY
Series Editor: Jane Ussher
School of Psychology, University of Western Sydney

This series brings together current theory and research on women and psychology. Drawing on scholarship from a number of different areas of psychology, it bridges the gap between abstract research and the reality of women's lives by integrating theory and practice, research and policy.

Each book addresses a 'cutting edge' issue of research, covering such topics as postnatal depression, eating disorders, theories and methodologies.

The series provides accessible and concise accounts of key issues in the study of women and psychology, and clearly demonstrates the centrality of psychology to debates within women's studies or feminism.

The Series Editor would be pleased to discuss proposals for new books in the series.

Other titles in this series:

THE THIN WOMAN
Helen Malson

THE MENSTRUAL CYCLE
Anne E. Walker

POST-NATAL DEPRESSION
Paula Nicolson

RE-THINKING ABORTION
Mary Boyle

WOMEN AND AGING
Linda R. Gannon

BEING MARRIED. DOING GENDER
Caroline Dryden

UNDERSTANDING DEPRESSION
Janet M. Stoppard

FEMININITY AND THE PHYSICALLY ACTIVE WOMAN
Precilla Y.L. Choi

GENDER, LANGUAGE AND DISCOURSE
Anne Weatherall

THE SCIENCE/FICTION OF SEX
Annie Potts

THE PSYCHOLOGICAL DEVELOPMENT OF GIRLS AND
WOMEN
Sheila Greene

JUST SEX?
Nicola Gavey

WOMAN'S RELATIONSHIP WITH HERSELF
Helen O'Grady

GENDER TALK
Susan A. Speer

BEAUTY AND MISOGYNY
Sheila Jeffreys

BODY WORK
Sylvia K. Blood

MANAGING THE MONSTROUS FEMININE
Jane M. Ussher

THE CAPACITY TO CARE
Wendy Hollway

SANCTIONING PREGNANCY

A psychological perspective on the paradoxes and culture of research

Harriet Gross and Helen Pattison

Routledge
Taylor & Francis Group

LONDON AND NEW YORK

First published 2007 by Routledge
27 Church Road, Hove, East Sussex, BN3 2FA

Simultaneously published in the USA and Canada
by Routledge
270 Madison Avenue, New York, NY 10016

Routledge is an imprint of the Taylor & Francis Group, an informa business

© 2007 Dr Harriet Gross and Dr Helen Pattison

Typeset in Sabon by Garfield Morgan, Swansea, West Glamorgan
Printed and bound in Great Britain by T J International Ltd, Padstow, Cornwall
Paperback cover design by Anú Design

This publication has been produced with paper manufactured to strict environmental
standards and with pulp derived from sustainable forests.

British Library Cataloguing in Publication Data
A catalogue record for this book is available from the British Library

Library of Congress Cataloging in Publication Data
Gross, Harriet.
Sanctioning pregnancy: a psychological perspective on the paradoxes and culture of
research / Harriet Gross and Helen Pattison.
p. cm.
Includes bibliographical references (p. 151) and index.
ISBN 0-415-21159-X – ISBN 0-415-21160-3 1. Pregnancy–Social aspects–Great Britain.
2. Prenatal care–Social aspects–Great Britain. 3. Pregnancy–Great Britain–Psychological
aspects. I. Pattison, Helen, 1955- II. Title.
RG556.G77 2007
362.198'200941–dc22

2006034908

ISBN: 978-0-415-21159-8 (hbk)
ISBN: 978-0-415-21160-4 (pbk)

To our fathers, David Gross and William (Bill) Pattison, who always encouraged us to follow our interests and sadly who were unable to stay until the long gestation of this book was complete.

CONTENTS

CONTENTS

x

CONTENTS

ACKNOWLEDGEMENTS

As always, the completion of a project, particularly one that requires time and relative solitude, is never exclusive to those engaged in the doing of the daily chores of writing and production. We would like to thank first our families, husbands Martyn Cornick and Anthony Johnson, and our children Daisy, Jack and Matilda, for their continuing support, patience and good humour. We also want to acknowledge the longer-distance support of our extended families who took on trust our non-appearance at events as the inevitable result of having an academic in the family. Other people have been important, in particular our immediate colleagues at Loughborough, Birmingham and Aston and especially our fellow researchers, Pam Quick, Penny Bee (nee Clarke), Elaine McWilliams, Charlotte Cast and Jasmine Bhagrath, without whom the material would not have been forthcoming. In this respect, we must also thank all the women who so kindly agreed to participate in the various studies and shared their experience with us and the professional colleagues who assisted us in our research. Thanks too to the Society of Reproductive and Infant Psychology for providing an initial and ongoing forum for discussion. Last, we must thank Jane Ussher and the publishers for their continuing interest and persistent support.

1

INTRODUCTION

Pregnancy in context

Pregnancy is a challenging topic for research: it is a normal and even essential part of everyday life. It is a natural biological event: a physical process underpinned by a complex physiology. It is a psychological event and a personal transition; its meaning is also socially and culturally determined. It is time-limited. Research may be concerned with any one or more of these co-existing and wide-ranging elements but in doing so it is inevitably drawn into contradictory and paradoxical conclusions. Our own starting point as pregnancy researchers was a personal observation of a major memory lapse that occurred at work during a pregnancy. This lapse was immediately attributed to the state of being pregnant. Why such an attribution should have been made was what led to our studies of cognition in pregnancy. In reflecting upon the material we collected, it was obvious that we could not simply describe a set of cognitive outcomes without placing these in the context in which they were reported and that this context was not simply 'being pregnant' but a sophisticated interaction of those elements described above. Hence, our interest and, ten years later, this book.

In the book we address the thesis that there are strong dominant socio-cultural constructions of pregnancy in modern society which influence what research is conducted into pregnancy, how such research is carried out and the way results are interpreted. Our intention is to explore perceptions and myths about pregnancy and the relationships between these and pregnancy research. We would argue that such beliefs affect the way pregnancy is experienced by women. Specifically, pregnancy allows the reproductive body to be a focus of legitimate surveillance and regulation, and research – largely biomedical in origin but psychological research is not exempt – has been instrumental in this process. We make use of material arising from our own studies of cognition, work, diet and exercise to illustrate how social constructions are influential in, and affected by, research which can act both to reinforce and to refute the myths about pregnancy.

We are particularly interested to examine the different ways in which women in the pursuit of their daily lives may themselves encounter

1

pregnancy research and cultural positioning of pregnancy. In this first chapter, we introduce briefly some of the issues that will be revisited in the following chapters and, in order to provide background for these later chapters, summarise the typical process of pregnancy and antenatal care.

News of a pregnancy is usually greeted with congratulations; pregnancy is seen as a joyous life event, concerning the personal and private hopes and desires of those directly involved. It is also a rite of passage, enacted in the public domain, carrying with it changes in perceived roles and responsibilities. Pregnancy is viewed as healthy and natural, both as a necessary component of the transition to parenthood and as a biological and physiological process. As with other natural (reproductive) transitions that occur in women's lives, such as menstruation or the menopause, pregnancy brings women into contact with health professionals and medical procedures to ensure the wellbeing of mother and baby.

However, natural or normal processes once constituted as health events carry with them a range of expectations and interventions. It has become customary to be highly solicitous of the processes of human reproduction. It is not enough to let pregnancy run its course. Women must be instrumental in a successful, problem-free pregnancy. Although different women experience their pregnancies in different ways, they are all recipients of professional advice, instruction and health education; the message that women receive when they are pregnant is that they must be vigilant of themselves on behalf of their baby. Once pregnant, women may find themselves treated differently by those around them. A pregnant woman is not only perceived as an individual who may require medical care and protection, but also as a person who must be guided or disciplined into the correct modes of behaviour, since something that is described as natural (arising from biology) also conveys a sense of being out of control. In this sense, therefore, women are expected to ensure that they are healthy and prepared for pregnancy and those who do not conform in this way are construed as being selfish and unconcerned about the health of their unborn child. Thus, during their pregnancies women become the subject of comment and, on occasion, their public presence has even been seen as unacceptable. Pregnancy could therefore be said to be highly visible; it certainly attracts attention, both positive and negative, and prompts women to behave in certain ways. It provides very public and visually salient evidence of femininity. Beliefs about pregnant women reflect wider beliefs about women generally, for example their emotional lability and women as the 'weaker vessel', whereas other beliefs reflect the uniqueness and strangeness of pregnancy. Moreover, pregnancy highlights the ambiguous and shifting positions of women in society and the complexity of the negotiations necessary for them to accomplish such a major life event in an acceptable fashion.

While pregnancy is represented as a natural and healthy state, the acceptance of biology also has the effect of pathologising normal female functioning and emphasising the unnatural and inherent problematic position of women being at the mercy of their physiology or hormones (Kristeva, 1997). This derives largely from the predominance of the medico-scientific tradition in pregnancy research, which arose from good intentions but has shaped not just pregnancy research but the beliefs associated with it. By this means, for example, explanations of behaviour and affect during pregnancy are couched in terms of physiological, neurological or endo-crinological change rather than psychological factors. Only recently has this powerful hegemony with respect to pregnancy been subject to marginal erosion in a faint awareness of the role of psychology in fertility. Pregnancy research itself both reflects and fuels the changing context of women's position in society and the nature of the areas that are attended to.

It is easy to assume that the medical intervention in pregnancy and childbirth has been a relatively recent phenomenon, deriving from changes in medical practice in the middle of the twentieth century. However, historically, pregnancy has been a topic of medically oriented research for several hundred years, as is well documented elsewhere (see, for example, Barker, 1998; Garcia *et al.*, 1990; Hanson, 2004; Murphy Lawless, 1998; Oakley, 1984; Tew, 1990). One major purpose of the initial involvement of the medical profession was to reduce the high rates of maternal and infant mortality. The development of public health measures and the devolution of technologies of practice to medicine and doctors arose from these demands for better maternal and infant health. The understanding of the nature of puerperal fever, previously the single largest killer of women in childbirth, cut maternal deaths dramatically by the end of the nineteenth century, although this was only finally resolved by the advent of reliable and easily available antibiotics and good antisepsis in the middle of the last century. Once this had been accomplished, women's health in pregnancy and childbirth could be reasonably assured and, although it remained an ongoing concern, it became largely secondary to the achievement of a healthy outcome. Thus, the baby's health became the focus of research attention and this has been the primary rationale for much research and especially research in the medical and biological tradition on pregnancy ever since. An effect of the transfer of attention was the relocation of pregnancy from the private and home-based domain, albeit with the intervention of usually male specialised assistance, to the public and health domain. This is where it has steadfastly remained, particularly with the advent of the new technologies of reproduction and monitoring, and despite the efforts of various groups concerned to place women at the centre of the process, such as the Radical Midwives, the Association for the Improvement of Maternity Services and the National Childbirth Trust.

As well as identifying and developing ways of improving mortality rates, medical research has included the development of the whole panoply of devices and services now considered routine in the process of pregnancy and childbirth, for example the identification of screening techniques and technologies of intervention, such as measurement of the foetal heartbeat, the invention of forceps and improved pain relief. In doing so, research has served to increase women's own reliance on external agents and expertise. More significantly, the medical tradition of research has also determined the way that research has been carried out in other domains. The attention to the baby has produced a range of studies using the same rationale of ensuring a healthy outcome and building on similar assumptions about women. Thus, research investigating risk factors for pregnancy has focused almost entirely on the outcome. For example, Da Costa *et al.* (1999), investigating psychosocial health and pregnancy complications, were concerned with how these might affect pregnancy outcome rather than with how they affect the woman's own experience of her pregnancy. Work within the medical tradition which does attend to the woman herself is clearly aligned with the pathologising of pregnancy, by representing psychiatric disturbances as inherent to pregnancy (Brockington, 1994).

A major impact of the medical tradition in researching pregnancy, which has formed the subject of discussions of pregnancy by feminist writers and researchers such as Julie Kristeva, Iris Marion Young, Susan Bordo and Jane Ussher, has been the instantiation of a metaphor of containment, whereby the woman is regarded as a vessel for the foetus, an essential but secondary role. This metaphor also places women as being at the mercy of elemental forces which may endanger the contents of the vessel (Smith, 1992). The metaphor can be seen in operation in research and publications on all areas of pregnancy and surfaces in medical advice and popular literature and in turn contributes to personal and social expectations of pregnancy. We return to this in subsequent chapters (particularly Chapters 4, 5 and 7). The medical focus on outcome is also utilising the same metaphor of containment, where the emphasis is on the effect of various individual factors or situational variables on the outcome of pregnancy (the baby), rather than on the nature of women's experience or interpretation of their situation. For instance, work on the effects of stress on preterm delivery (Hickey *et al.*, 1995), or activities such as standing and lifting at work and their link to rates of foetal growth or preterm delivery (Hatch *et al.*, 1997), attend to what women need to be told about these behaviours rather than how they might arise or relate to women's own experiences. The biomedical model of health is maintained and refreshed by such research.

Psychologically, pregnancy as a state is particularly interesting because it is a time of change. This change comprises the experience of the dramatic physiological alterations in women's bodies over a short period and the social and cultural construction of the change in role and identity. Such change carries implications for women's wellbeing during the pregnancy and beyond, and for the way they are viewed by others. Thus, a major psychological discourse of pregnancy, especially within a psychodynamic tradition, is on transition. In keeping with a primarily biomedical approach, however, such a discourse highlights the possible negative impact of transition on a woman's psychological wellbeing: pregnancy as a potential crisis state, involving shifts in identity and the move from non-motherhood to motherhood, as well as possible confrontations with unresolved issues (Breen, 1975; Deutsch, 1947; Raphael-Leff, 1991). In this view, pregnancy may be associated with feelings of loss as well as gain. Any realignment of identities associated with transition occurs in a personal and in a social context and a further significant psychological aspect of pregnancy is its public visibility. The visibility of pregnancy as an embodiment of reproductive fertility and sexuality can transgress boundaries between the personal or private and the public domains and affect both personal and public beliefs about pregnancy. Feminist psychological writing and research is concerned to elucidate the manifestation of these personal and public beliefs and examine further the paradoxes of the required passivity and agency that such beliefs engender. Importantly, in this context, pregnancy can be as an enabling state, offering the opportunity for shifts in women's presentation of self (Charles and Kerr, 1986; Oakley, 1980; Slade, 1977; Wiles, 1994). Much psychological research has operated within the prevalent biomedical discourses already discussed and has been focused on documenting the nature of changes during the period of pregnancy, for example in the alteration of affect or mood that might accompany the potential crisis state such as anxiety or depression, with particular concerns about the implications of such changes for women's longer-term mental and physical health. It is open to question how or whether the increasing focus on outcome and the accompanying requirement for vigilance impacts on psychological transitions, especially at a point in historical time when pregnancy is relatively infrequent and thus each pregnancy highly salient.

Arguably, partly because of falling birthrates and partly because of the increasingly public roles of women, not to mention the ubiquity of the media, the state of being pregnant in the early twenty-first century has become more visible rather than less. Since the twentieth century, women have been experiencing fewer pregnancies in their lifetime and there are fewer live births than ever before. Accordingly, more time and effort is devoted to ensuring that each one is healthy, leading to the highly desired positive outcome.

Certainly, in the eighteenth century, women might have expected to have as many as six or eight children from at least eight pregnancies. At that time, the predictability of outcome was low, maternal health was often poor, foetal viability was variable and confirmation of pregnancy was quite late – often around the time of quickening, at about four months. Thus, pregnancy was probably more frequent, often shorter and significantly riskier for all concerned, especially for the women, who frequently died in childbirth. This did not mean that there was little psychological investment in pregnancy. Just because it was not measured in the ways it may be now, there is no evidence that women were less anxious or concerned about each pregnancy (Hanson, 2004). However, the time available to attend to each pregnancy was probably somewhat diminished compared to the position today, when both frequency and the timing of confirmed status of pregnancy are very different.

Despite concerns about population growth in some parts of the world, figures show that rates of childbearing in Europe, the US and elsewhere have fallen significantly over the past fifty years, in some cases to well below the level considered adequate for population replacement (2.1 children per woman of childbearing age). For example, Italy has the lowest birthrate in the European Union (EU) at 1.32 and the most recent figures show the UK birthrate at 1.80 (Eurostat, 2005) and the Australian birthrate at 1.81 (Australian Bureau of Statistics, 2005). There are many possible reasons for the drop in the birthrate, one of which must be increasing female employment, in turn leading to a later age of first pregnancy. The mean age for first pregnancy in the UK is currently 27.5 years (ONS, 2006) (though this figure includes a higher fertility rate among women aged 30–34 than those aged 25–29). In Australia, the average age of first birth is now over 30 (Australian Bureau of Statistics, 2004). Whatever the derivation of the average age of first birth, the older it is, the more noticeable it makes the occurrence of pregnancy in much younger women, something we return to in discussions in Chapter 7.

Pregnancy itself lasts for approximately nine months, or 40 weeks. The expected due date is calculated from the first day of the woman's last menstrual period. The actual date of delivery, and the length of any individual pregnancy, may vary by as much as two weeks, depending in part on the length of the woman's usual menstrual cycle, but will typically be between 37 and 42 weeks. The sophistication of home pregnancy testing means that a pregnancy may now be confirmed before the first missed period, and does not necessarily require confirmation by a doctor. If it is possible to confirm a pregnancy before a menstrual period is missed, a woman's engagement with the physical status of pregnancy and the potential baby starts early on too. This apparent certainty about a physiological state raises a number of interesting considerations with regard to the woman's engagement with her condition and to the psychological preparedness for failure or termination and we consider this issue further in Chapter 2 on the paradoxes of pregnancy. Typically, the popularly anticipated symptoms of pregnancy such as nausea and extreme fatigue occur in the first phase or trimester (period of 14 weeks). The other popular representation of pregnancy as 'blooming' tends to be associated with the middle phase before the significant maternal and foetal weight gain, together with the often-described physical discomfort, of the final phase.

Current UK obstetric guidelines following medical research recommend that labour be induced at or around 40 to 41 weeks (NICE, 2003) in order to ensure that the woman and the baby are at least risk. The provision of antenatal and obstetric care emphasises the need to monitor health in order to reduce problems and minimise risk. When a woman is in good physical condition during pregnancy for example, the probability of complications during labour and delivery may be lowered (e.g. Dewey and McCrory, 1994; Simpson, 1993). The justification for medical involvement in pregnancy is the need to reduce any such complications and to identify and treat serious conditions of pregnancy which can significantly affect women's health, as well as that of their baby. These conditions include those associated with high blood pressure and hypertension, such as pre-eclampsia, which are some of the most important causes of maternal and foetal morbidity and mortality in Western countries since the demise of puerperal fever as a cause of maternal death. Other serious medical conditions include toxaemia, obstetric cholestasis and gestational diabetes as well as placenta previa, where the placenta may be positioned such that it is obstructed, preventing vaginal delivery. Babies born from the 37th week of pregnancy are counted as full term. Babies born before this time are considered to be premature, and the shorter the period of gestation, the more at risk the baby may be, with those born before 28 weeks likely to need considerable neonatal intensive care.

In the UK, antenatal care is provided by midwives and general practitioners as well as by obstetricians and specialist consultant doctors based in hospitals. Developments in the use of technology for antenatal screening mean more hospital-based tests. Routine antenatal testing can include: ultrasound scanning for anomalies; blood tests for rhesus status, blood group and rubella immunity; as well as indicators for spina bifida, which is also checked at later scans (approximately 20–23 weeks). Specialist additional tests may be carried out if considered necessary or appropriate, including nuchal scanning (for the identification of risk of Down's syndrome), chorionic villus sampling and amniocentesis. The provision of routine testing outside the UK varies, for example the Netherlands is reluctant to offer routine prenatal screening for conditions which cannot be effectively treated, such as Down's syndrome, although screening may be provided on request.

Women are encouraged to attend regular checkups with their doctors or community midwives to monitor the progress of the pregnancy and ensure that any deviations from the normal are identified, though the range of what is considered normal in antenatal encounters with midwives is quite broad. Studies of the conversations taking place during antenatal appointments highlight an overriding discourse on normality, whereby even irregularities are represented as normal (Linell and Bredmar, 1996). In addition to actual attendance at clinic, women's participation in public health activities may be monitored for compliance, for example through the use of patient-held records, which are updated on each visit. This resource has the dual function of making visible to the women the current status of their pregnancy and the baby's development and of permitting external sharing of the women's health status by medical professionals. On the basis of the information carried in this way, women can change or monitor their health or behaviour and advice can be given at appropriate times.

Despite recommendations that a greater emphasis should be placed on the social context of childbirth and the best intentions of those involved in women's care during their pregnancies, the level of technological and medical interventions in pregnancy and childbirth has increased, albeit within a rhetoric of normality and naturalness. This is perhaps inevitable when women of childbearing age have less experience of childbirth than at any previous time in history and when pregnancy is so obviously located in a medical context. Fewer than half of the women giving birth in England and Wales and less than two-thirds in Scotland do so without any form of medical or technological intervention (this includes the use of forceps, ventouse and caesarean section as well as pain-relieving strategies such as epidural injection and safety checks such as foetal heart monitoring). The rate of caesarean deliveries has significantly increased over the last 25 years, causing some concern among practitioners and healthcare providers. The most recent surveys of obstetric practice in hospitals put the UK, the US and Brazil in the top five countries for rates of caesarean delivery. Figures published for the last few years indicate a rate of about a fifth of all live births in England and Wales being by caesarean section (21.5 per cent, Thomas and Paranjothy, 2001) though the majority of these are emergency caesareans, rather than elective. World Health Organization guidelines indicate that 5 per cent is the minimum rate of caesarean delivery, and that anything over 15 per cent is considered excessive or inappropriate. Rates higher than 15 per cent suggest that the procedure is not being carried out on health grounds, since the benefit in terms of maternal mortality (from life-threatening conditions prompting the need for a caesarean section) levels off at this point. Reasons for higher rates may in part result from a perceived demand from women for elective surgery. This then compounds the rate increase, since one of the most reliable predictors of caesarean section is having had a previous caesarean, whether or not the need was medical or otherwise, and further increases the likelihood of its use as a routine procedure. For example, figures indicate that private health providers in Brazil deliver as many as 70 per cent of babies by this method (Potter *et al.*, 2001). Notwithstanding the high rate of caesarean section, many hospital delivery suites and midwives also support a more 'natural' birth, providing facilities for a more homely and family-friendly environment.

Women stay in hospital for a short time following the birth; in many cases they go home the same day or within two days. After a caesarean section, they may stay in hospital for longer to ensure post-operative recovery. Once at home, care of the woman and her baby is once again provided by the midwife and general practitioner in the community. Women who are employed at the start of their pregnancy may take maternity leave – the timing and length of leave available will depend on their country of employment with national minima and some qualifying requirements. In the EU, the statutory minimum period of leave available to women in all member states is 14 weeks, as recommended by the International Labour Organisation (2000), during which time jobs are held open. The leave can be taken both before the birth and afterwards. Some countries (Sweden is a well-known example) offer paid parental leave of up to 16 months. Elsewhere, leave is not necessarily so generous or automatically available. In the US, for example, while some states do have arrangements for short periods of paid leave, this is the exception rather than the rule and the pregnancy may have to be defined as a disability by a doctor before benefits can be paid. Otherwise, only women working in larger companies are eligible for a 12-week period of job-protected leave. The paucity of parental leave in the US puts it on a par with countries such as Lesotho, Papua New Guinea and Swaziland. In Australia, while job-protected leave of up to a year is available, there is no statutory minimum period of leave. In the EU, employers may also provide more generous leave of up to a year or longer, either of their own volition or in response to local legislation, some of which may be paid. The responses to pregnancy in the workplace are addressed further in Chapter 4, while the issue of how leave is embedded into a culture is also discussed in Chapter 2.

To summarise at this point, despite the relative infrequency of its occurrence and the significance of pregnancy as a life event, in looking at the research on pregnancy it could still be said to be a game of '*cherchez la femme*'. This paradoxical invisibility is not entirely new, rather it has been an emerging feature of the way that pregnancy has been viewed historically. Cultural shifts in the tolerance of risk and the recent expansion of technologies of reproduction have impacted on the way that pregnancy is managed and is incorporated into biological and legal domains. Despite the major scientific interest in these issues and the political rhetoric of choice, these phenomena also vary considerably in the attention they focus on the person of the pregnant woman. Thus, the effect of the relative infrequency of individual pregnancy has been to foreground the outcome of pregnancy and the woman's role in assuring that outcome. Such attention has tended to obscure the woman and the psychological processes involved and with these the mother. This is so not only in the wider social and cultural context but also in research.

In exploring the concepts of sanction and surveillance surrounding pregnancy, and in seeking the elusive woman at the centre of the event, it is inevitable that we will be revisiting a number of themes that have been addressed eloquently by others, most recently, for example, in Clare Hanson's book *The Cultural History of Pregnancy* (2004) and Jane Ussher's book *Managing the Monstrous Feminine* (2006). By using as a basis the research we are most familiar with, which has perhaps received less previous psychological attention, we hope to exemplify the complexities of normal experience for women when they become pregnant, especially for the first time. We should also state what this book does not do since it is clear that we cannot possibly address the full range of issues we raised at the start when describing pregnancy research as challenging. This is not only because of space constraints or the integrity of the case we would want to make, but also because there is already existing work that deals more than effectively with these issues and, since they do not form the substance of our own research areas, are better left to others. Furthermore, while we have spread our net as widely as possible in identifying research, we cannot provide cross-cultural comparisons. We are therefore drawing on the situations best known to us pertaining to the UK and Europe, most of which we consider have broader resonances in the treatment and experiences of all women when they are pregnant. More specifically, however, in talking about psychological perspectives, we are not addressing pregnancy and mood or women's mental health in pregnancy, or postnatal depression. We will touch on the issues of risk perception, the ethics of screening and the technologies of reproduction but there is no explicit discussion of infertility or even childlessness. These are all significant areas that concern women and for research; work by Lorraine Sherr, Paula Nicolson, Anne Woollett as well as authors already mentioned may provide some relevant material (see for example, Nicolson, 1998; Sherr, 1995; Woollett, 1991). Neither is this exclusively a feminist critique of psychological research into pregnancy although we are concerned to locate pregnancy as a personal and experiential event. And, last, although much of what we will discuss is pertinent to women's experience more generally, our focus is limited to the period of pregnancy itself, and excludes discussion of the serious issues concerning the period or process of labour and delivery and intrapartum care, and early motherhood.

The book that follows is the outcome of a series of research investigations by both authors, together and separately, on aspects of daily experience in pregnancy that intrigued us and that are the subject of women's vigilance and the potential focus for change as a result of pregnancy. Following a discussion of the various paradoxes of pregnancy and the concept of sanctions in pregnancy (Chapter 2), Chapter 3 addresses directly the way that psychological and other research has contributed to these in investigating cognition in pregnancy. Chapter 4 takes up aspects of the deficiency model of pregnancy and performance in the context of the workplace, and addresses the cultural beliefs and attitudes that impact on pregnancy and employment. Chapters 5 and 6 consider fundamental and topical issues of diet and eating and activity and exercise in relation to advice that emanates from research findings and the social expectations of pregnancy. Finally, in Chapter 7, we consider again the visibility of pregnancy and women's roles, by drawing analogies with the concepts of celebrity, and the book concludes, in Chapter 8, with a consideration of whether pregnancy can be considered 'special'.

2

PARADOXES OF PREGNANCY

The context in which pregnancy is experienced is laden with paradoxes; in the heart of our construction of pregnancy in the developed world at the beginning of the twenty-first century lie a set of apparently conflicting views. In this chapter we will explore these paradoxes and how they impact on the experience of women themselves and the way the research agenda has both determined and been shaped by these contradictions. In order to do this we draw on the theories and findings of research outside psychology, notably that of sociologists.

Growing safety and growing risk

In previous centuries, pregnancy and childbirth were fraught with danger. Poor pregnancy outcomes, in the form of miscarriage, the birth of disabled babies or even maternal and infant mortality, were relatively common. Importantly though, they were largely seen to be beyond the control of women themselves or even those with specialist knowledge: midwives and, increasingly, doctors. As discussed in Chapter 1, pregnancy was confirmed relatively late and mainly through the woman's experience of symptoms: missed periods, nausea, changes in the way her body felt and, eventually, quickening.

Nowadays poor outcomes for the mother or baby are relatively rare and pregnancy is confirmed and monitored by objectively measurable signs. The expectation is that most women will seek help and advice at an early stage and any problems with the pregnancy can be detected and acted on.

Scientific and medical research has led to greater understanding of the physiological processes of pregnancy and preventable threats. With that has come a much lower risk of women experiencing the traditional hazards, but this does not seem to have been accompanied by a commensurate lessening of the expectations of risk. Josephine Green (1990) in her major study of the experiences of women undergoing antenatal screening in the UK, *Calming or Harming?*, points out that for the pregnant women some degree of worry about whether or not the baby will be alright is still

12

the norm, with only 10 per cent of the women questioned indicating that they are not at all worried about the outcome of their pregnancy. This worry is largely unrelated to the tests that a woman undergoes or to her knowledge of such tests (Green *et al.*, 1993). One factor that seems to underlie these perceptions of risk is a change in the perception of the role of human agency in pregnancy. The old certainties that nature would take its course, or that what happens is God's will, have been replaced by notions of individual and social responsibility for the hazards that we may experience.

Sociologists have drawn attention to the experience of societies in the developed world becoming increasingly aware of hazards that may affect them yet at the same time becoming increasingly distrustful of those experts who traditionally have been relied upon to protect society from such hazards. Indeed, much of contemporary society distrusts those groups of experts who have drawn attention to the risks of such hazards: scientists, and medical and environmental experts. Ulrich Beck (1992) has termed this concept the 'risk society': a term which is used interchangeably with that of another sociologist, Anthony Giddens, the 'climate of risk' (Giddens, 1991). In his book *The Risk Society: Towards a New Modernity* Beck delineates the central dilemma of 'the risk society' thus:

> In contrast to all earlier epochs (including industrial society), the risk society is characterized essentially by a lack: the impossibility of an external attribution of hazards. In other words, risks depend on decisions, they are industrially produced and in this sense politically reflexive.
>
> (Beck, 1992: 183)

The risk society brings together a suspicion of scientific innovation with the irresistibility of using such innovation to make choices at an individual and societal level. In obstetrics, the ability to quantify the risk level of individual women and their babies, mainly through the extrapolation of epidemiological data, has been used to justify the use of technological interventions (e.g. caesarean section) by both health professionals and women themselves (Lankshear *et al.*, 2005).

Alongside the risk society, or maybe as a function of it, we see other currents which have an impact on the experience of pregnancy. Even in Europe, which traditionally has adopted a social-medicine model in the allocation of resources, government policy interventions to redefine patients as consumers of a public service, and funding pressures for health services, have encouraged the emergence of a self-care culture. In this context, people are taking more responsibility for their own health and adopting more consumerist attitudes to healthcare (Lupton, 1997). In the UK we can also perceive the process of 'de-professionalisation' whereby organisational and managerial change brings about a reduction in professional control, demystification of expert knowledge and indeed a disembedding of that knowledge (Elston, 1991). This is linked to suspicion of the competence and ethics of doctors.

In pregnancy care, technological innovation has undoubtedly brought greater safety and a higher likelihood of a safe delivery. Ultrasound scanning and various other forms of screening as well as diagnostic tests help to reveal conditions in the foetus (e.g. heart defects, Down's syndrome) and the mother (e.g. gestational diabetes, pre-eclampsia). The value of this information is seldom questioned but the benefit of screening for foetal health in illuminating risks for individual women has to be weighed against the risk of harm from seeking that information. Most women will have screening for foetal health for reassurance that nothing is 'wrong'. Indeed, Marteau (2002) has pointed out that many women do not realise that ultrasound, for example, can detect foetal anomalies, or that many screening tests are not diagnostic and produce results which are not definitive but probabilistic. Some results of tests are difficult to interpret even for the professionals conducting the tests as they reveal anomalies which may be signs of serious conditions or which may resolve themselves during the pregnancy. There is high morbidity associated with both false negative and false positive results and the raised awareness of risks itself raises anxiety.

At the level of behavioural advice, women are expected to act on information presented to them by midwives and general practitioners, but also respond to information which is often presented in a sensationalist manner by the media, including, increasingly, the internet. What is a 'risk behaviour' may be defined not by scientists who collect the data but by the media who present those data. As we explore in several of the following chapters, information about what is harmful or beneficial to women and their babies may be presented as black and white with apparently little concern for the impact this has on women's decision making during pregnancy, or their emotional wellbeing. What is more, the behavioural advice presented will often come too late for many women to act on it, relating as it does to preconception or early pregnancy. Thus, the concept of the 'good mother' extends back to before the baby is actually born. In weighing up current scientific opinion with the views of social commentators presenting a position in opposition to conventional medicine, women are accepting that the locus of control is within themselves.

As psychologists we seek to understand these feelings of uncertainty and risk at a time of increasing certainty and safety by considering the individual processes which underlie such feelings. Two areas of research, in psychology and in the social sciences more generally, seem to be relevant here. The first area is concerned with individual perception and assessment of risk, and the second with the social amplification of risk through the mass media.

We now understand a great deal about how people judge the likelihood of an event or their risk of experiencing a particular outcome. Early work on decision making in health assumed that people consider how pleasant or unpleasant outcomes of certain courses of action are and weight them by how likely each outcome is. So they will, consciously or unconsciously, choose the course of action with the highest weighted score. This is known as 'subjective expected utility theory'. The empirical evidence that people do not necessarily make decisions in this way, even when encouraged to do so by 'decision support' systems, has led many professionals, particularly economists and doctors, to the conclusion that people are not good decision makers. However, we can show that the mechanisms that people use most of the time will lead them to decisions which are best for them, with the least cognitive effort. In understanding these mechanisms we can understand the way that women use the information presented to them, and act upon it. Of key importance to the experience of pregnancy is, first, the perception of categorical safety or threat, so behaviour is perceived as either risky or not (Redelmeier *et al.*, 1993). This influences not just the way in which information is perceived but also the way it is presented. Second, people have difficulty in distinguishing between very small probabilities, and the value of following one course of action rather than another may appear obvious to an epidemiologist considering populations but not to a lay person considering only their individual risk status. Finally, outcomes that are easier to bring to mind are judged to be more likely; this has been termed the 'availability bias' (Tversky and Kahneman, 1981). The ease with which an outcome is brought to mind is influenced by how frequently or recently a person has been aware of it and also by strong emotions being associated with it. So, media coverage of a particular hazard or event makes it seem more likely. The literature in this area has been dominated by these cognitive mechanisms, however, more recently researchers have returned to considering the ways in which emotions such as 'anticipated regret' influence perceptions of risk and concomitant decisions. For example, Wroe *et al.* (2005) have shown that parents' decisions on vaccination are influenced by emotion, and particularly that risk associated with inaction is perceived as more acceptable than positive actions.

In recent years both researchers and political and social commentators have become increasingly interested in the way in which risk is propagated, particularly by the mass media. This 'social amplification' of risk not only makes people aware of hazards they may face but also tends to encourage a distrust of experts and organisations involved in risk management. This leads to uncertainty and feelings of danger. Different types of media, even different types within media (e.g. tabloid and broadsheet newspapers), produce different narratives of risk (Murdock *et al.*, 2003). So, women are confronted both by 'official' information produced and disseminated by health professionals and information produced by a wide range of media, which command varying degrees of trust.

How then do individual women respond to the risks presented to them by different sources? Joffe (2003) has suggested that, when presented with the likelihood of hazards, individuals use the ways of reasoning and the values common to the groups with which they identify. Thus, the source of the threat and how that source is viewed, and the way the threat is linked in to group identity, will determine how an individual will respond. If women are relying more on external representations of risk and less on their embodied experience then it is likely that their decisions and actions are better understood by examining the values of the group to which they belong rather than the scientific evidence presented. If we accept that individual actions are guided by cultural and subcultural values then screening technologies and information presented with a view to guiding women to one course of action (e.g. terminating pregnancies where the baby would be born with a life-limiting condition) may lead to unexpected effects on a large scale. These might include a growing opposition to the termination of pregnancy because of its use to prevent the birth of children with what to most groups would seem not to be a serious condition (e.g. cleft palate), or, conversely, the distortion of population, e.g. through sex-selective abortions, which has led to a shortage of girls in some states where boys are more highly valued.

This leads us to another paradox of pregnancy. Reproductive technologies and risk interventions while reducing uncertainty at one level appear to make individual pregnancies more uncertain.

Being a little bit pregnant

The change between being not pregnant and being pregnant has long been used as an example of a quantum change in colloquial English. The sentence 'you can't be a little bit pregnant' is used to challenge a position of uncertainty. However, the earlier detection of pregnancy itself or problems with the pregnancy and the possibility of preventing the birth of babies with serious health problems have led to what Barbara Katz Rothman (1986) has memorably termed the 'tentative pregnancy'.

Pregnancy testing kits were first actively marketed for home use in the 1970s, a development of near patient testing used by health professionals to test patients without recourse to laboratory facilities. Manufacturers and suppliers are driven by commercial concerns, albeit tempered by ethical and social considerations. The use of this technology was for some time treated with suspicion by doctors and pharmacists (Stim, 1976). However, home pregnancy testing has been absorbed into routine antenatal care, and has improved in reliability and ease of use as demand for it has increased. Its use has been further sanctioned in the UK by the evaluation of over-the-counter tests by the Medical Devices Agency. Self-testing may be seen as part of the development of a 'self-care culture', discussed above, with patients as 'consumers' taking more responsibility for their own health, and having rights over information about their bodies (Lupton, 1997). NHS Direct, drop-in health centres on the high street and health sites on the internet are other manifestations of this movement. The use of these technologies in the home must be set against the wider social and cultural context in which a changing healthcare system impacts on patient behaviour and relationships between patients and healthcare professionals (Rose, 1990). Most importantly here, pregnancy testing allows women to confirm a pregnancy long before the signs and symptoms of pregnancy appear and without confirmation from health professionals who hold privileged knowledge. At once a pregnancy becomes a reality at a much early stage and also is less likely to result in the birth of a baby: a pregnancy which ends early can no longer be regarded as a 'missed period' but has to be regarded as a failed pregnancy and the pregnancy test is just the first of many tests which will lead to decisions about whether the pregnancy should continue or not. Lewando-Hundt and her colleagues (2004) discovered that 37 per cent of women who were receiving antenatal care in a UK centre which did not offer first trimester screening for Down's syndrome paid to have this screening done privately.

Barbara Katz Rothman in her book *The Tentative Pregnancy: How Amniocentesis Changes the Experience of Motherhood* (1993) suggested that the introduction of amniocentesis irrevocably changed the way that pregnancy was viewed both by pregnant women themselves and their partners, and by those others not directly involved. Rather than the birth of a baby with, for example, Down's syndrome being regarded as a family misfortune, it is now regarded as a personally avoidable mistake. Thus, the ability to test the health of the foetus has led to the possibility of embarking on a pregnancy which will not necessarily have to be seen to term.

The case of amniocentesis was complicated by the danger inherent in the procedure itself, particularly in the early days. So the risk of terminating a wanted pregnancy through this invasive procedure had to be weighed against the possibility of giving birth to an 'unwanted' baby if the procedure was not undertaken. The assumption was made that if a woman chose to have an amniocentesis she must be willing to terminate the pregnancy if the result was positive. Nowadays, not only is amniocentesis much less likely to lead to an unintended termination, but also it has largely been superseded by other technologies which provide more or less definitive results on the health status of the foetus without any risk of termination, being based on blood samples or imaging techniques. However, the assumption still seems to be made that if a woman is willing to undergo testing she must be willing to act on the basis of the information provided to terminate a foetus that is not 'perfect'. This is particularly the case when technologies provide this information very early in pregnancy, that is, when the woman is only 'a little bit' pregnant.

Jenny Hewison and her colleagues (2004) have posed the question of who sets the agenda for technological development in antenatal testing. They have investigated the views of mothers living in the north of England from Pakistani and white European ethnic origins, on the range of antenatal diagnostic tests which could become available and the value of the information afforded by them. Using a set of scenarios which described, but did not name, various conditions, women were asked first whether they would test for each condition and second whether they would terminate a foetus discovered to have this condition. There was considerable agreement on the conditions which women would most want tests for and for which they would seek termination of pregnancy: anencephaly, trisomy 13 or 18 (which lead to death within months of birth), quadriplegia and Duchenne muscular dystrophy. However, fewer than 25 per cent of the women questioned would consider a termination for most conditions and there was great divergence in what conditions would be so severe that the woman would feel that termination was better than continuing with the pregnancy. These include conditions for which tests are currently widely available, such as Down's syndrome. Furthermore, the percentage of women who wanted antenatal diagnosis for each condition was far higher than the percentage of women who would consider termination.

So the development of antenatal testing services seems to be being driven by the technology. However, this is not to say that the women studied by Hewison and her co-workers were not very much in favour of these developments, but that what they want from testing is information, not a way of ensuring a perfect baby. Giddens (1991) talks of 'colonizing the future' by attempting to predict risk of hazards and preventing them; however, for women contemplating the health of their children the prediction seems to be far more important than the prevention, at least at any cost.

The secret made visible

We have discussed above the impact of antenatal scanning and testing on the individual choices that women now have to make about their pregnancy. However, there is another important aspect of this technology and that is that testing is taking precedence over the private lived experience of the mother. As we have said, pregnancy was formerly confirmed and monitored through the embodied experience of the mother. Now that experience is made public through technological means. Foremost among these technologies is ultrasound scanning, which provides pictures of the foetus.

Ultrasound scanning is the most commonly used screening technology in antenatal care and is taken up by the overwhelming majority of pregnant women in the developed world. It has long been used to check that the foetus is alive, has no major abnormalities and to check that the date of conception estimated from the mother's account fits with the growth of the baby. As the technology has become more sophisticated it is possible to produce very high-definition pictures and to detect more signs of abnormality at an earlier stage, for example nuchal fold abnormalities seen in foetuses with Down's syndrome.

Parents generally welcome the chance to see the foetus. Indeed, the visual record of a baby's life is now likely to start with the first ultrasound picture. The visual representation is a very powerful mechanism which turns a foetus into a baby. Both parents, and indeed others, are able to experience the foetus and therefore bond with it, rather than just the mother. In 2004 Stuart Campbell released 3D and 4D pictures and 'films' of foetuses from 12 weeks, showing the development of behavioural routines such as 'stepping'. The pictures were incorporated in a book *Watch Me Grow!* (Campbell, 2004), which has become a bestseller. However, the release of these pictures, particularly real-time depictions of the movement of foetuses, fuelled debate on termination of pregnancy and led to calls to restrict the ability of women to terminate pregnancy even in the first trimester. High-definition ultrasound has made the foetus appear more like a person not only to the mother carrying that foetus, but to the public at large.

Through ultrasound scanning the foetus is literally put under surveillance, without any input from the mother other than her consent and presence. The mother in the ultrasound picture is a container, or rather a frame, for the subject. The primacy of her intimate and private experience of the growing foetus has been overtaken by the distanced and public scrutiny by health professionals and others. Rather like a wedding where more time is spent on capturing the event in photographs than on the ceremony, the visual record of the foetus is given more credence than the account of the person who is present at the event.

So far in this chapter we may have appeared to take a rather negative view of the consequences for pregnancy of the information age. So before going on, let us reiterate here that advances in technology and understanding of the processes of pregnancy and birth have undoubtedly improved the experience of pregnancy and childbirth for many women. Although the onus of decision making has shifted to the individual, many women would welcome that empowerment. And although pregnant women are now bombarded with information and advice, many women welcome, desire and seek them out. From the pregnancy test which allows them to confirm their own pregnancy, through the web pages and magazines which allow them to learn about pregnancy for themselves, the first ultrasound picture which takes its place in the family album, to the prior warnings of difficulties with the baby's health or birth which allow action to be taken and preparation, many women feel that the greater control and reassurance offered now is a price worth paying for the rise in responsibility and anxiety which may accompany them.

Absence of women in research on the most feminine of states

The research reviewed above in relation to women's experience of, and response to, reproductive technology is largely atypical of research on pregnancy in that the views and motivations of women have been sought and studied; though even in this area, such views are seldom sought before the technology is introduced. In most of the research we will be reviewing in this book, the women themselves, as actors, seem curiously absent. Most research concentrates on the outcome of pregnancy related to the baby. While the behaviour of women may be mapped and linked assiduously to particular pregnancy outcomes, and women judged on the basis of their behaviour, the motivations and beliefs of individual women are seldom sought. Rather, their health, behaviour and even state of mind are regarded as characteristics of the container of the foetus. In the chapters that follow we will return to this theme and we hope that it will become clear that one of the motivations of our own research on pregnancy is to put the psychology of women back at the centre of this uniquely feminine experience.

Pregnancy as an exceptional normal state

There are several senses in which pregnancy is simultaneously regarded as a normal and exceptional state. As we commented in Chapter 1, pregnancy is becoming an increasingly uncommon event for individuals, especially in Europe, where the birthrate has long been below replacement levels for the majority ethnic groups. Yet pregnancy is regarded as a commonplace experience. This is particularly the case in the workplace, where pregnancy may be a common event among the staff of a large employer. Any individual woman on that staff, however, is likely to only experience being pregnant at that workplace once. This may help to explain the level of prejudice that women experience when they announce that they are pregnant. As we have found in our own work, fellow workers and employers may regard pregnant workers as a group as incapable of carrying out their jobs and as unfairly entitled to special treatment and benefits. At the same time they may have very positive views of individual pregnant women they have worked with (Pattison et al., 1997).

In this chapter we have concentrated on the construction of pregnancy and the implications of that construction in the developed world. One of the reasons for this is that although pregnancy is a universal experience, it is seldom studied or even considered from a cross-cultural perspective. Simultaneously, two positions are held, sometimes by the same researchers.

The first is that all women are basically alike in their reproductive processes and that pregnancy can be defined by the physiological changes women undergo. If this holds, then cross-cultural comparisons will add little to the studies of participants readily available to researchers in their local environs. We will see this perspective dominating the research on cognition in pregnancy in Chapter 3. The second perspective is that resource availability and social conditions vary to such an extent across the world that information needs to be gathered on women who are alike in these regards. This is the perspective that dominates research on pregnancy and work covered in Chapter 4. However, where cross-cultural comparisons are made the results can be illuminating in understanding the interplay between the physiological and the psychological. For example, studies of dietary habits of women from different cultures could be interpreted as showing that the basic motivations of women are the same, which is that physiological changes and demands prompt behaviour to improve the health of the baby. However, depending on the cultural beliefs, these may be manifest in eating earth in one culture or vitamin pills in another (Henry and Kwong, 2003). See Chapter 5 for a further exposition of this point.

Another sense in which pregnancy is both normal and exceptional is as a natural process which is still highly medicalised for most women in the developed world. In recent decades organisations such as the National Childbirth Trust in the UK have supported pregnant women by providing information and education, and attempting to limit the amount of medical intervention that women experience. However, the National Childbirth Trust itself brings together unlikely allies. It was founded in 1957 to champion the position of doctors, notably Grant Dick-Read, who felt that middle-class women were being put off childbearing through poor preparation for birth, leading to fear, particularly of the pain involved. This eugenic motivation is far from the motivations of feminist champions of natural childbirth who see the medical model of pregnancy and child-birth as an example of the way that patriarchies control women. The natural childbirth movement has led to changes in the way women are treated and certainly to the way that many women now give birth. At the same time, though, the reproductive technologies described above, the fear of litigation if a baby is not born healthy and the trend for women to have fewer babies have led to the medicalisation of pregnancy on an unparalleled scale.

Is there never a good time to be pregnant?

Women in the developed world now have unprecedented control over the timing of childbearing. Advances in contraception, fertility monitoring devices and assisted reproductive technology have meant that most women can choose to have children and choose when to have them. However, the timing of pregnancy is hedged around by conflicting cultural mores. Teenagers, older women, women without a job and women with careers are all publicly criticised for choosing to have children when they do. Similarly, white European women are criticised for having single children; the natalist policies of many European countries, notably France, provide considerable welfare support for families with several children. A similar natalist approach to benefits is taken in Australia by the current Conservative administration. However, at the same time, and in the same countries, minority ethnic women are criticised for having several children and benefiting from that welfare support. Central to this general disapproval seems to be the assumptions that women are exercising choice and that once again the avoidance of risk is a matter of personal decision making. Furthermore, though, the belief is held that in exercising choice women are pursuing their own selfish ends. So older women are assumed to be putting their career first, and younger women are portrayed as avoiding earning a living by having children at the times they do. Little credence is given to the view that when heterosexual women choose to have children is influenced largely by the presence and willingness of men to act as fathers. Indeed, the role of men in the creation of families is rarely considered in these discourses. The importance of the presence of a suitable and willing putative father in the choice to have children was highlighted in Fiona McAllister and Lynda Clarke's (1998) study of childlessness in Britain. They found that those childless women they interviewed who were living alone held conventional views on partnerships and would not contemplate becoming a single parent. In general, decisions to remain childless, and, by extension, to delay childbearing, were not made in a vacuum but rather crucially depended on relationships with partners and the perceived suitability of women's circumstances for parenthood.

At the extreme, the view of women caring for their own interests over the interests of their children leads to policies which curtail the rights of pregnant women over their own bodies. Sheena Meredith (2005) in her book *Policing Pregnancy: The Law and Ethics of Obstetric Conflict* makes a powerful case that in recent case law in the US and the UK pregnant women are denied the rights of self-determination and bodily integrity which are enshrined in law for all others. Such cases arise when health professions do not agree with the women themselves on best courses of action or behaviour. Thus, the pregnant woman finds herself in legal conflict with her foetus, or rather others who regard themselves as more suitable guardians of the foetus.

The debilitated nurturing

In reviewing the research literature on pregnancy, one could be forgiven for questioning whether women are fit to be mothers. We suggest that beliefs

22

about pregnant women reflect wider beliefs about women generally, perhaps because pregnancy provides such clear evidence of femininity. Traditional beliefs about women in Western society are characterised by beliefs about the weakness and vulnerability of women. So women are seen as the 'weaker vessel', prone to debilitation, in need of protection from men and governed by irrational and emotional thinking. As reproduction most clearly delineates sex if not gender, these stereotypical views of women tend to be most clearly connected to women in aspects of reproduction: menstruation and the menopause, but above all pregnancy. We are left, then, with the view that women are at their most vulnerable when they are responsible for the wellbeing of unborn children. Researchers seldom discuss or engage with this anomalous position, yet it is a strong influence on the kind of research which is carried out and how results are interpreted.

Sanctioned behaviour

The word 'sanction' in English has contradictory meanings. It refers both to the approval or authorisation of behaviour and the punishment for behaviour which is seen as not obeying the rules. We can see women's behaviour during pregnancy as being sanctioned in both ways, and women often have the feeling that they are always somehow in the wrong. Research on pregnancy, as we will show, is largely concerned with authorising women's behaviour by providing rules which will lead to the best outcome for the baby, the family and for society at large. However, the fluid nature of these rules, and the conflicting interests of different researchers, mean that research findings effectively define individual women's decisions and behaviour as beyond the pale. Thus, pregnant women face sanctions in both senses of the word.

In conclusion, it is puzzling that women are treated with such distrust when they undertake this fundamental task of procreating. Pregnant women can expect to be criticised, lectured and harassed by those closest to them and by complete strangers. How fortunate, then, for those women and their families and even their critics, that nevertheless most continue to find pregnancy such a fascinating, fulfilling and joyful experience.

3

COGNITION IN PREGNANCY

I went to get a drink in the night and opened the freezer and found
a tea towel in there that I had mislaid earlier in the week.

(Gross and Pattison, 1995: 24)

Anecdotes such as the one quoted above are common in discussions with
women about the experience of pregnancy. Many women report that
during pregnancy they suffer episodes of forgetfulness, difficulty in concentration or planning, and making errors in tasks they were previously able
to accomplish with ease. The prevalence of accounts of this type and the
repetition of these accounts by midwives, other health professionals and
the media have led to a general belief that women are less cognitively able
during pregnancy. Such experience has been labelled, in the psychology
literature, cognitive failure (Broadbent et al., 1982). On the face of it, it
seems curiously non-adaptive that women who have responsibility not only
for themselves but also for their unborn offspring should be vulnerable in
this way. Only an assumption of an association between pregnancy and
debilitation would lead to the a priori prediction that pregnant women will
have general problems with memory, attention and learning. However, as
we shall show in this chapter, the picture is complicated and the research
literature contradictory.

The phenomenon of cognitive failure in pregnancy has been investigated from a number of perspectives and in a number of ways. Studies
range from informal self-report studies of pregnant women (e.g. Poser
et al., 1986), to more formal self-report studies (e.g. Gross and Pattison,
1995), to assessments of cognition in laboratory experiments often
combined with self-report (e.g. Brindle et al., 1991), to behavioural and
neuro-physiological studies of animal models (e.g. Kinsley et al., 1999).
In this chapter we will critically review the research of psychologists
and others on cognition in pregnancy and particularly consider how
stereotypes and constructions of pregnancy have influenced what research
is carried out and published, and how the results of that research are
interpreted.

24

Theories of cognition in pregnancy

Broadly there are two groups of theory of cognition in pregnancy. The first sees cognitive change as a function of pregnancy *per se*, particularly the concomitant neuro-endocrinal changes. The second type sees cognitive change as a function of the psychological and social events which accompany pregnancy, leading, for example, to stress or cognitive overload. Both types of theory could lead to predictions of problems with cognition, though there are also some grounds to anticipate an improvement in cognition or at least in some cognitive tasks.

One of the most marked signs of pregnancy is the rise in circulating hormones, for example progesterone levels rise sharply in early pregnancy and continue to rise steadily until by the end of pregnancy they are typically more than 20 times the levels outside pregnancy (Tulchinsky *et al.*, 1972; Willcox *et al.*, 1985). This rise is subject to only minor fluctuations and individual variations, and is markedly different from any changes occurring outside pregnancy. Brett and Baxendale (2001) give a full review of pregnancy hormones in relation to memory performance.

The links between hormones and women's behaviour are, of course, a popular area of investigation; women are often seen as being at the mercy of 'raging hormones' (Vines, 1994). Research has particularly focused on cognition during the menstrual cycle and post-menopause. However, the evidence does not suggest a link between fluctuating hormone levels over the menstrual cycle and fluctuations in cognitive performance (Richardson, 1992; Walker, 1995) or between hormone change in the menopause and cognitive function (Henderson *et al.*, 1996).

Research on cognition in pregnancy has concentrated on the direct effects of changes in four hormones: progesterone, glucocorticoids, oxytocin and oestrogens. Progesterone is known to increase neural inhibition and decrease arousal and therefore may have a sedative effect. Memory performance on a paragraph recall task of non-pregnant women volunteers was significantly impaired after large doses of oral progesterone (Freeman *et al.*, 1992, 1993). Therefore, the effects of the rise in progesterone may be a decrement in performance occurring early in pregnancy and continuing until after the birth, unless women adapt to the problems and compensate, in which case initial problems should improve. Glucocorticoids also rise steadily in pregnancy. The glucocorticoids, particularly cortisol, have been linked to a reduction in cells in the hippocampus and this reduction correlates with memory impairment in people with Cushing's syndrome, a condition marked by an overproduction of cortisol (Mauri *et al.*, 1993; Starkman *et al.*, 1992).

Oxytocin rises gradually in pregnancy until just before the birth when the levels increase sharply as it triggers birth contractions and milk production. Oxytocin has been linked to low arousal level and fatigue (Pietrowsky *et al.*, 1991). However, it also appears to have effects on the hippocampus that improve memory and learning. The hippocampus is a region important for learning and memory. Tomizawa *et al.* (2003) have reported that injecting oxytocin into the brains of female mice improved their long-term memory and injecting oxytocin inhibitors into the brains of mother rats led to impairments in memory-related tasks. In any case it would be expected that oxytocin would have more of an effect in new mothers than pregnant women and there appear to be individual variations in levels (Drewett *et al.*, 1982).

Changes in the final group of hormones studied, oestrogens, are the most marked, with serum levels in the third trimester some many times the levels outside pregnancy. However, the effects of oestrogen on cognition seem to be different to those of the other hormones studied in that oestrogen seems to lead to unqualified improvements in cognition. High oestrogen levels are associated with high levels of neuronal excitability and increases in dendritic spine density in the hippocampus (McEwen *et al.*, 1995, 1997). Interest has grown over recent years in the neuro-protective properties of oestrogen. Research with post-menopausal women, whose levels of oestrogen have fallen, seems to show that low levels of oestrogen are associated with problems in cognition (Henderson *et al.*, 1996). Studies of female rats have shown that removal of the ovaries leads to a reduction in the number of synaptic contacts on hippocampus neurons, which is reversed by oestrogen replacement (Woolley and McEwan, 1993). Oestrogens seem to be particularly important for verbal memory. Phillips and Sherwin (1992) found that in women who had had both ovaries removed for benign disease, performance was significantly worse on memory for story paragraphs and this deficit was reversed with subsequent oestrogen replacement. There is some speculation in the psychology literature that very high levels of oestrogen may be harmful to cognition but Keenan *et al.*'s (1998) work on in vitro fertilisation showed that high doses of oestrogen did not impair memory.

Changes in synaptic contacts are associated with apoptosis, defined as programmed cell death. Apoptosis is an adaptive response to changes occurring in animals, enabling the breakdown of old patterns of behaviour and the formation of new neural pathways to support behaviour appropriate to the changed circumstances. Simulations of apoptosis and neurogenesis in neural network models have demonstrated that these processes can lead to adaptive changes in cognition and emotion to meet new and stressful demands (Chambers *et al.*, 2004). In the case of pregnancy, this would suggest changes appropriate for parenting. So this should give rise to improved cognitive performance, though the ability to carry out previously learned tasks may be impaired. If this is happening, cognitive performance should change over the course of pregnancy, and a smaller effect should be observed in multiparous women as adaptation to mother-hood should have already occurred in previous pregnancy.

The effects of hormones on cognition are complicated by the indirect effects which may be caused by concomitant changes in mood. In parti-cular, raised levels of vasopressin and oxytocin, such as are seen during pregnancy, have been linked to raised levels of anxiety. We have argued elsewhere that raised anxiety can be seen as adaptive during pregnancy, showing preparation for childbirth and parenting (Pattison and Gross, 1996), however anxiety may also have a detrimental effect on learning. Raised levels of cortisol have been linked to depression which in turn is associated with poor cognitive performance (Veiel, 1997). However, the impact of the rise in free cortisol is mediated in pregnancy by the effects of progesterone. The impact of mood on cognition is considered further below.

Another, less direct effect of physiological change on cognitive function may be due to deficiencies common during pregnancy, most notably iron. Pregnancy often leads to iron deficiency and anaemia, and iron deficiency has been shown to be important in the cognitive development of children (Lozoff et al., 1982a; Oski, 1975). Oski and Honig (1978) have shown that this can be reversed by intramuscular iron supplementation, but Lozoff et al. (1982b) showed no such effect with oral iron supplements. The relevance of these studies to adults is questionable. Studies have shown a link between iron deficiency and depression in women of childbearing age (Bodnar and Wisner, 2005). A less clear-cut relationship between iron status and cognition, together with depression and stress, was found in a study of women immediately post partum, though there was no significant difference between anaemic and non-anaemic women (Beard et al., 2005).

Another factor contributing to cognitive change may be the effect of fatigue. Sleep disturbance and sleep deprivation are commonly experienced by women later in pregnancy as a result of physical changes and the activity or positioning of the foetus. Both sleep disturbance and deprivation have been shown to affect performance on tasks which make demands on attention and memory, which seem to be a function of fatigue (Horne and Pettit, 1985; Horne et al., 1983). For example, the cognitive performance of junior doctors on work-related tasks is poorer when they have spent the previous night on-call (Deary and Tait, 1987). So it would be predicted then that cognitive dysfunction may be experienced by women whose sleep is disturbed during pregnancy.

So far we have considered the impact on cognition of changes brought about directly or indirectly by pregnancy per se. However, the literature on cognitive failure suggests it could be the psychological changes associated with pregnancy that have an effect and there are several ways in which this could be happening. Pregnancy itself can be regarded as a stressor. The stress may be a result of concern about the process of pregnancy and birth itself or concern for the baby's health; a woman's state of health is closely monitored throughout pregnancy both personally and by others, and this closer involvement with their own functioning could result in a heightened awareness of other behaviours. In addition, a woman's body is undergoing tremendous and rapid physical change, which could be experienced as stressful. Stress leads to depression and anxiety, and has been shown to be linked to cognitive dysfunction (Buckelow and Hannay, 1986), as indeed have high levels of depression and anxiety regardless of the cause (Veiel, 1997). Furthermore, most pregnant women, especially during a first pregnancy, are fulfilling the requirements of a job as well as meeting other cognitive demands resulting from their pregnancy, for example keeping antenatal appointments, receiving new information about pregnancy and childbirth as well as planning how to accommodate the changes to their lifestyle that will follow the birth. These competing demands might create 'cognitive overload'.

As we discussed in Chapter 1, pregnancy can be regarded as a time of transition, carrying with it both positive and negative implications, for example the prospect of new responsibilities and loss of independence or the marking of adult status as a parent. Support for the psychological effects of transitions on cognition comes from work investigating young people entering university. Fisher and Hood (1987, 1988) found that students suffering from homesickness reported higher levels of cognitive failure and also had higher levels of stated depression and anxiety than those who did not report being homesick. While leaving home to go to university is not directly analogous to the experience of pregnancy, the same range of emotions as those described by the homesick students could also be described during pregnancy – feelings of loss, feeling that life had changed forever, feelings of inadequacy and uncertainty about the future.

Yet another explanation of cognitive change is that proposed by psycho-analytic theory. This posits that women during pregnancy change their cognitive 'style' from thinking which is characterised by logic and evaluation to a more intuitive and less rational style (Condon, 1987; Condon and Ball, 1989). As a consequence they are likely to have difficulty when remembering or attending to material which is not directly relevant to themselves or their unborn babies. One of the problems with this theory is that it also predicts changes in mood and, at the extreme, psychiatric disturbance. So it is difficult to ascertain whether problems of memory and attention result from the change in cognitive orientation or from mood changes directly.

Finally, we have to consider that the expectation of changes in cognition during pregnancy could affect both feelings and performance in cognitive tests. This is an effect seen in older age, when people expect their memory to become poorer and this is reflected in self-reports (Jorm *et al.*, 1994). The expectation of debilitation is also often accompanied by depression in older people (Cockburn and Smith, 1994). This could account for self-reported cognitive failure in everyday life, but what would be the effect of expectations on performance in a more controlled setting? The answer will very much depend on how women respond to that expectation. Rodin (1976) showed that women who reported pre-menstrual symptoms reattributed the feelings of anxiety to their menstrual cycle when being tested. Therefore they performed better in the pre-menstrual part of their cycle because anxiety tends to interfere with memory, learning and attention. If pregnant women reattribute their anxiety from the experience of being tested to the somatic symptoms of pregnancy, one would predict they would actually do better. Similarly, women who believe their performance is likely to be poorer because they are pregnant may achieve a better performance through more 'effortful processes', that is, consciously trying harder. However, the picture is more complicated because these factors are balanced by the effects of self-efficacy (Bandura, 1989): a belief in one's ability to complete a task well becomes a self-fulfilling prophecy. So, conversely, believing you are not going to do well will lead to a poor performance through increased anxiety and less effort being devoted to the task.

In summary, there are many theories which would account for cognitive change in pregnancy. Neuro-endocrinal change could bring about both enhancements and decrements in performance of cognitive tasks. It should be noted that these theories are not mutually exclusive. However, theories other than those to do with hormones would mainly predict decrement but also would predict more variation between people.

Self-reports and performance on cognitive tasks

The medical and professional literature is littered with anecdotal accounts of cognitive failure during pregnancy. Some of these accounts are written by women themselves, who report having experienced this during their own pregnancy (Baildam, 1991; Burgoyne, 1994; Welch, 1991). Since all these accounts are written retrospectively, most do not clearly distinguish between what they perceive as the effects of pregnancy and those of caring for a young baby.

There are a number of more systematic studies of self-reported cognitive failure during pregnancy. Poser *et al.* (1986) carried out a retrospective interview survey of 51 female colleagues. Most of these were professional/middle-class women, and were colleagues of the researchers. Twenty-one of the women (41 per cent) said that they had suffered from cognitive dysfunction of one kind or another, with the most common symptom, reported by 81 per cent of the women, being forgetfulness. The symptoms were not related to age, percentage weight gain, alcohol consumption, sleepiness or the severity of other symptoms of pregnancy such as morning sickness or anaemia. The authors also stated that the forgetfulness was not related to depression or sleep deprivation.

Responding to these findings, Purvin and Dunn (1987) pointed out that a significant change during pregnancy in the women in their small survey (of six women) was the reduction of caffeine intake and they suggested that the reduction in intake of a central nervous system stimulant may have produced the symptoms described by the subjects in both studies. However, our own work has shown that even when women deliberately reduce caffeine intake by cutting down their coffee consumption, their self-reported consumption of other caffeine-containing drinks, for example tea, increases (Gross and Pattison, 1995). It seems unlikely that changes in coffee consumption would produce significant cognitive change in the majority of women.

Parsons and Redman (1991) conducted two studies of self-reported cognitive change during pregnancy. In the first they surveyed 236 primiparous women within three days of giving birth. The participants were asked to compare their concentration, memory and absent-mindedness before pregnancy to the experience in the previous three months (that is, during pregnancy). In total, 79 per cent of the women reported one or more problems, with 37 per cent reporting all three. It is worth noting that the timing of this survey very soon after giving birth to a first child may have influenced how women reported their experience during pregnancy. However, their second study of 48 women interviewed during pregnancy found similar results. Interestingly, Parsons and Redman found that most participants attributed these problems to changing physiology.

In our own study (Gross and Pattison, 1995) we tried to overcome some of the shortcomings of previous self-report studies. First we used a standardised measure of self-reported cognitive problems: the Cognitive Failure Questionnaire (CFQ) (Broadbent *et al.*, 1982). This has been shown to be sensitive to individual differences in levels of cognitive failure (Broadbent *et al.*, op. cit.) unrelated to intelligence and trait anxiety and other psychometric measures. More importantly, high scores do correspond to a true liability to make such slips of action and experience memory failures rather than simply report them (e.g. Maylor, 1990) and susceptibility to cognitive failure under stress (Broadbent *et al.*, 1982; Martin and Jones, 1983). A second important characteristic of our study was that it was longitudinal, so that we could investigate change across pregnancy; we studied women from, on average, 11.7 weeks of pregnancy to just before the birth. At four-weekly intervals our participants completed the CFQ and measures of mood, social, psychological and physical factors. They also completed diaries of cognitive events where they noted down any unusual aspects of memory or attention, including cognitive lapses. Thirty-one women remained in the study until the final measurements were taken. We were principally interested in observing variation within the pregnant group; however, we did have 17 matched women for the CFQ as we were using a different time period for reporting from the norms. What we found was that CFQ scores in pregnancy, on average, were not significantly higher than the general female population, though some women did report abnormally high levels. For all pregnant women in the study, CFQ levels were higher between weeks 12 and 20 of pregnancy and this was true of the diary entries too. High levels of cognitive failure were related to higher depression and anxiety, poorer reported psychological and physical health prior to pregnancy, changes in sleep pattern and lower-skilled maternal occupation, making the reasons for failures difficult to isolate. These findings were partially replicated by Morris *et al.* (1998) who also used the CFQ in their study of 38 employed women, in their late second trimester or early third trimester. As we had found, they reported no difference in scores between pregnant and non-pregnant women.

In our study the strongest association was to whether the women reported experiencing Pre-Menstrual Syndrome (PMS). Women who reported PMS reported more cognitive problems both on the CFQ and in their diaries. This finding, that there is variation in report of cognitive problems related to non-pregnancy factors, has been shown in other studies. Using a rather dubious statistical procedure, which involved categorising women according to the number of problems they reported, Parsons and Redman (1991) found that complaints about poorer cognition were more common in women who were older and better educated. In an earlier study by Poser and his colleagues (1986), it was the physicians and psychologists in the group who reported most problems. Poser *et al.* suggested that this was because these groups would be more sensitive to and aware of change, though it is not clear why this should be the case. Our own findings fitted better with the literature on transitory cognitive symptoms in that women from less-skilled occupations reported the most problems, rather than highly educated and skilled women. However, the most striking finding from our study was the difference between women who reported experiencing PMS and those who did not. One explanation of the findings of all these studies is that some women are more sensitive to change. Alternatively, they could have a higher expectation of change and debilitation associated with reproductive events (including the menstrual cycle) and this is reflected in their self-report.

Many cognitive psychologists are highly critical of self-reported assessments of cognitive performance, such as those described above, believing that people do not have sufficient insight to accurately report their cognitive abilities and that self-report is influenced by mood and other factors (Morris, 1983). So in an attempt to obtain a more objective perspective of cognition during pregnancy, researchers have tested pregnant women on a variety of standard psychological tests of attention, memory and learning. These tests are widely used in experiments on cognition or in assessing

31

people who are thought to have some cognitive deficit, for example following stroke.

One of the earliest studies which compared the performance of pregnant and non-pregnant women on controlled tests of cognition was conducted by Jarrahi-Zahed and his co-researchers in 1969. They investigated emotional and cognitive change in 86 pregnant women in the third trimester and post partum. Participants in the study were asked to comment on their own mental functioning and 'fogginess', but only a small proportion (12 per cent) reported this symptom during pregnancy. The researchers found that there was some reduction in attention in the pregnant women as compared to control subjects, measured using mazes and trail-making tests. The authors suggest a range of possible explanations for this change, though none of these was explicitly tested, including biological factors such as corticosteroid changes, hormonal effects and the attendant emotional changes measured over the period. They concluded that the poor test performance was due to emotional disturbance rather than any 'real' alteration in mental functioning.

Several studies have looked specifically for deficits in implicit and explicit memory. Put simply, implicit memory is memory for material which has not been deliberately learned, whereas explicit memory is memory for material which the person has been instructed to learn or has tried to learn. Blaxton (1989) suggests that these two types of memory rely on different types of processes which can be selectively impaired. Indeed, people who have long-term amnesia as the result of some neurological damage or disease usually have very poor explicit memory but have relatively intact implicit memory. If neurological impairment, particularly in the hippocampus, causes cognitive problems in pregnancy, then from these other studies we would expect pregnant women to have more problems remembering things they were overtly trying to learn and remember.

However, one of the most widely cited studies found completely the opposite of this prediction. Brindle et al. (1991) studied memory impairment in 32 pregnant women using laboratory testing of explicit and implicit memory as well as self-report. All the women expecting their first baby (15 women) showed deficits in implicit memory, especially those who were in the second trimester (six women). Their performance on this task correlated well with their self-report. There were no problems with explicit memory and multiparous women performed no differently from non-pregnant women. A later study by the same group of researchers (Sharp et al., 1993) seemed to contradict these findings. In this study, all the pregnant women showed a deficit in implicit memory, which again correlated with self-report, but there was no effect of trimester or of whether the women had already had children. However, here there was a difference between pregnant and non-pregnant women on explicit memory, with multigravid women especially affected.

Contradictory findings such as these, from the same group of researchers, using similar tasks, with similar participants, cast doubt on the reliability of the findings, and make it difficult to draw any conclusions about possible causes. We shall return to this point below. However, there is also the issue of the unexpected impairment in implicit memory since other studies have failed to show a deficit in implicit memory during pregnancy. These include a study by Keenan *et al.* (1998) which did report a problem in explicit memory later in pregnancy (see below), whereas Janes *et al.* (1999) failed to find a deficit in either implicit or explicit memory in pregnant or recently delivered women, though both of these groups reported more problems than women who had never been pregnant. A further study by this research group also showed no difference between non-pregnant women and either multigravid or primagravid pregnant women (Casey *et al.*, 1999). Again pregnant women reported more problems but this was not reflected in their performance. This was also the finding of Christensen *et al.* (1999). Janes *et al.* (1999) suggest as an explanation that perceptions of memory impairment are related to perceptions of sleep quality and other life changes.

Research has focused on the type of memory and the tasks used to assess memory performance. McDowall and Moriarty (2000) were particularly struck by Brindle *et al.*'s (1991) finding that implicit memory was impaired in pregnant women but memory for deliberately learned material was unaffected. They therefore attempted to replicate and extend this finding using more discriminating tasks, but still found no differences in either implicit or explicit memory between a group of 32 pregnant women and a matched group of 32 non-pregnant women. However, as in other studies we have reviewed above, the pregnant women reported their memory as being worse. Both Christensen *et al.* (1999) and McDowall and Moriarty (2000) criticised the tasks used by Brindle and his co-researchers to test implicit and explicit memory, and particularly proposed that their tests of implicit memory may allow some deliberate learning of material. Nevertheless, despite overcoming this problem in their own studies, neither group found deficits in pregnant women.

So most published studies report no impairment in implicit memory, but what are the findings when pregnant women are explicitly instructed to remember material? Keenan *et al.* (1998) used a longitudinal design to compare memory in women throughout pregnancy and in the postpartum period with matched non-pregnant women. They found a decline in memory in the pregnant group between the second and third trimester, whereby both immediate and delayed recall of paragraphs was impaired. The poorer performance did not seem to be related to depression or anxiety: although the pregnant women were more depressed and anxious on average over the period of the study, the occasions when their memory performance was impaired did not coincide with those occasions when they were more depressed or anxious.

Lurie *et al.* (2005) also found deficits in late pregnancy, but in this case the comparison was to the women's own four months after the birth. No measures were taken earlier in pregnancy. By contrast, de Groot *et al.* (2003b) tested 71 women much earlier in pregnancy (at 14 weeks) and compared their performance with that of matched non-pregnant women. They found small deficits in intentional learning and in memory which involves processing the meaning of material (both aspects of explicit memory). We have discussed above the hypothesis that cognition might improve during pregnancy, and a few studies have found a cognitive improvement. Schneider (1989) studied women's performance prior to conception and weekly during pregnancy. Not only was there no evidence of impairment but all improved during pregnancy. Christensen *et al.* (1999) also found that their participants recognised more pregnancy-related words.

Another aspect of cognition which has been studied is attention. Poor attention may be the basis underlying problems with learning and memory, since people have to attend to material, whether consciously or unconsciously, in order to learn and remember it. In contrast to most studies, Ros Crawley (2002) found little evidence of self-reported deficits in cognition. In reports of changes experienced by 198 women during pregnancy, only 2 per cent spontaneously included cognitive changes. When questioned specifically on this, the majority reported no changes. Crawley concludes that for most women such problems are not a salient part of pregnancy, though women could readily provide incidents of cognitive failure during pregnancy and after the birth when prompted to do so.

However, in a prospective longitudinal study conducted by Crawley *et al.* (2003) self-assessment ratings showed that in the second trimester the pregnant women rated themselves as more impaired than before compared to the non-pregnant women. No deficits in performance were found on tests of memory or attention.

In a second longitudinal study (Crawley *et al.*, 2003) the researchers compared 25 pregnant and 10 non-pregnant women using daily ratings over a period of one week on four occasions during pregnancy and the first year post partum. In this study it was women in the third trimester who reported mild impairments in their focused and divided attention and memory. Taken together the results of these two longitudinal studies show that there are perceived cognitive impairments during pregnancy. Crawley and her co-researchers suggest that the objective tests may not be sensitive enough to reveal these mild impairments, because the women are able to complete them successfully by making more effort. However they also suggest that the self-report may result from depression or expectations of lower performance rather than from actual impairments.

De Groot *et al.* (2003b) also studied women longitudinally. They found that selective attention, that is, the ability to concentrate on one aspect of the environment or task to the exclusion of others, was impaired in pregnant women late in pregnancy (i.e. at 36 weeks) when compared to non-pregnant women and their own performance 32 weeks after the birth. Studies conducted by Woodfield (1984) and by Silber *et al.* (1990) found that pregnant women's performance in attentional tasks improved more over the time following childbirth than non-pregnant women over the same period. They interpret this as meaning that performance is depressed during pregnancy, though the results could show that women's attention improves after childbirth. On the other hand, Harris *et al.* (1996) tested women in the last month of pregnancy, and two days and four weeks after delivery. Compared with a group of non-pregnant women matched on age and IQ, they performed worse on digit symbol and paced auditory serial addition tests, but only 48 hours after delivery (i.e. not when they were pregnant). However, the women who had been recruited when pregnant were all more depressed throughout the study and cognitive impairment was correlated with the severity of depression: all differences became non-significant when the effect of depression was controlled.

Most studies which assume that memory and other cognitive impairments are caused by hormonal change do not actually measure those changes directly. This may be because researchers assume that the changes are so large that there will be little inter-individual difference. However, all studies of self-reported cognitive dysfunction find variation between women in the extent to which they report such problems. There are some studies which have attempted to link changes in cognition to changes in measured circulating hormones.

Silber *et al.* (1990) linked cognitive performance to oxytocin levels; these rise slightly throughout pregnancy but then rise sharply just before the birth. In their study, 20 pregnant women were tested five times: towards the end of pregnancy and then four times in the 12 months post partum. On each occasion, memory and attention were tested and oxytocin concentrations were measured in blood samples. Twenty non-pregnant women were given the same test schedule. Pregnant women's performance actually improved more than controls when results at 6 and 12 months after delivery were compared with those from the end of pregnancy and up to three months after birth. Oxytocin concentrations were obviously higher in pregnant women than in non-pregnant women up to three months post partum. However, there was no association between test performance and oxytocin levels, suggesting that this is not a primary cause of changes in cognition.

Keenan *et al.* (1998) investigated changes in oestrogen and progesterone and their relationship with mood and cognitive change. They found that pregnant women were poorer on remembering learned paragraphs in the third trimester, and they reported more depression and anxiety (though only on the somatic symptoms). However, although oestrogen and progesterone levels were much higher in the pregnant group, the variation within that group was not accounted for by differences in these levels. And indeed the authors point out that their own work on in vitro fertilisation showed that high doses of oestrogen did not impair memory.

Buckwalter *et al.* (1999) also measured progesterone levels in women in the third trimester and then shortly after delivery. On a battery of tests the participants showed deficits in some aspects of verbal memory during pregnancy and reported poorer mood. Although higher progesterone levels were related to mood, neither progesterone level nor mood related to memory deficits. So again hormonal change appears not to be a direct cause of changes in performance.

Various other hormones have been linked to cognition in pregnancy. Shetty and Pathak (2002) found decrements in memory in women in the second trimester compared with non-pregnant women. They also measured levels of epinephrine, norepinephrine and serotonin. Since levels of these hormones also dropped in the second trimester, they suggest that memory performance is linked. Taking a different approach, Vanston and Watson (2005) investigated cognitive performance in women from early pregnancy until after the birth. They found an effect of foetal sex whereby women pregnant with boys outperformed those pregnant with girls on difficult tasks requiring working memory and spatial ability.

There are other physiological changes during pregnancy which may have psychological implications, though these have received less attention. Immature red blood cells, which are less efficient carriers of haemoglobin, normally account for 1–2 per cent of the total; however, in late pregnancy the proportion rises. Lurie *et al.* (2005) hypothesised that this may lead to decrements in cognitive performance. They measured explicit and auto-biographical memory in women in late pregnancy and then four months after the birth. Only explicit memory was poorer antenatally than post-natally, and the difference was correlated with the difference in haemo-globin. Although a link has been made between the proportion of immature blood cells and cognition in older people, given the differences between levels during pregnancy and other times, it is not clear whether Lurie *et al.* were simply measuring a sign of pregnancy rather than a causal factor. However, research by Groner *et al.* (1986) suggests that anaemia may underlie memory deficits in some women. In this study, teenagers at about the 16th week of pregnancy received either iron supplements or, as a control comparison, vitamins without iron. The group which received iron supplements for a month improved slightly on sensitive measures of short-term memory.

Several studies reported above speculated that changes to sleep patterns may be related to cognitive deficits. Although many women find that their sleep is affected by pregnancy, there is variability both between women and with the stage of pregnancy, such that increased tiredness and longer time spent sleeping is reported in early and late pregnancy, and more interrupted sleep closer to the birth. As far as we are aware, no researchers have measured sleep patterns in pregnancy in relation to cognition, rather they have collected self-reported changes to sleep. Some have found a relationship between self-reports of sleep changes and of cognitive problems, but they are not usually an independent predictor of performance on cognitive tasks. Casey *et al.* (1999) found that sleep loss was related to self-reported memory change, but not any memory test performance. They suggest that changes in sleep may contribute to a perception of memory change. The same group (Janes *et al.*, 1999) found that women who had had their first baby reported more sleep disruption than pregnant and non-pregnant women, and this predicted self-reports of memory difficulties. However, the few differences they found in performance on objective tests were between non-pregnant women and both pregnant women and women who had newly delivered. The decline in explicit memory performance that Keenan *et al.* (1998) found in late pregnancy was not related to sleep deprivation.

We suggested in the introduction to this chapter that cognitive failure may accompany changes in mood, not directly the result of pregnancy but of the stress that pregnancy brings for some women. Keenan *et al.* (1998) found that pregnant women scored higher on both depression and anxiety scales; however, this was on the somatic items (i.e. referring to bodily experiences) rather than cognitive items accounted. Fluctuations in mood did not coincide with changes in memory. This study highlights the problem with measuring both depression and anxiety during pregnancy. Some symptoms of pregnancy would at other times be interpreted as symptoms of depression or anxiety. So measures of mood include items which pregnant women may endorse, even though their mood has not been affected. However, in our own work we excluded somatic symptoms of depression and anxiety from the instrument we used and found that high levels of cognitive failure were still related to higher depression and anxiety, as well as poorer psychological health prior to pregnancy (Gross and Pattison, 1995). Harris *et al.* (1996) explicitly tested the hypothesis that cognitive impairment was secondary to depression and found that cognitive dysfunction was explained by depression in their sample. However, impairment in cognition was only displayed immediately after birth, that is, not during pregnancy.

As mood is generally lower during pregnancy, several studies have controlled for depression rather than studying it as a predictive variable (e.g. Parsons *et al.*, 2004). It has also been considered as part of the adaptation or maladaptation of cognitive style to pregnancy. Affonso *et al.* (1991, 1994) have shown that attitudes to pregnancy and motherhood and cognitive adaptation to stress predict depression. More positively, Christensen *et al.* (1999) have suggested that cognitive adaptation leads to a greater focus on issues relevant to pregnancy; they found that women were better at recognising pregnancy-related words.

Of rats and women: neurological research

We reflected at the beginning of this chapter that cognitive failure during pregnancy would be curiously non-adaptive. It seems that most of the neurological research on animals supports this view. Far from finding that pregnancy is a time of cognitive degeneration, most studies find that it is a time of adaptation to the demands of parenting. Neural adaptation in rats, through the action of pregnancy hormones, results in enhancement of foraging abilities and reduction of fear responses, which lead to mothers being better able to nurture and protect their young. In contrast to the research reviewed above, the assumption of this research is not that pregnancy will be a time of cognitive debilitation, but rather a critical developmental period for essential parenting skills.

A review of the work in this area, carried out in their own and others' laboratories, is given by Craig Kinsley and Kelly Lambert in their *Scientific American* paper 'The maternal brain' (Kinsley and Lambert, 2006). They posit the argument that two essential factors for a successful rodent mother are foraging skills and a reduction of fear responses to new environments and predators. So it would make sense if brain changes during pregnancy were related to the enhancement of these. Given this, they searched for evidence of enhanced cognitive skills in rats and the neurological changes that underlie these.

Several studies have now shown that mother rats display better spatial learning and memory than matched non-mothers (Kinsley *et al.*, 1999; Love *et al.*, 2005). They learn their way around a maze more quickly and are better at remembering the location of food rewards. Work by Hester, Karp and Orthmeyer (cited in Kinsley and Lambert, 2006) has also shown that mother rats are faster than non-mothers at capturing live prey. However, the picture presented by Galea *et al.* (2000) is more mixed. They found that rats in the early and middle stages of pregnancy found their way around a water maze more quickly than non-pregnant rats, but that in the last stage of pregnancy they performed worse. It should be noted that most of the studies on rats have continued to study the mothers after they have given birth. It has been found that the improvements in foraging-type behaviour continue after the birth, seemingly stimulated by the presence of pups. Non-mothers, when given other rats' young to look after, also perform better on foraging, which Kinsley and Lambert (2006) suggest means that simply the presence of offspring can provide a boost to spatial memory, either by providing cognitive stimulation or by prompting the secretion of oxytocin. These changes can be observed long after the birth.

In understanding these improvements in skills important for successful foraging, researchers have concentrated on changes in the hippocampus, as the area of the brain underlying memory and learning. Kinsley *et al.* (1999) showed that the brains of pregnant rats, and females given pregnancy hormones, display alterations of the hippocampus. They found the concentrations of hippocampus spines to be denser. They suggest that this rise is linked to the enhanced ability of rats to navigate mazes and capture prey because these spines directly input to their associated neurons. However, Galea *et al.* (2000) reported a decrease in the volume of the hippocampus in late pregnancy.

Studies of the morphology of rats' brains have relied on post-mortem dissection. This means that comparisons are made between individuals rather than of changes in the same individual at different points in time. Developments in brain imaging have allowed researchers to study morphological changes in women's brains during pregnancy and after giving birth. Holdcroft *et al.* (1997, cited in Moore, 1997) and Holdcroft *et al.* (2005) reported a decrease in brain size in the latter stages of pregnancy, but an increase after the birth. They conclude that the implications of these changes are not clear, but Moore's article on the earlier study in the *New Scientist* (1997) started a flurry of interest in the media. The findings were broadly interpreted by non-scientists as meaning that pregnancy shrinks women's brains and that therefore their cognitive skills become permanently impaired from pregnancy onwards.

Another aspect of adaptation to motherhood predicted in rats was a reduction in fear which would enable new mothers to explore new environments and protect their young. Douglas *et al.* (2003) and Bosch *et al.* (2005) showed that pregnant rats have reduced stress hormones. And Wartella *et al.* (2003) observed that mother rats spent more time investigating new environments and were less likely to freeze. In addition, the areas of the brain that regulate stress and emotion were less active in rats after they had given birth. DiPietro *et al.* (2005) produced similar behavioural results in women. They showed that pregnant women reported finding a cognitive task (the Stroop test) more difficult but their stress response was reduced when measured by, for example, heart rate and respiration, as well as self-reported mood.

Methodological issues

The literature on the effect of pregnancy on cognition in women has grown considerably in recent years, but it has failed to produce definitive results which contribute to a body of evidence. Reviewing this literature, it is obvious that one cause of the variability in results is the quality of the research, which limits the generalisability of findings. In this section we will consider how methodological limitations may lead to the contradictory findings that we have reported, but first we will consider the issue of publication bias.

It is well recognised that the published scientific literature is biased in favour of papers that produce results which accord with the predictions of the authors and can be explained by the theories put forward in the paper. Exceptions to this are papers which can disprove commonly held beliefs, or, more commonly in the psychology literature, papers which produce convincing reasons for doubting the current canon. In this chapter we have seen several papers which fall into these categories. For example, Brindle *et al.* (1991) produced evidence that pregnant women have problems with memory (a commonly held belief) and Christensen *et al.* (1999) produced evidence that challenged this belief, that is, that pregnant women actually performed better in some cognitive tasks. More rarely published are studies which fail to find evidence for the theories the authors expect to explain behaviour. An example of this type of paper is McDowall and Moriarty's (2000) study which set out to show that Brindle *et al.*'s results were artefactual, and that during pregnancy women are impaired in explicit rather than implicit memory tasks. However, they found support for neither type of impairment. The failure of journals to publish more papers of this type runs the risk that papers which fail to show cognitive change of any type are simply not published and therefore theory is not developed on the basis of all the evidence.

Turning now to methodological issues, one of the most striking aspects of papers in this area is the low number of participants. For example, Harris *et al.* (1996) used only 20 pregnant and 20 non-pregnant women, Silber *et al.* (1990) had similar numbers and Parsons *et al.* (2004) based their findings on a comparison of seven women expecting their first baby and nine multigravid women. One of Brindle *et al.*'s (1991) main findings was that women expecting their first baby are more likely to show cognitive deficits and particularly those who are in the second trimester. However, the total number of women expecting their first baby in this study was 15, and, of those, four were in the first trimester, six in the second and five in the third. This would not be so much of a problem if these studies only involved a few variables, but multiple comparisons of several variables with few participants makes it more likely that the analyses will produce one or more significant results by chance (i.e. 'type 1' errors). This may help to account for why some researchers find that pregnant women have a particular cognitive deficit while other researchers find a different impairment.

Many studies only make comparisons between women, usually a group of pregnant women and a group of non-pregnant women, or women at different stages of pregnancy, rather than comparing a woman's performance, behaviour or perceptions at different times. The danger here is that the underlying differences between women may be larger than any that are brought about by pregnancy. Unless participants are very carefully matched on relevant factors such as intelligence and age, this design of study can lead to real differences being undetected, and spurious differences between groups being reported. Systematic bias can creep in when comparisons are made between groups that have some underlying difference.

Since so many factors can affect a person's cognitive performance and their perception of their own cognitive skills, quantitative research should either employ large numbers of participants (see above) or study participants longitudinally.

Self-report studies, where women are asked about their own perceptions of their cognitive state during pregnancy, are often retrospective. In the case of Poser *et al.*'s (1986) study, for several of the participants it had been years since the birth of their children. At the opposite end of the spectrum, the first of Parson and Redman's studies (1991) was carried out within three days of the women giving birth. Most psychologists would caution against retrospective research because the findings are likely to be contaminated by what has happened since the period being reported on. Accounts of pregnancy collected after a woman has given birth are likely to be coloured by the experience of the demands of motherhood, when sleep disturbance is much closer to that experienced by junior doctors on call, and the physical demands of feeding and childcare often lead to fatigue.

However, there is one aspect of pregnancy research which almost inevitably leads to retrospective data collection. This is the gathering of information about women's cognitive functioning and health before pregnancy. Conducting prospective research with women prior to conception in order to follow them through to delivery is usually prohibitively expensive. Very large numbers of women are needed if a representative sample of pregnant women is to be recruited. Advertising for women who are intending to become pregnant will result in a biased sample of women who are planning their pregnancy. Such people are likely to differ in important ways from women who simply do nothing to avoid pregnancy, or who become pregnant through contraception failure. So it is necessary to rely on women's recollections, as we did in our study, or to use proxy variables (e.g. age, educational attainment) to match women who are likely to experience the same level of cognitive problems, as in Parsons *et al.* (2004).

A major source of bias in the studies of women we have reviewed in this chapter is that in many studies participants are told not only what the researchers are investigating, but what they are expecting to find. An example of this is given in Poser *et al.*'s (1986) paper. The researchers recruited women by sending out a questionnaire with an accompanying letter describing in detail one woman's experience in order to illustrate what kinds of cognitive change they were investigating. The account given in the letter begins as follows:

> In the most general terms, I felt incredibly stupid. My concentration was poor, my secretaries noted that they had to remind me of things more often, and that I was prone to omitting words in writing and dictation.

and concludes:

> Associate thinking must have been a problem, as one of the first
> things I noticed was an inability to complete the Sunday *New York
> Times* crossword puzzle.
>
> (Poser *et al.*, 1986: 40)

There are two effects of recruiting people in this way. First, women who
have not experienced such problems are unlikely to participate as they
assume they have nothing to contribute, leaving aside those for whom
having several secretaries and completing the *New York Times* crossword
are such alien concepts that they would assume the researchers are not
interested in people like them. The second effect is that women are likely to
attribute any problems they can remember to pregnancy, rather than other
factors, and if asked to complete a cognitive test they will expect to do
poorly. In other areas of research on cognition, for example ageing, self-
scrutiny of performance with the expectation that it will be worse than
expected leads to more lapses being noticed and attributed to the factor in
question, and/or a reduction in self-efficacy. Clearly this is not a problem
with rodent participants, but the situation is complicated in women by the
reflexivity of the participants. Expectations and beliefs about performance
can affect performance in apparently objective tasks. Telling women that
you expect them to perform worse during pregnancy or even that you are
investigating cognitive performance during pregnancy sanctions women to
perform poorly in tests that require effort to complete successfully.

As psychologists, ethical concerns demand that we should inform prospective participants of the nature of our research, the reasons why we are
conducting it and the type of study or experiment for which they are
volunteering. Researchers from other disciplines are bound by similar
guidelines issued by professional bodies. Commendable though this practice is in its aim to protect the wellbeing of those we study, it undoubtedly
leads to bias in recruitment to the study and in the way in which women
respond to questioning and tasks they are set.

Concluding remarks

We have found that the literature on cognitive change in pregnancy is
inconsistent, and has failed to produce a convincing body of evidence
that such change occurs. However, there remains a persistent belief that
women's memory, attention and ability to plan deteriorate to such an
extent during pregnancy that everyday tasks are affected. Indeed, it is this
belief that has driven much of the research covered in this chapter rather
than the predictions of theoretical models of mechanisms which would
account for such deterioration.

Many studies are essentially a-theoretical, looking for more convincing evidence of anecdotal reports and investigating the nature of deficits. Hypotheses about explanatory mechanisms may be added as an after-thought in a paper's discussion (e.g. Woodfield, 1984) or in the introduction to studies, but with no subsequent measurement of salient variables (e.g. Brindle *et al.*, 1991). The most common hypothesis, certainly in earlier work, and whether or not it was tested, is that pregnant women's cognitive functioning is affected by raised levels of circulating hormones. This hypothesis helps us to understand the nature of the research that has been conducted and the interpretation of results. As levels of the key hormones (progesterone, oestrogen and, at the end of pregnancy, oxytocin) are so much higher during pregnancy than at any other time, most studies simply look for differences between pregnant and non-pregnant women. The assumption that changes in behaviour and psychological health during pregnancy must be hormonally driven is pervasive. This is reminiscent of research on the menstrual cycle and particularly PMS. Anne Walker has written about research on PMS:

> PMS has been seen as so obviously hormonally related that explicit theorising is not a requirement for research [. . .] this failure has resulted in poor integration of findings and inconclusive data.
> (Walker, 1995: 799)

Theories which link behavioural change in pregnancy to hormonal change are in danger of being tautological, because describing women as having raised levels of pregnancy hormones is usually simply another way of describing women as pregnant. The crucial underlying belief here, though, as we suggested at the beginning of this chapter, is that pregnancy is synonymous with debilitation. It is all the more striking then that evidence from studies with animals suggests that pregnancy hormones, particularly oestrogen, actually have a positive effect on learning and memory. Research with women is conducted largely in the expectation of cognitive failure; research with rats is conducted largely with the expectation of cognitive enhancement. Contrast the following extracts:

> It is important to investigate scientifically such anecdotal reports (of memory loss) since pregnancy is experienced at least once by a large sector of the population. Memory loss in pregnant women could adversely affect their compliance with medical instructions: pregnant women are a particular target for health education.
> (Sharp *et al.*, 1993: 209)

> When a female mammal makes the transition from virginity to motherhood, she is forced to refocus her activities dramatically.

43

She must adapt to a multitude of new demands by her offspring
[. . .] The performance of these tasks may depend on a sharpening
of her cognitive abilities.

(Kinsley *et al.*, 1999: 137)

We cannot, of course, dismiss the reports by women themselves that
pregnancy is a time when they feel cognitively challenged. With a few
exceptions, most studies found that a high proportion of women reported
their cognitive abilities to be worse than before pregnancy or reported
more symptoms of cognitive failure: 59 per cent (Brindle *et al.*, 1991), 82
per cent (Parsons and Redman, 1991), 91 per cent (Schneider, 1989). The
proportion reporting these problems does not seem to link with whether or
not impairments were found on cognitive tasks: the women in Schneider's
study actually improved on cognitive tasks from the beginning to the end
of pregnancy. However, it should be noted that in all these studies women
were directly asked about cognitive impairments. As Morris (1983) has
pointed out, one of the problems with self-reports of memory is acqui-
escence, with some people more likely to agree with statements which are
couched in positive terms. One notable exception to the general trend of
high levels of reported problems is Ros Crawley's (2002) work, which
showed that only 2 per cent of the 258 women questioned spontaneously
mentioned cognitive changes when asked about any changes they had
noticed in themselves during pregnancy. Nevertheless, the psychology
literature offers several hypotheses which would predict this impairment
during pregnancy. Two in particular seem apposite. First, we know that
people are more likely to notice cognitive failures when they are under
stress, and particularly if they have a tendency to report cognitive failures
generally. Although the evidence is mixed, women who report being
stressed or depressed do tend to report more incidences of problems during
pregnancy. Second, we know that the reporting of cognitive failure is more
common among people who are more self-conscious and self-orientated.
Pregnancy is a time when women who have these cognitive styles may
monitor their own behaviour and feelings particularly closely. In our own
study (Gross and Pattison, 1995), we found that women who reported
experiencing PMS before pregnancy were the women who were more likely
to report cognitive failure during pregnancy. We know of no other study
which has specifically measured this, but we suggest that women who
report PMS may be either more aware of subtle changes or have an
expectation of change associated with reproductive events and therefore
attribute any cognitive failures to their pregnant state.

These types of explanations go some way to understanding individual
differences in self-reports and the discrepancy between self-report and
objective tests. Are there other reasons for these, and why does research
with women generally find deficits in cognition whereas studies with other

animals generally find improvements? Striving to understand cognitive skills, particularly memory, through carefully controlled, objective tests, psychologists and other researchers seldom study the kind of memory failures that are regarded as important by lay people. Although attempts are made to make findings relevant and applicable to everyday life, psychologists are still more likely to be found testing memory for lists of words than the ability to remember an antenatal appointment. The development of questionnaires such as the Cognitive Failure Questionnaire, and the use of cognitive diaries, was in part an attempt to tap the kind of cognitive impairment that has an impact of people's everyday lives. So perhaps tests of cognition such as explicit memory tests are not close enough to real tasks to reveal deficits of which women are aware.

The belief that women experience cognitive impairment during pregnancy has a real effect on women's lives. As we and others have shown, such beliefs affect the way that women are treated by employers and fellow workers (Pattison and Gross, 1996; Pattison, Gross and Cast, 1997). Jackson et al. (1996) found that up to 30 per cent of registered midwives have negative attitudes to women's ability to learn during pregnancy.

Several of the studies we review here found no evidence of cognitive deficits during pregnancy. The following quotations are taken from two such studies:

> Pregnant women and new mothers generally should be confident of performing to their normal cognitive capabilities, but may be more affected than usual by a high cognitive load.
>
> (Casey et al., 1999: 158)

> It is argued that the cognitive efficiency of workers is not compromised by pregnancy but steps should be taken to ensure that work load is adjusted to take account of the self-reported reduced arousal that may arise.
>
> (Morris et al., 1998: 377)

As the above quotations illustrate, even when researchers find no evidence of cognitive deficits, their conclusions or recommendations may suggest that women should assume that they have. The strength of the expectation of an association between pregnancy and cognitive debilitation seems to override research findings to the contrary, and leads the researchers quoted here to undermine their own research.

4

BEING PREGNANT AT WORK
Pregnancy and employment

Work is one of the predominant components of everybody's daily life. Employment is not only a means of achieving economic security or independence; it has psychological importance. At its best, work can provide opportunities for self-fulfilment, self-identity, creativity, social engagement and the success of shared goals, skills or activities. At its worst, the money helps. Statistics show that the majority of women are in employment and women of childbearing age are therefore likely to be working when they become pregnant for the first time (Eurostat, 2004). Immediately, however, the conjunction of pregnancy and work (by which we mean paid employment) invokes a variety of potential discourses concerning the role of women in the public domain. Thus, the topic of work, and the research on women, work and pregnancy, refer directly to the debates we have alluded to in the discussions of the medicalisation of pregnancy and childbirth and the normalisation of pregnancy through the predominance of the bio-medical tradition. Furthermore, the issues of cognition and performance we discussed in the previous chapter can be regarded as integral to perceptions of women when they are pregnant in the workplace.

To examine these issues, we review some of the work on the associations identified between pregnancy, work and health, particularly the health of the baby, and we examine aspects of women's experiences at work when they are pregnant, with a view to explaining how pregnancy is perceived in the workplace. In so doing, we will raise a number of issues which characterise the discourses of pregnancy and pregnancy research and which are revisited through the book. First we look at the impact of pregnancy on the workplace by reviewing evidence describing women's experiences of announcing their pregnancy and being pregnant at work. We go on to explore how these experiences might be explained. We then consider whether or how employment affects pregnancy, and the relationship between pregnancy, employment and pregnancy or birth outcome. Finally, we examine the products of research described, in terms of the advice and information about working that women may encounter and their behaviour in response to it. In the process of looking at how pregnancy affects work, we make use of a range of research arising from a perceived need to address social policy and employment practices as well as psychological or health concerns addressed through academic studies of the topic. In considering the way that work may affect pregnancy, we draw on the epidemiological and physiological literature on factors influencing pregnancy outcome as well as that examining the relationship between work and health.

Information on working during pregnancy comes from qualitative surveys of women and their employers investigating the implementation and experience of maternity rights, such as those by Rodmell and Smart (1982), O'Grady and Wakefield (1989), McRae (1991, 1996) and a report from the National Association of Citizens Advice Bureaux (NACAB, 1992). There are some experimental studies of pregnancy and employment, including our own (Corse, 1990; Halpert *et al.*, 1993; Pattison *et al.*, 1997), together with some more anecdotal work, for example Baildam (1991). Popular women's magazines, and publications aimed at pregnant women, also address these issues (Gross and Pattison, 2001). In other work of our own we have interviewed pregnant women about their experience at work and we will give some examples from these interviews. The largely quantitative literature on outcomes is extensive and could form the substance of an entire book; only a sample of this is discussed here. There are a number of other texts that address similar issues from different perspectives, which are not reviewed here but provide fascinating additional material on the tricky work/life balance that has come to represent modern working life in the twenty-first century (Brannen and Moss, 1988; Devlin, 1995; Humphries and Gordon, 1993). Our particular interest is on the period of pregnancy itself rather than on the related concerns of managing childcare and returning to work. These are significant concerns in their own right which naturally follow from pregnancy but are not the focus of this book. Nevertheless, it is likely that pregnancy irretrievably affects women's relationship with paid employment.

Announcing a pregnancy at work

Given women's current employment participation rates, it might be assumed that pregnancy would be unremarkable in the workplace. But this is not necessarily the case: in 2003, a news item covered the outcome of an industrial tribunal that had found in favour of a lawyer who had been dismissed from her job while pregnant (*BBC Radio News*, 2003). McGlynn's (1996) concern appeared to hold true: 'advances so far gained in relation to pregnancy dismissals do not yet reflect a cultural shift in attitudes and consequently vigilance and continued campaigning is required to improve the real situation of women in the workplace' (McGlynn, op. cit.: 229). Recent statistics confirm this (Dunstan, 2002; EOC, 2005; James,

2004). Of the 440,000 working women who become pregnant in Great Britain each year, almost half can expect to experience some form of disadvantage at work and as many as 30,000 will be forced out of their jobs while they are pregnant. Such figures clearly demonstrate that for a significant number of women being pregnant at work is seen as unacceptable in some way, prompting commentators to liken such treatment to outdated Victorian values rather than suited to the twenty-first century (*The Guardian*, 2 May 2003). Women's experiences of responses to pregnancy announcements catalogued by research findings show that these can take several forms.

Rodmell and Smart (1982) interviewed 30 pregnant women at work in London about their experiences. The women represented a range of non-professional work where women were and still are commonly employed: as carers, in catering or in clerical jobs. Although women found work physically tiring, most felt able to cope well and said that they preferred to be at work rather than sitting at home. This was despite the fact that when asked how their managers had responded to the news of their pregnancy, the women indicated that attitudes had varied from positive, through indifferent, to some cases where they were described as contemptuous. The women also talked about the responses from their direct colleagues; this was reported as more positive from female colleagues than male ones, with women saying that by and large their female colleagues were really pleased for them. In contrast, several women reported that men used the fact that pregnancy was not an illness but a normal event as an excuse not to be helpful or even pleasant, and were resentful that the women were going to be paid to take time off. Interestingly, some participants were sympathetic to their colleagues' feelings of resentment and acknowledged the difficulties that follow for all workers when someone is going to be off work for a length of time.

In their survey published seven years later, O'Grady and Wakefield (1989) highlight similar findings. Their survey involved 250 women and they summarise the responses of managers and colleagues to the news of a woman's pregnancy as generally positive. Women also reported a neutral response to the news from their boss as a good response, perhaps suggesting that negative comments are so obviously unpleasant that anything less than overt hostility is seen as positive. Overall, these women too reported that their female colleagues were more interested in their pregnancy announcement than their male colleagues. However, as in Rodmell and Smart's (1982) study, men's negative comments and responses often centred around the rights of pregnant women to pay and particularly to leave, on the grounds that maternity pay was a woman's benefit not available to them and that maternity leave was seen as basically a paid holiday. Some older women were resentful that they had not had the chance to benefit from newer maternity provisions themselves. Hence, it is not only the pregnancy itself but also the consequences of the pregnancy for the rest of the employees that may create tensions in a workplace, and both their own current and future state have to be managed by pregnant women while they are working.

In Europe there are formal health and safety requirements, involving risk assessments, to move women to less dangerous working environments when they are pregnant. There are also institutional policies with regard to pregnancy and alterations to working conditions, as well as rights for pay and reinstatement following leave. Rodmell and Smart's (1982) findings suggest that arrangements to reorganise work or to change jobs to take account of more risky activities, for example using heavier cleaning equipment, or to cover during maternity leave, were frequently the result of informal arrangements with fellow workers rather than with their managers. Informal arrangements can break down through no fault of the individuals concerned and any arrangements can mean, of course, that women are not necessarily taken out of dangerous or physically demanding jobs, even when they should be. A further problem with informal arrangements was that the women concerned felt that their colleagues were doing them favours and this in itself caused the women anxieties about not letting fellow workers down, not being fair to them or getting them into trouble. Even when formal arrangements are made in an organisation, they are not always helpful. The relationship between the rhetoric of the legal requirements and the practice is exemplified by the case of a nurse, considered to be at risk working within a radiology department when pregnant, who was moved to a job involving anaesthetic gases, even though these carry as great a risk as radiation. It is also the case that changes in the employing organisation can effectively be used to ease women out of jobs while on maternity leave. Though this is against the law, there are many cases in literature where employers' responses have been aggressive and discriminatory, seeking to prevent women from working long enough to claim their rights to maternity benefits or to create grounds for dismissal. For example, 'When the client discovered she was pregnant, her employer indicated his "moral outrage" at her unmarried state . . . and told her that he will reduce her salary by 40% on the grounds that she is not doing her job satisfactorily' (NACAB, 1992: 9).

Taking such an unhelpful line in response to a pregnancy announcement is not the only way that the experience at work can be affected. The women in Rodmell and Smart's (1982) survey said that personal comments increased: comments about their appearance or their size that would not otherwise have been made. 'I mean, I got a lot of comments about my bum or my body looking like some revolting blob' (op. cit.: 104). They also had to cope with some people's embarrassment, particularly younger people. In O'Grady and Wakefield's (1989) survey, they reported that men who were not directly unpleasant nevertheless behaved in ways that would normally be considered unacceptable or even as harassment, such as patting a woman's stomach and making comments on fertility, on size and shape. Comments on appearance are a common finding, even a ground for dismissal, as in the case of a care attendant dismissed by her proprietor who told her 'it isn't very nice having someone with a big belly working here' (NACAB, 1992: 9). O'Grady and Wakefield (1989) showed that marital status was another factor that affected how women were treated at work. Like the client in the quote above, some single women reported that their colleagues were 'shocked' that they were pregnant and not planning to marry: 'All my difficulties stemmed from being unmarried – but my pregnancy was deliberate. I was expected to marry straightaway. In fact I only returned to my job through lying and saying I am now married' (ibid.: 7). In our own interviews with pregnant women there were similar comments about marital status, especially addressed to the youngest women: 'people at work said I was too young' (Kirsty, age 17). The most recent Equal Opportunities Commission (EOC) survey (EOC, 2005) found that disabled women who became pregnant were dismayed to be asked questions that colleagues had no right to ask, such as how they became pregnant and whether they should have.

Rodmell and Smart (1982) summarise their findings as demonstrating that the responses of co-workers and management to the presence of a pregnant woman in the workplace were experienced by the women in the study as implicitly dismissive, even where ridicule was not intended. In order to explain away what they obviously found upsetting or disconcerting responses from people they regarded as friends or colleagues, some women resorted to blaming themselves. They suggested that they were being oversensitive and therefore reacting to situations in an atypical way. Indeed, in an attempt to distance themselves further from the personal criticism they felt they had attracted, they accounted for their own sensitivities as the effect of their hormones. Pregnancy can hardly be considered routine in the workplace, when women have to negotiate this complex positioning of both their colleagues and themselves.

Women's experiences at work when they are pregnant are not solely the result of personal interactions. In a study of 2,250 pregnant women, Cherry (1987) examined the physical demands of work during the last three months of pregnancy. She found that 20 per cent of the women studied were required to stand for four hours or more every day, some with their back bent over work or handling loads with a twisted position. In most cases women could take a break when they felt it necessary but 8 per cent (still nearly 200 women) had to sit or stand for two or more hours at a stretch. The incidence of fatigue, varicose veins, back problems and breathlessness were all found to be related to general or specific job demands like these. Very few women in Rodmell and Smart's survey of pregnant women had regular and permitted access to rest facilities; many were not allowed to sit down during the working day, and this refusal has been the basis of employment tribunal cases for constructive dismissal over a number of years. Women in the 2005 EOC survey also reported that although they were told they were allowed to sit down regularly by the health and safety assessor, managers overrode this permission because by sitting down 'they didn't look busy'. Furthermore, for some women who were expected to wear a uniform or protective clothing at work, there was not always an alternative version available for pregnant women. Indeed, many workplaces, workstations and much equipment and protective clothing are adaptable for overweight people but not for pregnant women. Not having appropriate work clothes made the women feel self-conscious and drew attention to their state, making comments more likely.

The emphasis so far has been on negative experiences, since it is these that give such cause for concern. However, it is important not to automatically assume that all women will be treated the same way, since all the studies mentioned also found that women had had a positive experience, with colleagues and managers being extremely supportive and thoughtful. A small survey of maternity policy in practice in Eire found that during their pregnancy women were treated well; the difficulties arose when they returned to work (Brady *et al.*, 1999). Importantly, however, the difficulties that women encounter in the workplace do not necessarily detract from the benefits that women gain in working. One woman in Rodmell and Smart's (1982) survey commented that she found her work easier, because she felt 'centred' and 'calm'. The emotional high of pregnancy can thus carry women through the more negative aspects of their working experiences during this 'special' time.

Nonetheless, an extremely important issue raised by women in several of the studies was that they no longer felt that they had the same employment status as they had done before they were pregnant (and this has implications for return to work too). Women found themselves excluded from training courses or promotion-linked activities, and this they felt was 'not exactly direct discrimination' but a form of exclusion. One woman quoted in the summary report of the EOC survey (*Greater Expectations*, EOC, 2005: 2) said that she felt treated like an 'outsider' the minute that she found out she was pregnant. O'Grady and Wakefield's (1989) earlier study reported very similar comments together with some incidents of demotion or problems with promotion. There seemed to be an expectation that, once pregnant, women would no longer be as interested in work as before, and would probably not return to their job after maternity leave. In some cases this was taken to the extreme of appointing a permanent replacement before any final decision had been made about a woman's return to work following her leave. Kate Figes, in her book *Because of Her Sex*, also gives examples of harsh treatment, for example the dismissal of a woman, who had taken a week's annual leave following the announcement of her pregnancy, because the employer did not like the woman's attitude (Figes, 1994).

It is usually the case that by looking at a series of findings over time, it is possible to demonstrate a change for the better. This is not so in the treatment of pregnant women at work. Depressingly, the experiences described by Rodmell and Smart's study published in 1982 and the EOC surveys of 2005 are almost interchangeable, whether this is the negative responses to pregnancy announcement, the feelings of exclusion and lack of opportunities or the intrusive personal comments. While many women do report a positive experience, given the extent of possible negative treatment, it is perhaps not entirely unexpected that pregnancy also provides some women with an opportunity to give up work that they have disliked (Harris and Campbell, 1999). The consistency of the comments and findings over time suggests that there is nevertheless a persisting resistance to pregnancy in the workplace.

The frequency of pregnancy discrimination highlighted by these studies draws attention to the different ways in which pregnancy continues to be represented in different domains, as we alluded to in Chapter 2. As we have discussed, pregnancy can be seen as a normal event that is treated in many ways as an abnormal one, and women are treated accordingly. The explanations appear to draw on not only social and cultural norms and expectations of women and of women when they are pregnant but to incorporate knowledge which arises in part from research on pregnancy. Such research, in turn, depending on its rationale or theoretical position, both colludes with and challenges these representations. As with the other topics we are addressing in this book, the area of pregnancy and employment is a good example of how conflicting and confusing evidence can be and how entrenched attitudes and beliefs about pregnancy remain.

Why is pregnancy still so stigmatised within the workplace?

There are a number of explanations that might provide pointers to the way that pregnancy is situated within the public perception and why it continues to provoke such negative responses in the workplace. As the evidence suggests, treatment may reflect current socio-political and cultural attitudes to women in the workplace more generally. Discourses of femininity brought into play by the crossing of private and public boundaries through the visibility of pregnancy may present difficulties for women wishing to maintain their role as worker, and for employers and colleagues (Gross and Pattison, 2001). Alternatively, the persistence of negative treatment may result from the cultural perception of pregnancy as an ambiguous health state, falling between a natural healthy experience and a health state requiring medical attention. This is emphasised by the legislation which allows time off for visits to hospital and clinics, as well as maternity leave itself. The association of pregnancy with sickness can lead to problems (Hanlon, 1995), since the ideology surrounding pregnancy as a healthy or sick state may affect women's own views of themselves as competent workers or as responsible mothers and their colleagues' expectations of pregnant women's performance (Pattison *et al.*, 1997). The various explanations proposed are not mutually exclusive but represent a means by which the complexity of the issues, which are not exclusive to employment, can be explored.

Private life/public activity boundaries

The first of these concerns the overlap between the private and the public. At a fundamental level, pregnancy very obviously brings into the workplace aspects of a person's private life that are normally restricted to conversations between close friends or family (though they may create the subject for jokes and gossip at work). The working environment comprises a mix of managers, subordinates, colleagues and friends, all of whom may have different responses to this visible transgression of privacy. The visibility of pregnancy as the representation of reproductive fertility and of sexuality can transgress boundaries, here between home and work, which may normally be carefully policed. For example, workers may wish to display their commitment and adherence to the hegemonic male model of work.

An interesting anthropological study of a North American working environment, referred to as The Laboratory, demonstrates the way that home and work boundaries can be created and maintained by different types of workers and artefacts (Nippert-Eng, 1996). Nippert-Eng points to the variety of ways that such boundaries are represented, for example by the restriction of personal telephone calls, the availability of places to put personal effects and the degree of freedom to carry work equipment between home and workplace, as well as the integration of domestic and work items, such as keys or addresses, onto combined keyrings or home address files, and socialising with work colleagues out of work time. She describes both individuals and workplaces as integrative or segmenting, that is, those that encourage or allow a crossing over of the private into the public arena and those that do not. In this context she says: 'it is hard to imagine anything more fundamentally, undeniably integrating than a visibly pregnant worker. A pregnancy is a powerful souvenir of home life. It brings the very essence of home into the workplace in its most sacred form' (Nippert-Eng, 1996: 213).

In an integrative workplace, pregnancy may enhance a family-friendly environment and Nippert-Eng describes the experience of three women who became pregnant around the same time within The Laboratory's personnel section. For them, pregnancy was a highly positive experience, with the women sharing notes and discussing their progress with each other and other members of their group. In addition, they became more friendly outside work than they had been before their pregnancies. However, significantly, such harmony was not the case elsewhere in the same organisation and by contrast 'it [pregnancy] seriously, undeniably challenges . . . more segmentist groups. More than anything else, the varying treatment of pregnant women in the workplace shows that "pollution" is in the eye of the beholder' (op. cit.: 214). In clarifying this position, Nippert-Eng cites the case of a worker who found that on announcing her pregnancy not a single departmental member commented on it throughout the ante- and postnatal period and most avoided her altogether. This extreme response, which might in other circumstances be described as discrimination, chimes with reports in the EOC study (2005) of the ways that women were treated, which included not speaking to them and ignoring their presence. Clearly, pregnancy can really create problems in maintaining boundaries for others and calls into question the way that women are perceived and how they are able to function in their work roles when at work.

One reason that this public/private distinction is so powerful may be because of continuing strongly held beliefs that it is a woman's primary duty to care for her family. Working during pregnancy may be seen as simply inconsistent with that belief. Furthermore, the boundary shifts between the personal/private and the workplace, and the associated links with taboo images of women, can mean that it is seen as inappropriate, offensive or embarrassing to have pregnant women in the workplace at all. In part this may arise from the physical changes in body size and weight in pregnancy, which become increasingly visible as the pregnancy progresses and which may be accentuated through current fashions in maternity clothing (see also Chapter 7). This is borne out by evidence from the surveys described above, whereby women reported that they had had to change their role from receptionist to office work behind the scenes, and of having to give up working at the counter in a bank because of the potential embarrassment to customers and fellow workers. The physical changes in women's appearance can provoke a range of responses from employers and colleagues, which may affect women's experiences of working at this time, and lead to the perpetration of discriminatory behaviours by employers and colleagues.

Workplace cultures

An alternative approach to explain the findings relates to the culture of organisations. The corollary of falling birthrates is that pregnancy is less common in the workplace than it used to be. Faludi's (1992) discussion of the 'infertility epidemic' among 30-something middle-class career women suggests that the proportion of working women becoming pregnant may be very small in some types of workplace. There is some evidence from our own study of the perceptions and beliefs of fellow workers (Pattison *et al.*, 1997) that negative attitudes are more likely to be expressed by those who have no direct experience of working with or alongside pregnant women and that there are gender differences in attitudes. The findings do suggest that women are generally more positive than men about women's rights at work and pregnant women in the workplace. Even in these circumstances, however, if pregnancy is uncommon then the likelihood of poor treatment may be greater.

The relevance of the workplace culture is illustrated by findings reinforced by the EOC survey (2005) that the women most affected by discriminatory acts at work were those in lower-paid, less secure jobs, in routine occupations such as sales or customer services. More importantly, they very often worked in smaller workplaces (less than ten employees) but this does not prevent individuals in large organisations also feeling dismayed by their treatment or under pressure to perform once they have announced their pregnancy, and professional women are by no means exempt from discrimination. In Rodmell and Smart's (1982) survey there appeared to be no difference between the type of employer and the nature of their response, though the number of women in the study and therefore of employers was small. McRae (1991) suggests that there are differences whereby employers in the public sector tend to be better informed about maternity policy and rights, which have in the past caused problems for some employers, for example replacement of staff while on maternity leave or holding jobs open (Callender *et al.*, 1997). Other factors contribute to poor experiences, as research shows that refusals from employers to grant favourable arrangements during pregnancy were actually more frequent when working conditions were tiring and that taking sick leave was more common when working conditions were hard and job adjustment was not made by employers to accommodate pregnant workers (Saurel-Cubizolles *et al.*, 1991; Strand *et al.*, 1997).

Employers' attitudes are by their own admission in part driven by the need to balance the requirements of legislation and their costs with running a competitive business: 'If you have a list of people with equal merits, I might be more inclined to employ a bloke as he is not going to get pregnant' (EOC, 2004: 22). This is despite findings that where employers and organisations provide a supportive environment, they appear to take their women workers seriously and regard good support as a sound business investment in their workforce. This is especially important given that women who feel badly treated during their pregnancy are less likely to return to work and those who feel supported are more likely to return to work (Killien, 2005; Lyness *et al.*, 1999). Some very small businesses have trained every member of staff to do another person's job so that one person's absence does not cause disruption to the business. Evidently, it is possible to create a supportive culture and it makes economic sense to do so. It requires a willingness to see women as equal partners in the workplace and pregnancy as a normal and manageable event.

The difficulties highlighted by workplace culture may reside in the gap between policy and practice. The danger would seem to lie where women lose the confidence of their manager or colleagues if they become pregnant. In an organisation where a time limit operates on work completion, so that a project ends after the individual running it is on maternity leave, it is not difficult to see how misunderstandings can arise. The resolution of such issues is undoubtedly one that causes problems even in the most positive working environments and means that even within them the experience of pregnancy is less than ideal. Figes (1994) suggests that because of the hostility expressed in the context of work, women are likely to become secretive and guilt-ridden about what should be a significant and positive life event. However, as we have seen, this may be more prevalent in certain types of organisations or sections of organisations than others. The integrating environment is able to absorb the violation of the boundaries whereas the segmenting one finds difficulty in adjusting to the visibility of such an intrusion.

Reinforcing stereotypes

An additional explanation for the treatment of women once they become pregnant could be straightforward stereotyping. Not only might the publicly held beliefs about a woman's public role as family carer impinge on the perception of her suitability in the workplace, but also on her recently acquired status as a worker. By this we mean that the working pregnant woman seems to provide for some colleagues and employers the opportunity to compound negative attitudes held more generally about working women. These attitudes typically characterise female workers as suited only to particular types of work (nurturing roles), as being interested in jobs rather than having careers, as unreliable workers – because they have more time off than men to have children or look after children – and as displaying certain types of behaviour, such as showing more emotion, being more conciliatory and submissive at work (e.g. Rosen and Jerdee, 1978; Wilson, 1995). While we can dismiss these stereotypes, pregnancy remains as a visible marker for the perceived lack of commitment: that women are not, and will not be, as committed to their jobs as they were before their pregnancy, in particular that they are less hard-working, (Bistline, 1985) integral to the stereotype. Added to this, the pregnancy stereotype itself also carries with it some assumptions about women's behaviour (see Chapter 2), in particular that they are more emotional and that their brains shrink, and hence may be less effective at work. These myths are supported not least by pregnant women themselves and by anecdotal reports. However, studies investigating cognitive processing, in particular cognitive failure, do not generally endorse this, as we have already discussed in Chapter 3. A study by Nicholls and Grieve (1992), investigating the relationship between performance and posture, found that although women typists in the third trimester felt that their physical discomfort at work was affecting their work efficiency, the measures of their performance, in terms of speed and accuracy, showed this was not the case. Even in the face of contrary evidence, pregnancy is aligned with the female stereotype, making it even more difficult for women to be regarded as effective workers and increasing the expectations of others that women will behave in a stereotypically feminine way (Taylor and Langer, 1977). If businesses are using economic arguments to justify their attitudes and behaviour, investing in women's skills and careers of women who are regarded as likely to leave is certainly bad economics and adherence to such a stereotypical representation allows unfair treatment to be maintained. The significance of the stereotype in determining responses is examined by some experimental work by Halpert *et al.* (1993) and by Corse (1990).

In some of the limited psychological research on this topic, Halpert and her colleagues (1993) used an attitude questionnaire which covered issues of pregnant women as employees, the treatment of pregnant employees, emotional stereotyping, physical limitations of pregnancy and choosing career or family. The findings of this part of their study were that, particularly among the men who responded, there was substantial negative stereotyping in attitudes to pregnant employees. A second part of the study asked the participants to view a videotape of a pregnant or a non-pregnant woman carrying out assessment centre tasks and to rate her performance. The pregnant employee was consistently rated lower compared to the non-pregnant employee, and the analysis of the interaction showed that men assigned lower ratings than women and were more negatively affected by the pregnancy condition. There are some problems with this study, the main one being that the people doing the rating were undergraduate students. But, a worrying aspect of Halpert *et al.*'s findings is the implication for appraisal of pregnant women's performance at work and the role of young male managers in this activity. Bragger and colleagues (2002) found a bias against pregnant job applicants and, as recommended in any strategy to minimise discrimination, suggest that it is possible to reduce the impact of negative bias against certain groups of applicants for posts by using structured interviewing and attention to equal opportunities policies.

Corse (1990) used postgraduate MBA students in a role play exercise with two women managers, one of whom was apparently pregnant and the other who was not. Participants had more negative impressions of and lower satisfaction with the pregnant manager than with the non-pregnant manager. Interestingly, they (the subordinates) initiated more conversation with the pregnant manager than with the non-pregnant manager, that is, they were more social in their comments. The data from the interviews with the participants suggest that the reasons for the negative impressions of the pregnant manager were because they had expected her to be 'passive, nice and giving' and were surprised by her authoritative behaviour. The author relates these findings to work gender expectations and sex-stereotyping, for example Taylor and Langer's (1977) finding that people like pregnant women better when they behave passively and Butensky's (1984) finding that they are evaluated more favourably when they occupy a stereotypically feminine rather than masculine work role. However, the issue remains a complex one.

In attempting to explain why pregnant managers are viewed so negatively, Corse (op. cit.) suggests that they may evoke images of the Great Mother, one of the three archetypes of femininity (Neumann, 1955), the other two being the Good Mother, representing our culture's view of desirable femininity (and which we also discuss in its various forms in Chapter 7), and the Terrible Mother, who is devouring and aggressive. The Great Mother combines aspects of both the Good and Terrible Mother, having creative and destructive powers. The female stereotype conveyed by pregnancy combines these elemental aspects of femininity and the challenge it presents, via the Terrible Mother, to masculinity. Thus, the image of the pregnant manager creates discomfort, confusion and hostility in subordinates whose cultural stereotypes and feelings of vulnerability lead them to want her to behave like the Good Mother – nurturing, giving and caring. Pregnancy is uniquely a time when women can demonstrate visibly the evidence of their creative power; and coupled with an institutional sanction of power in the managerial context, the image evoked may be too threatening. One way of dealing with this is for subordinates to reframe their position by using social contact rather than work contact. Corse suggests that there may be dangers in the relationships between a pregnant manager and subordinates or other workers who may limit their style or content of communications so that pregnant managers may find themselves excluded from certain types of information, something that has been raised by a number of women interviewed in studies. Corse raises, too, the general issue of diversity in the workplace, of which pregnancy is one aspect, and which cannot just be ignored or regarded as a female-only issue.

Pregnancy as sick role

Finally, as the surveys suggested, an explanation for negative attitudes may stem from the linking of pregnancy with illness, something which has been strongly resisted but in which some forms of legislation have been complicit.

In our study of attitudes (Gross *et al.*, 1997), the most negative responses were given in the *physical limitations* category and the *emotional stereotypes* category, and these give credence to the idea that pregnant women are perceived as invalids, conforming to the most extreme feminine aspects of the female stereotype, and are not capable either emotionally or physically of fulfilling the demands of their employment. This aspect of pregnancy is addressed at some length in a paper by Taylor Myers and Grasmick (1990) in which they highlight the social rights and responsibilities of pregnant women (the title of their paper). Their case is that because of the anomalous position of pregnancy as a healthy and as an illness state, the beliefs held by the general population have the effect of ascribing the sick role (described by Parsons, 1951) to pregnancy. While the sick role is presented as a set of rights and responsibilities for individuals, rather than the equation of pregnancy with illness in the legal context, it is their contention that the adoption of this role actually prevents women being accorded adequate healthcare during pregnancy, and particularly those women who are least able to access such care. This is because they are held responsible for their own condition and it is their duty to manage it. Taylor Myers and Grasmick are concerned about publicly held beliefs, which their study confirmed, and access to healthcare in the US, not specifically with employment, though of course many of the same issues arise. Clearly, the issue of pregnancy as an illness has repercussions for both social and legal treatment (Tavris, 1992) and Hanlon (1995) explores the notion of pregnancy as sickness in relation to pregnancy discrimination in employment and considers the way that pregnancy has been treated in law.

Hanlon, like Tavris, argues that, ironically, attempts to establish equality at work had actually reinforced stereotypes of men's and women's work and created further distinctions rather than equality. His view is that pregnancy discrimination has its roots as long ago as the Industrial Revolution, and represents a paternalistic desire to protect women from heavy jobs in the emerging coal and steel industries. This initial notion of protection is now one of the two ways in which pregnancy has been treated in law: the comparative (same/different) or the protected status approach. The comparative approach requires that where situations are alike they should be treated alike but that where they are different they should be treated differently. Leaving aside the extensive room for debate about sameness and difference that this implies in relation to definitions and criteria, this of course fails to recognise that some inequalities arise from gender differences and that gender is about power relations and the persistence of structural inequalities. So previously, the comparator for a pregnant woman was a sick man, thus ensuring that the same structural inequalities were reinforced. Moreover, analogies with the treatment of sick men are misleading because pregnancy is a healthy state (Rubenstein,

1992). Rulings in the appeal courts and the European Court of Justice challenged this approach, and the concept of 'protected status' – effectively a gender-specific approach – has taken over. Its strength is that women have uniquely to be protected in order to prevent them being discriminated against in the labour market and it does not require them to be compared with men. While Hanlon is concerned that the protected status approach is not entirely free of gendered stereotypes, for example that women are responsible for parenting, he considers that having treated pregnancy as a form of sickness is tantamount to the dismissal of women's role in society.

However, the provision of this gender-specific status is not without problems when women find themselves pregnant in the workplace. In this sense, therefore, the advances in the law and the protection for women have not necessarily overcome the persistent willingness to ascribe the sick role to pregnancy as described by Taylor Myers and Grasmick (1990). In terms of women's experiences at work, it is perhaps inevitable that the notion of protected status enshrined in law as maternity rights to time off and leave can create resentment among fellow workers. It is seen as unfair treatment, although as the legislative approaches had previously conceded, employees are entitled to sick leave, but it remains the case that a colleague who has time off because of a broken leg is regarded quite differently from a woman having time off to have a baby. How leave or time off is perceived is very much in the eye of the beholder. As Goode and Bagilhole (1998) point out in their study of university academics and gender, men who leave work early to pick up children are viewed positively while women are not. Similarly, going to test drive a car or have a game of golf may be considered acceptable or even enviable but staying at home to look after sick children is not. A pregnant woman has the responsibility of remaining a good employee at the same time as being given time off when they are healthy. Not only is this an issue of pregnancy but also of women having responsibility for children, which contributes to the perception of women as unreliable workers. Regardless of the legal position, the equation of pregnancy with sickness is still prevalent: 'The problem is the archaic perspective of what pregnant women can do in the workplace. They see it as an illness. It wouldn't have affected the way I do my job, but I wasn't given the chance' (EOC, 2005: 2). As we have discussed, responses in the workplace are likely to reflect the culture of that workplace as well as individual internalisations of public attitudes and reference to female stereotypes. Employers' responses to pregnancy may be related to beliefs about women's role at work, coupled with the beliefs of women and their fellow workers about the competence and commitment of pregnant workers. Effectively, therefore, when in the workplace pregnant women are in a double bind, if pregnancy is a normal event then they should not receive special treatment, which is regarded as unfair; if it is an illness then they should not be at work and the negative treatment is justified and can persist.

In summary, therefore, whether women's experience can be accounted for by the prevalence of stereotypes and the expectations of the sick role, or whether the violation of the boundaries between home and work is too explicit in pregnancy, we can conclude that the exclusively female demands of pregnancy appear to exacerbate conflicts around these issues concerning the role of women and the relationships between work and home. Pregnancy could be said to provide a focus for all these concerns that at other times may remain unexpressed. The very visibility of a pregnancy makes the woman the target of resentments unassociated with the specifics of pregnancy itself. At this point, having looked at what pregnancy seems to accomplish in the workplace, we move on to look at the other side of the relationship between pregnancy and employment, whether and how work, and their treatment at work, affects women and their pregnancy.

The effects of discrimination: work and wellbeing

We have seen that there are a number of possible ways of accounting for the negative attitudes expressed towards pregnant women in the workplace. Whatever the merits of these various accounts for negative treatment, the fact of its existence has the corollary that it impacts on women's experience at work, for example making it less likely that women will return following maternity leave. As we have already discussed, extreme treatment might have a negative effect on women's future employment and also on their psychological wellbeing. The impact of such treatment and anxieties may not be psychologically trivial, as a quote from one of the women surveyed by the EOC indicates: 'It's appalling that someone I had worked with for so long – had a good relationship with and had no complaints from – should treat me like this. It was extremely traumatic. I had stress related hospital treatment' (EOC, 2005: 2). The impact of this treatment is undoubtedly compounded by anxieties about fairness, or anxieties about working conditions or the health of their baby.

The complexity of the social and political dimensions of the issue of pregnancy and employment is highlighted by Karen Messing (1999), who points to the way that women have been excluded from examination of reproductive hazards in the workplace in favour of the foetus, even by feminist-oriented research concerned to place pregnancy as a normal event and yet to identify reasons for increasing rights at work. Messing suggests that legal pressure is necessary to protect women's employment and their health at the same time. The possibility that work and aspects of women's experiences at work might cause stress-related health problems raises a related issue of how women respond to the demands of their employment during pregnancy and how they are able to combine advice and information about the progress and management of pregnancy within these demands. There is a long tradition of research investigating the impact of employment on pregnancy and on pregnancy outcome specifically, which pays less attention to women's experiences and the value of employment. A further issue that we have already raised concerns the research methods used in examining the impact of work on physical and psychological wellbeing as well as on pregnancy outcome. Looking at women remaining in work during their pregnancies may be sampling from a restricted population (see Chapter 2; Bramwell, 1997). This makes any conclusions about the impact of work in general without reference to other aspects of women's experience inconclusive and confusing.

Some evidence that pregnant women find life to be more stressful during pregnancy comes from a study by Nicholls and Grieve (1992). They found that just under 50 per cent of 200 women asked directly whether they found life to be more stressful during pregnancy reported that they did and that most of this stress came from work rather than from home, though it is important not to exclude the possibility of some response bias. In particular, however, and in keeping with the findings we have outlined above, work-related stress was associated with negative attitudes of both supervisors and colleagues, a lack of flexibility in the working schedule and pressures of time. Of course, it is not necessarily the case that the presence of a stressor equates with feelings of stress (Dewe *et al.*, 1993) or poor health outcomes. Care must be taken in interpreting findings in this area, especially since many of the studies looking at potential stressors in the workplace have as the primary focus their impact on the baby, or birth outcome measures, rather than women's concerns about working during pregnancy. Also, the attention focused on women working during pregnancy and the outcome of pregnancy emphasises the rhetoric of risk; thus, employment is presented in research terms as a potential source of risk, as dangerous. The results of many large epidemiological and cohort studies are thus represented within the context of danger avoidance or protection. It goes without saying that no one would advocate that women be required to work in environments which could cause direct harm either to themselves or to their baby and health and safety guidelines do exist to provide protection for pregnant women. However, the role of work in women's lives, as well as their work role, is rarely accorded the same level of attention as those potential risks.

As we shall see from our discussions below, all available evidence over the past 30 years has indicated that women in stressful occupations or carrying out low-grade jobs, for example on production lines, with poor working conditions, are more likely to suffer from pregnancy-related problems such as preterm delivery, lower birthweight and to give up work earlier. These are also the women most likely to suffer from pregnancy discrimination. In considering the impact of work on women's health, it is, of course, essential to be aware that the health impact of job tasks is not restricted to women during pregnancy but may affect all workers carrying out that job. In this regard, therefore, problems and discomforts faced by pregnant women are frequently the result of poor work practices that affect the whole workforce and may reflect a poor attitude to work design and conditions. Typically female jobs, including clerical or shop work, childcare and assembly line work, as well as waitressing and hairdressing, are done either standing up or sitting for long periods, may be repetitive and may require to be done at speed, regardless of whether the woman is pregnant. Such jobs are associated with poorer health at all times. For example, Cherry (1987) collected data on the experience of fatigue and nervous tension in the first and third trimester of pregnancy and found breathlessness, back problems and varicose veins increasing throughout the pregnancy. However, she also collected information on health states in the 12 months before pregnancy. Though the two time periods are not directly comparable, the number of women reporting back pain was higher in the 12 months before pregnancy than in the two trimesters of pregnancy under study and more women reported nervous tension in that earlier period than at any stage of pregnancy. This cautions us against attributing health problems during pregnancy to pregnancy *per se* and also highlights the prevalence of health problems among working women more generally.

It is not unreasonable that women exposed to negative attitudes or doing stressful jobs might experience poorer health. The mechanisms by which this occurs and the extent of the effects are probably too involved to tell a simple tale of cause and effect, even within the positivist biomedical tradition: hence, the proliferation of studies seeking to identify which factors at work determine what outcomes. Given what we have already said about women remaining in work and their reasons for doing so, there is a high likelihood of a range of responses in health terms to their circumstances. However, it is important not to fall into the trap of considering women to be especially vulnerable, and pregnant women even more so. As we shall see, the evidence for pregnant women suffering distress is equivocal, despite many compelling anecdotes.

If we continue to address issues of women's health and wellbeing rather than that of the unborn baby, we find similarly ambiguous relationships though often this produces positive relationships between working and mental health, particularly for part-time workers. Comparing workers to non-workers, De Joseph (1992) found that there were no significant differences in mental health between the groups in measures of distress, including depression, state and trait anxiety and perception of negative life events. Like Homer *et al.* (1990), Saurel-Cubizolles and Kaminski (1987) emphasise that it is other factors rather than working by itself which can lead to poorer mental health among women working during pregnancy, and these tend to be the factors over which women have little control, such as socioeconomic status and working conditions. De Joseph (1992) admits that there were large demographic differences between her groups in that homemakers were younger, less educated and had lower incomes and the study groups were not subdivided according to whether they already had children. Once more it seems likely that working during pregnancy is confounded with other factors that are associated with distress (Mamelle *et al.*, 1987).

It is also important to be aware that women may feel differently at different stages of pregnancy. In a study carried out in the Netherlands, Kleiverda *et al.* (1990) found positive effects of working on pregnant women's psychological wellbeing at 18 weeks of pregnancy, but at 34 weeks the relationship was more complicated: higher job satisfaction predicted an increase in psychological wellbeing and was related to lower anxiety. Leaving work earlier in pregnancy was related to a decrease in depressive symptoms, and more hours of paid employment correlated with an increase in anxiety. But, low job satisfaction, leaving work later in pregnancy and working longer hours were all associated with low occupational level and, as the authors point out, socioeconomic variables might be more important as determinants of psychological wellbeing than work itself. The picture is complicated by the fact that unless women are in a position to give up work without financial penalty, unemployment is likely to bring a lower standard of living, which in turn is related to an anxiety state and depression during pregnancy.

In a study of women working in law firms Schenker *et al.* (1997) found that women lawyers who were working long hours (more than 45 hours per week) were five times as likely to report high stress than those working less than 35 hours per week. Those women lawyers who worked longer hours during the first trimester of their pregnancy were also more likely to report high stress at work during pregnancy overall. This was probably not special to pregnancy *per se*, but to do with the nature of the job, the culture of the workplace and the expectations of work colleagues. In some cases, such expectations may be more imagined than real, and relate to their own concerns over poorer performance. In other cases, the comments and behaviour of others may add to the demands of the job. The findings suggest that though pregnancy does create some special problems at work, results are not all explained by the pregnancy alone. Work ethos and working patterns are likely to be a factor in how levels of stress are reported. In some (mainly white collar) jobs, suggesting that a job is highly stressful may be a way of enhancing self-esteem, and being able to cope with a highly stressful job can be regarded as evidence of work commitment, despite expressing complaints about long working hours and pressures of time. It is also a way to justify time away from work when leave is due. Few people complain about the stresses of having too easy a job, for example. Nevertheless, highly stressful jobs may have a knock-on effect on other parts of people's lives, and on lifestyle. It is some elements of lifestyle and behaviours resulting from stressful events, such as smoking, that are associated with preterm delivery (Petridou *et al.*, 2001).

The work on distress during pregnancy does not tell us whether those who did not suffer distress did not appraise pregnancy as stressful or whether they coped with the stress effectively. There has been little if no direct research on the way in which women appraise the stress of working during pregnancy or cope with work-related stress during this time. Hees Stauthamer (1985) described a process beginning in the first trimester, whereby some of the women she studied reorientated from work to motherhood. Such women found that they were unable to integrate motherhood with their profession despite being highly committed to their careers before pregnancy. The women did not give up their long-term career goals but saw the reorientation as temporary. Rodmell and Smart (1982) reported that women relied on emotional support from friends and family and the most dramatic form of coping with stress at work was to absent oneself from the workplace and it is clearly the case that women who do not get better working conditions or better working arrangements are more likely to go on sick leave or to take up maternity leave earlier.

We can conclude from this survey of the literature, that most women adapt well to working during pregnancy inasmuch as levels of psychological distress are not found to be significantly raised, using the kinds of measures available. There are changes in psychological state during pregnancy but working while pregnant *per se* does not account for significant changes in psychological health. However, it is clear that some groups of women are more vulnerable, notably those who are unskilled, poorly educated, on low incomes and who have little job satisfaction or commitment. Working women who suffer psychological distress during pregnancy seem to differ from those who do not, mainly on variables that are outside their own control and that are not exclusively associated with pregnancy, since these factors map closely on to those identified as causing psychological distress in non-pregnant working women (Cooper *et al.*, 1988) and they will undoubtedly be confounded. If it is indeed the case that employment only rarely causes health problems for women, what of the other major issue, the impact on pregnancy outcome?

Work and pregnancy outcome

Pregnancy is about having a baby. Whatever cultural overlay might be operating in stereotyping women as primary carers, as female workers or in discriminating against women when they are pregnant in the workplace, it is difficult to deny that women's concern during their pregnancy is that their healthy baby will arrive safely. In this context, the prolific research identifying the risks of certain jobs for pregnancy outcome cannot be ignored. This section is by no means a thorough review of this research literature. It is intended to provide a flavour of (a) the way that such research has been conducted, (b) the rationale for such research activity and (c) the nature of the findings regarding pregnancy outcome and maternal health.

A classic text, Chamberlain's book *Pregnant Women at Work* (1984), focuses heavily on teratogenic aspects of work without necessarily considering the role of work, the economic value of work and the women's psychological health or wellbeing. Because of the protective model operating in the workplace, the effect of the discourses of risk is not necessarily encouraging or sympathetic to women and, as we have seen, can mean that women are removed from their jobs or the workplace to make things easier for employers, rather than changing working practices. As Queneau and Marmo (2001) point out, women have to manage the tension between employment, pregnancy and health concerns for themselves and their child, and their economic position. The relative balance may mean that women are prepared to undertake risky work. In addition, research on paid work rarely takes into account the range and quantity of unpaid work done in the home or elsewhere, nor, as both Karen Messing and Patrizia Romito point out (e.g. Romito, 1989), the extreme physical demands of work that is traditionally undertaken by women, including waitressing, laundry work and cleaning. Except in cases of major illness, medical advice rarely includes suggestions that pregnant women should give up either paid or domestic work, whether paid or unpaid (Frazier *et al.*, 2001; McKechnie, 1984), nor that teachers or nurses give up their jobs when pregnant.

In addition to the work we have already referred to in looking at the impact of pregnancy in the workplace as a social and political phenomenon, which has pointed to some of the psychological effects of working, there has been wide-ranging research investigating links between work and pregnancy outcome in particular. Like much of the work on pregnancy and employment, the research is rarely undertaken from a purely psychological perspective even if it frequently invokes psychosocial measures as a factor. These studies are attempting to address several different questions, though one could be forgiven for not recognising the subtle differences between them. They include, for example:

- Is paid work itself related to poorer outcomes for women and babies?
- Is it the type of job that produces an association with poor maternal or foetal outcome in pregnancy?
- Are routine aspects of carrying out a job task, including lifting or carrying, standing for long periods or walking, related to outcome?
- And finally, are the findings on types of jobs and job tasks explained by the extent of physical activity or work effort involved in those tasks?

A positive answer to the first question, that is, work has detrimental effects for women and babies, has enormous political ramifications, particularly at a time of high female employment, and risks an outraged response on behalf of all those who have campaigned for equality of opportunity and women's presence in the public domain. Thus, while the question has been addressed, it has also usually moved swiftly from a macro to a micro level. As we have discussed in describing the impact of announcing pregnancy at work, there is some suggestion that stress or aspects of psychological wellbeing, possibly affected by experience in the workplace, may be associated with poorer outcomes for women. This is a complex issue but is likely to be an indirect effect in this case. Studies are more concerned to identify whether it is work itself that causes the problems, rather than the attitudes and beliefs of work colleagues or managers. For example, Higgins *et al.* (2002) suggest that work is associated with higher blood pressure and pre-eclampsia though not with lower infant birthweight.

The question is, therefore, is this increased risk of raised blood pressure the outcome of being pregnant in the workplace or is it due to other factors? It is this question that is the focus of many of the physiological and epidemiological studies. Savitz *et al.* (1997) indicate that working during pregnancy is not associated with miscarriage either early on or at seven months. Henriksen *et al.* (1994) found that working women and students had the most favourable demographic risk factors for gestational outcome, while unemployed women had the least favourable, but they conclude that work *per se* had little if any detrimental or beneficial effect on the risk of giving birth to a small for gestational age (SGA) infant or of preterm delivery (PTD). A study by Dooley and Prause (2005), seeking to understand how underemployment might be associated with lower birthweight (LBW), indicates that despite the risks associated with working, in fact adequate employment is protective in terms of LBW. Already, therefore, the picture becomes unclear, and depends to some extent on whether this is being investigated at aggregate or individual levels.

As far as the second question is concerned – what types of jobs are more risky – we have already identified a number of factors in jobs that have an impact on women's health. Since women need protection from adverse work environments and change will only happen when there is evidence to justify it, there have been many studies investigating the question of what jobs have what impact. Examples of research are: that done by Farrow *et al.* (1998), using British data from the Avon Longitudinal Study; Messing (1992) and Moss and Carver (1993), reflecting on the gendered nature of working and the need to take account of what women's work entails; and Saurel-Cubizolles and her colleagues (1991, 2004), using large epidemiological surveys of European women to investigate the impact of employment on pregnancy and pregnancy outcome.

These types of studies do point to the dangers of particular sectors of employment. The sectors include not only those obviously involving chemicals like dry cleaning (Doyle *et al.*, 1997; Solomon, 1997), but also jobs in the textile trade, electronics and welding (Farrow *et al.*, 1998). Typically, the association is with poorer perinatal outcomes: LBW and PTD. However, while we can clearly identify occupational sectors which carry higher risks for women during pregnancy and in which health and safety guidelines are needed, the outcome findings are not always consistent, with some reporting LBW, others higher miscarriage rates and yet others PTD. These inconsistencies may depend as much on the type of study and measurements as on the type of employment. In order to try to clarify further what aspects of work make it risky, the studies usually attempt to address additional elements of the working experience.

The question of what the job task entails is often addressed within the same studies as those indicated above (such as Gabbe and Turner, 1997; Hatch *et al.*, 1997; Saurel-Cubizolles, 1991, 2004) and it is here that, for example, job demand and physical components may be relevant. The findings from studies addressing this level of detail are more consistent. In pregnancy, women's increased weight and size are concentrated in the abdominal area, shifting their centre of gravity. At the same time, the ligaments in the lower back soften. Therefore, long periods of standing or sitting in a poor position can lead to backache, in both the short and longer term, and heavy lifting can do permanent damage (Ostgaard and Anderson, 1992), whether or not there is any direct impact on pregnancy outcome.

One of the potential mechanisms for poorer outcome is high blood pressure (hypertension). A number of studies have clearly identified standing for long periods as a major factor in raised blood pressure, together with carrying heavy loads and performing heavy cleaning tasks (Henriksen *et al.*, 1995; Myllinen, 1991; Saurel-Cubizolles *et al.*, 1991, 2004). In a large sample of 4,292 women, infants of women who were standing for more than five hours a day at work were an average 49g lower in birthweight than those of women standing for less than two hours, with adjustment for confounding variables and gestational age at delivery (Henriksen *et al.*, 1995). Standing and walking combined gave the lowest birthweights of the sample though, conversely, walking on its own seemed to be positive in its effect. Because hypertension is closely monitored during pregnancy, it is not entirely surprising that it is also associated with higher anxiety levels.

Studies attempting to link job strain (i.e. stress) with pregnancy outcomes rather than women's health have concluded both that working in a high strain job, that is, one with high demand and low levels of control, may not be associated with poor outcomes, such as PTD or infants being SGA, and also that it may be associated with such outcomes, albeit weakly

(Brett *et al.*, 1997; Hickey *et al.*, 1995; Henriksen *et al.*, 1995). Bramwell (1997) points out that such ambiguous, conflicting and non-significant results cannot be considered surprising given the methodological complexities of researching the impact of job stress on pregnancy outcomes, which include the variability of measuring both job/work stress and perinatal outcome. Oths *et al.* (2001) do find an association between job strain and LBW, but only in one subgroup of their sample. Henriksen *et al.* (1995) allowed four exposure categories for job strain: relaxed jobs with low demands and high control; active jobs with high demands and high control; passive jobs with low demands and low control and high strain jobs with high demands and low control. They analysed the responses of 3,503 women working at least 30 hours per week during the first trimester of pregnancy and related these to pregnancy outcome. Their results suggest that women with relaxed jobs had the lowest risk of SGA and PTD, and that risks were consistently increased in women with low job control (i.e. passive jobs and high strain jobs), though social class must have been a confounder here. Homer *et al.* (1990) showed that work-related stress as measured by high job demands and low control, assigned according to job title, was not associated with PTD/LBW on delivery. Importantly, however, for women who were working but did not want to remain in the workforce, stress was associated with an increased risk of LBW and PTD. Homer *et al.* (op. cit.) emphasise the need to consider personal motivation to work and not just physical efforts required when considering the impact of job characteristics on pregnancy outcome.

Further factors contributing to the impact of job tasks on outcome include long hours of work (Hatch *et al.*, 1997), which relates not only to hours per day but also length of time working while pregnant. Whenever there is an accumulation of the possible risk factors, the likelihood of poorer outcome, as measured either through increased rates of hypertension or through rates of LBW and PTD, is significantly raised. As discussed in Chapter 2, the way that studies are carried out on pregnancy effects may have bearing on the findings of such studies. There are fewer prospective studies of the effects of working on pregnancy outcomes, largely because of the expense and complexity of setting them up, than there are retrospective studies. The size of the study sample may also be relevant, in either producing positive associations or in adding confounding variables. Because of this, although statistically significant, the size of effects is sometimes small. For example, a difference of 80g between babies born at term to women working part time and full time is probably not a major risk to infant health or to future health. The more preterm the birth, however, the more significant such weight differences may be, once combined with other risk factors such as poorer maternal health, family circumstances and job demands. It is of more relevance, however, that studies emerge in a piecemeal fashion, thus health professionals and any advice they provide are affected on an incremental basis, making the inconsistencies both less visible and paradoxically more confusing. This is something we have already alluded to in Chapter 2 and refer to again in the chapters on diet and exercise (Chapters 4 and 5).

The final question being addressed by the research – the amount of physical effort involved – has produced research looking at both physiological responses to work and reminds us, however, that on top of the demands of paid employment many if not most women also have to work when they get home (Newell, 1993): the classic 'double shift', though double is perhaps an underestimate of the many different roles women must take on inside and outside the workplace. Not being in paid employment is no guarantee of not carrying out strenuous or physically demanding tasks and any research on employment must also take this into account in any conclusions about the relationships with outcome, something that is often missed in controlling for confounding variables in the large cohort studies.

In Erkkola's (1976) prospective study, work effort was measured on a cycle ergometer for a sample of women followed from the end of the first trimester to the 38th week of their pregnancy. Physical work capacity measured in this way had no influence on the duration of pregnancy, duration of induced labour nor on infant APGAR scores, a measure of neonatal health immediately after delivery (scores on five vital functions: respiration, colour, muscle tone, reflexes and heart rate). However, those women who were at risk of premature labour and were treated for this also had lower work capacity at 38 weeks, though the direction of this relationship is not clear from the data, that is, whether the lower work capacity was a result of the threatened early labour and treatment or that reduction in capacity was predictive of it. Mothers with higher work capacity (than non-pregnant controls) had shorter labours. So we can see evidence for some relationship between effort, capacity and the woman's experience in labour and infant outcome. One of the difficulties is the variability in the measures taken, the focus of the study and the differences in populations studied. Florack *et al.* (1993) found that while intensity of activity and fatigue levels were not related to the occurrence of spontaneous abortion, work that involved lifting and bending was related to that outcome. Specific elements of the job task do seem therefore to present risks of poorer outcome while physical activity itself is largely beneficial. Data collected by Magann *et al.* (1996, 2002) on employment, exertion and outcome in Australian women suggest that women who were least active, in either employment or other physical activity, were at most risk of pre-birth admission to hospital and of PTD, and another study points to the benefits of non-sedentary employment, together with leisure time physical activity, particularly in reducing risk of pre-eclampsia (Saftlas *et al.*, 2004) (see also Chapter 5). Once again, the message in terms of women's ability to respond appropriately in relation to their work practices is difficult to interpret. Clearly, some women are at risk, with those in the highest exposure category at risk of giving birth prematurely. The highest risk category means that they would have prolonged standing, considerable physical exertion and long working weeks. In these cases, women might be advised that continuing in employment might be putting themselves and their baby at risk.

A major consequence of research into outcomes has been the development and content of advice for pregnant women, at work and elsewhere, on activities to pursue, maintain or avoid. We address this topic at some length in Chapter 6 on exercise but in the context of this chapter on pregnancy and employment we open the discussion here by examining how prevailing discourses of responsibility present in research are translated into practice through advice.

Enacting responsibility: responding to advice

The nature of advice provided is that women should avoid or maintain certain behaviours in relation to paid work, with standard advice to take more rest, to sit down regularly, to avoid heavy lifting and bending and to avoid working with chemicals, lead or x-rays. The prevailing biomedical discourse of pregnancy serves to locate advice as authoritative and reassuring. However, advice about working is often contradictory or ambiguous, and though it stops short of dictating how women behave, it is often hectoring or patronising in style. As might be expected in the light of the extensive literature on the links between employment, aspects of job tasks and adverse pregnancy outcome, the advice is centred on the avoidance of risk and makes use of the literature we have discussed above. This has the effect of positioning work as one of the 'elemental forces' (Smith, 1992). Paid work is presented as potentially dangerous for the baby and, in order to minimise the danger, the expectation is that women will manage to accommodate their need to work and simultaneously to extricate themselves from its risky components. Of course, this discourse of riskiness is also available to others in the workplace who may be able to use it to their advantage by pressuring women to behave in ways that might appear concordant with their own expectations but are in fact disadvantageous. Representations of advice, however, fail to make connections between the discrete elements of research evidence that have emerged, for example that women may suffer stress at work, which is risky for the baby, but that it is others who are responsible for creating the stress, not the women themselves. Emphasis throughout is on how the woman can adjust her lifestyle and behaviour to reduce exposure to stress or other conditions that might be harmful.

The contradictory coverage of the risks associated with working incidentally acts to separate public and private activity. As we have highlighted above, discussion of paid work rarely transfers into the private domain and domestic work in the home is largely ignored, with some exceptions. Features on the demands of working and being responsible for home life are addressed occasionally, and indicate that women should avoid the double demands, though how this might be done is less well defined.

Specifically, advice requires women to be proactive on their own behalf and that of their baby. As we have seen from the studies of women's experience at work, this is not always easily accomplished because of considerable opposition to providing flexibility or even of conforming and responding to policy requirements. The difficulty some women encounter is addressed in ways that make it sound as though it is merely a matter of being clear about needs and calling on legislation for back-up. As the various EOC surveys have shown, this is hardly helpful in many situations where pressure from others is significantly greater than an individual might be in a position to confront.

A fascinating way in which women may respond to the demands to be proactive and to avoid risk is exemplified in our prospective study of women's changes in activity over the course of pregnancy (Clarke and Gross, 2004a; Clarke et al., 2005; Rousham et al., 2006). In this study, whose other findings are discussed again in Chapter 6 on exercise activity, women's daily activity was measured through the use of activity monitors and through self-report. The findings indicate that overall activity levels declined across the course of pregnancy. When this was broken down into the differing realms of activity, a similar pattern was demonstrated with mean self-reported total occupational activity levels decreasing over time. Even prior to maternity leave, the mean number of hours worked per week decreased significantly between 16 and 34 weeks of pregnancy. The women in our study were fortunate enough not to experience discrimination, and were generally treated well by their employers. Though, of course, as others have indicated, those who felt they might encounter difficulty may have left work earlier, making the group of women involved in the study in some ways atypical in this regard. Most of the women reported that they had made adaptations to their work, nevertheless.

Most interestingly, given the advice to rest as much as possible but also to maintain activity, women undertook a neat shift in their activity, whereby a significant decrease in the mean total length of work breaks was observed, but the frequency of work breaks increased. In response to restrictions on the time available for breaks – something women often reported – the women managed their time differently in order to conform to the need to take more or at least adequate rest. The physical aspects of work, including working posture or stairs climbed, did not change significantly (though most women's jobs were largely sedentary) since these were mostly fixed components. What women did report was that they changed the behaviour that was under their control, even if the activities did not form part of the women's daily routine, such as reducing lifting and carrying or bending: 89 per cent of the women reported not lifting although only 27 per cent had originally indicated that their job required them to lift heavy loads. However, this involved a subtle combination of behaviours in an attempt to minimise the impact on their role in paid employment and to undertake appropriate responses to the risks to maternal and foetal wellbeing. The adaptations were unlikely to impinge on productivity or performance and were under the women's individual control. This included the number of trips made around the office environment, recruiting others to do small tasks for them, such as taking things to other offices when they are passing and taking paper to the photocopier.

Such subtle changes may be a reflection of how pregnancy may legitimate opportunities to relinquish roles or responsibilities that are considered irksome, boring or unnecessary. Alternatively, they may be represented as a woman's engagement with the perceived responsibilities of motherhood. The decision to maintain workplace activities, on the one hand, yet change the more flexible elements of their job, on the other, may reflect cultural attitudes too. As other studies describing women's experiences at work have demonstrated, women have to conform to the role of responsible mother and as an individual with agency. By announcing that they have changed behaviour they are conforming to the explicit demands to minimise risks. At the same time they are maintaining agency through their judgement of the potential impact of their changes on their working day.

Concluding remarks

In general terms, we can conclude from the available research that for most pregnant women work is not a source of serious problems, either in psychological terms or in terms of pregnancy outcome. Nevertheless, for some women, notably those in positions with less control and poorer working conditions or in smaller workplaces, the experience may not be as positive. As the case of pregnancy discrimination in the workplace demonstrates, pregnancy retains a potency that is perhaps unexpected in the early twenty-first century. The issues raised by the negative treatment described appear to revisit a continuing ambiguity in societal or public beliefs about the divisions of labour and essential roles and about women and femininity. These are very fundamental beliefs that cannot easily be dismissed by the presence of policies and laws designed to prevent their impact. Moreover, the protective framing of pregnancy legislation, together with the research striving to isolate the precise sources of harm, positions women and their babies as at the mercy of risks arising in the public world of work. The treatment of women in the workplace is simultaneously accounting for and making women accountable to those risks. The construction of pregnancy as a risky endeavour emphasises the metaphors of containment which are inherent in the discussions that follow concerning diet and exercise.

The willingness of individuals to offer up their relinquishing of activities identified as appropriate in the advice they receive suggests to us that it is possible to manage the demands created by the conflicting and confusing evidence in a personally meaningful way. It is possible that where treatment at work is less positive, this controlled adjustment and accountability is more difficult to accomplish and, paradoxically, in being attempted may even reinforce attitudes and beliefs about pregnancy in colleagues and employers. The pregnant woman in the workplace could be said, therefore, to provide a focus for all these beliefs that at other times remain unchallenged.

5

EATING FOR ONE OR EATING FOR TWO

Diet and eating behaviour in pregnancy

Changes in diet and eating behaviour are an essential part of the stereo-typical image of pregnancy, but surprisingly little research has concentrated on what women actually eat and why. Pregnant women are typically depicted as being plagued by strange and irresistible cravings as well as having aversions to certain foods. Nausea, familiarly, though inaccurately, known as 'morning sickness', is seen to be characteristic of pregnancy and in popular culture is regularly depicted as the earliest somatic symptom.

The regularity of the reporting of somatic symptoms across the world suggests that these symptoms and dietary change in pregnancy are driven by physiological and endocrinal factors. Certainly research in this area routinely assumes that these are the only drivers but it is likely that other, psychological factors may be as important. In the case of eating behaviour, a combination of dietary beliefs, an association of symptoms with diet in the past, and past dietary behaviour may be used to guide behaviour and interpret experience. There are many traditional beliefs about what and how women should and should not eat during pregnancy, some of which appear to be common across cultures, for example that women should increase their food intake at least in the early stages, as summarised in the phrase 'eating for two'. Other dietary beliefs seem to be very culturally specific and derive from belief systems relating to the body and the development of the foetus, for example pica – the craving for and eating of non-food substances such as earth and clay, as Walker *et al.* (1997) investigated in South Africa.

Although the adoption of stereotypical beliefs may limit women's choices, it also sanctions behaviour that is otherwise not regarded as acceptable in young women, for example satisfying 'cravings' allows high calorie eating patterns. Many young women restrict their calorific intake in pursuit of the current ideal feminine body shape in the developed world and concern is often expressed in the popular press in the developed world about children and young girls as young as seven years old restricting their food intake. It has been estimated that on any given day approximately 45 per cent of American women are on a diet. Eating disorders, principally anorexia and bulimia nervosa, are largely afflictions of women (Andersen,

75

1995) and women of all ages express dissatisfaction with their body (Stevens and Tiggemann, 1998). Estimates of the prevalence of eating disorders in women of childbearing age have been found to be between 1 and 2 per cent (Fairburn and Beglin, 1990).

Further pressures on pregnant women come from external sources. As we have shown in Chapter 4, and as David-Floyd (1994) points out, the pregnant body can be seen as inappropriate. In Chapter 7, we see how pregnant celebrities are currently usually depicted in the media as remaining slim during pregnancy and rapidly regaining their pre-pregnancy shape. Therefore, for many women, pregnancy, with its accompanying change in body size and shape, may be seen as a personal challenge.

To add to these pressures, pregnant women are often the target of food scares in the media. In some instances this is because a link has been posited, by epidemiologists or basic scientists, between particular foodstuffs and foetal wellbeing (for example, there were reports in 2002 on the possible risks of drinking too much coffee and the dangers of mercury in tuna fish). In other cases, targeting arises because pregnant women are generally regarded as a vulnerable group, alongside older people and the very young. So if a foodstuff is discovered, or thought, to pose some health risk, then vulnerable groups are advised to avoid it. This was the case in the UK when there were reports on the risks of Salmonella in chicken eggs, which originally appeared in the 1980s and reoccurred in the late 1990s. How women respond to these scares is less frequently reported.

And it is not just the potential risk of poor foetal outcome; the diet of women during pregnancy has a significant impact on their long-term health. The most rapid rise in obesity and overweight in women occurs during the peak childbearing years (Department of Health, 2002) and obesity is a major factor in ante- and perinatal maternal deaths (Lewis and Drife, 2004). Importantly, for long-term health, 14–20 per cent of women are 5kg or more heavier 6–18 months post partum, compared to their pre-pregnancy weight (Keppel and Taffel, 1993; Ohlin and Rossner, 1990). As has been regularly documented, obesity and overweight are increasingly important health problems and are associated with a number of diseases including hypertension, type II diabetes, cardiovascular disease and some types of cancer (NIH, 1998).

Despite the known impact of diet on the health of women, it has taken the results of long-term studies of its impact on the health of offspring into adulthood to prompt the interest of mainstream medical researchers in maternal nutrition during pregnancy, outside underdeveloped countries where even basic nutrition is problematic. Poor maternal nutrition has long been linked to foetal and child ill-health. This effect is due not only to insufficient energy intake overall but also to the incorrect balance of food types and nutrients, leading to restricted intrauterine growth, low birthweight, prematurity and other perinatal morbidity (Kramer, 1993). More recent research suggests that several diseases of later life also originate from impaired intrauterine growth and development, leading to permanent effects on structure, physiology and metabolism (Godfrey and Barker, 2000; Mathews *et al.*, 1999). This is known as the 'foetal origins' or Barker hypothesis, named after David Barker who studied the records of 16,000 men and women born in Hertfordshire, England from 1911 to 1930 and whose records can be traced to the present day. The birth records on which these studies were based came to light as a result of the Medical Research Council's systematic search of the archives and records offices of Britain. The Hertfordshire records were maintained by health visitors and include measurements of growth in infancy as well as birthweight. Death rates from coronary heart disease fell two-fold between those at the lower and upper ends of the birthweight distribution. Barker concluded: 'The fetal origins hypothesis states that fetal under nutrition in middle to late gestation, which leads to disproportionate fetal growth, programmes later coronary heart disease' (Barker, 1995: 171). Similar results have been reported in other European countries, India and the US. More recently, excessive maternal weight gain has also been related to perinatal problems in babies (Kabiru and Raynor, 2004) and to childhood obesity (Whitaker, 2004). Higher levels of obesity and of infant mortality and morbidity (associated with poor maternal nutrition) are seen in more disadvantaged groups in the UK (Department of Health, 2002; Macfarlane *et al.*, 2000). This work prompted an ongoing large-scale survey of the lifestyle and dietary behaviour of 20- to 34-year-old women in Southampton in southern England. Three thousand of the 12,500 women surveyed became pregnant during the course of the study, and their dietary behaviour is being closely monitored.

Such surveys and monitoring research will add considerably to our knowledge of what women eat during pregnancy and how their diet changes. However, we still know little about what prompts women to change their diets during pregnancy and what external pressures, personal beliefs and habits underlie the dietary choices they make: for example, whether women who eat healthily prior to pregnancy make more changes than those who do not. In this chapter we consider the research on various aspects of dietary behaviour during pregnancy and reflect on research perspectives. On the one hand these perspectives take pregnancy out of the context of women's lives and, except in the extreme case of eating disorders, disregard previous eating behaviours. On the other hand they fail to take account of the influence of women's culturally embedded beliefs about pregnancy as a different and specific physical experience.

Dietary beliefs and dietary change

There seems to be general agreement among those with expertise in nutrition and women themselves that diet should change during pregnancy.

At the very least, the extra demands on the body call for increased calorie consumption of about an extra 200 calories a day. Beyond this consensus, however, there seems to be wide variation about what exactly is an appropriate diet during pregnancy, with competing information from the media, health professionals and pregnancy manuals and from family and friends. Beliefs about changing one's diet during pregnancy may be associated with the wellbeing of the mother, with the wellbeing of the baby or with a desirable weight gain. Such beliefs may be rooted in the woman's own past eating behaviour, in antenatal health education or may have been transmitted from generation to generation within a particular culture or subculture.

One of the first questions we should ask is whether women do deliberately change their diet during pregnancy for either their own or their child's wellbeing. The answer, from our own and others' work, suggests that they do, and that the changes seem rather more motivated by concern for their child than themselves.

Two early studies of US women looked at how they reported changing their diet (Norman and Adams, 1970; Orr and Simmons, 1979). In Norman and Adams' (1970) study, approximately two-thirds of the women reported adjusting their diet. Such adjustments included adding, reducing or eliminating foods. Greater intakes of dairy products together with fruit and vegetables have generally been reported as usual dietary additions. High sugar foods such as desserts, chocolates and biscuits were the items most commonly reported to be reduced or eliminated, as were foods with a high salt or fat content. Orr and Simmons (1979) found that most of the women they studied believed diet to be important for both mother and baby, though a substantial number did not recognise its importance for mothers. However, they did report that they were prompted to change their diet on the basis of advice from health professionals, who may have placed more explicit emphasis on change.

Most studies rely on women's reports of how they change their diets rather than measuring actual food intake. In a study we carried out we examined the eating patterns of a demographically mixed sample of 102 women during their first or second pregnancy by exploring specific changes that they made to their diet, as well as how somatic symptoms associated with pregnancy, such as nausea, affect food choice, and how dietary beliefs influenced women's food choice (Pattison and Bhagrath, 2003, 2004). We found that 79 per cent of women reported that they should increase consumption of certain foods and 82 per cent reported trying to avoid certain foods. The foods increased were fruit, vegetables and dairy products whereas the foods avoided were foods high in sugar and fat and those that health professionals and other advisors had suggested were dangerous, such as soft cheeses. However, when we measured the actual frequency of consumption, no significant difference was found between when women last consumed the food they felt they should increase or avoid and their current reported intake, suggesting that other factors are at play.

In a study in the US, Pope *et al.* (1997) studied dietary changes in pregnant adolescents. Their results indicated that the pregnant girls' diets were more nutrient dense than a matched sample of non-pregnant girls. Since becoming pregnant, a majority reported that they had increased the amount of food eaten, specifically milk/dairy products, vegetables, fresh fruit/unsweetened juices, breads/cereals and chocolate. Health professionals' influence was cited for increased intake of vitamin supplements and milk, but not for changes in food intake. The major motivations for increasing food intake during pregnancy seemed to be food cravings, increased appetite, improved taste of food and concern for the baby.

So there is evidence that women report changing their diets in such a way as to increase their calorific intake, and specifically increasing certain foodstuffs and reducing intake of others. However, what they actually eat is not simply motivated by dietary advice from midwives or nutritionists. One interpretation of our own findings is that the women in our sample knew what foods their midwives would recommend them to eat, but that somatic symptoms such as nausea, or other beliefs about diet, affected their food choices as well as presumably personal preferences. Traditional beliefs may significantly influence dietary patterns and many are not consistent with recommended guidelines for nutrition during pregnancy. Examples of these include eating for two, not mixing certain foods, taking vitamins to overcome an inadequate diet and eating only a few selected foods.

The impact these traditional beliefs have on dietary behaviour in developed countries may be limited because of increasing access to resources, for example formal education, the internet and pregnancy magazines as well as positive media attention promoting healthy eating and regular contact with health professionals, which would subsequently encourage a different attitude towards diet to be established. In our own work in a UK population, belief in traditional eating patterns varied with educational level so that more highly educated women were less likely to endorse such beliefs and less likely to report suffering cravings (Pattison and Bhagrath, 2003). However, in this sample educational level was confounded with socio-economic status, as it is in many studies.

In a sample of 6,125 non-pregnant women from the Southampton study, mentioned above, Robinson *et al.* (2004) examined the influence of socio-demographic and anthropometric factors on the quality of the diets of young women in the UK. They found that educational attainment was the most important factor related to the quality of the diet consumed. In all, 55 per cent of women with no educational qualifications had scores in the lowest quarter of the distribution, compared to only 3 per cent of those who had a degree. Smoking, watching television, lack of strenuous exercise and living with children were also associated with lower diet scores. After taking these factors into account, no other factor including social class, the deprivation score of the neighbourhood or receipt of benefits added more than 1 per cent to the variance in the diet score. The significance of these findings is that they suggest that poor diets in general in this group are not simply a result of the level of deprivation, but reflect a more general pattern of health behaviour that is linked to poor access to information sources through education.

Some support for this thesis comes from our study (Pattison and Bhagrath, 2004) where women who reported making changes to their diet were also more likely to have made additional changes to their lifestyle. Although there was no variation on alcohol intake (all women who previously drank alcohol reported cutting down or abstaining from alcohol consumption during pregnancy), more educated and younger women were more likely to have attended antenatal classes and changed their exercise levels. In our study, women who increased exercise and women who decreased exercise were classified together as having made a change. As we shall show in the next chapter, exercise seems to be an area where pregnant women respond in different ways.

In considering how women respond to pregnancy we should not forget that people's belief systems are complex and they can simultaneously hold beliefs which are conflicting and contradictory. A study carried out by Carruth and Skinner (1991) found that a substantial proportion of clients of the 1,771 practitioners they surveyed had beliefs about physiological needs during pregnancy, practices related to a healthy baby and alcohol and caffeine consumption that were not significantly different from those endorsed by the American Dietetic Association. However, they also held beliefs, particularly about cravings, which showed strong regional differences, and which represent traditional views not supported by dieticians (e.g. eating for two, eating only a few selected foods, restricting salt intake, taking vitamins to overcome an inadequate diet and deciding that pregnancy is a good time to lose weight). This study was performed in the US. However, few similar studies have been done elsewhere to assess whether similar beliefs exist and if so to what extent. Nevertheless, as we discuss below, advice given by midwives and in publications for pregnant women is often vague, recommending a 'healthy diet' and being open to interpretation within the woman's own belief system. Many traditional beliefs about diet in pregnancy revolve around cravings, aversions and somatic symptoms of pregnancy, particularly nausea and vomiting, and we will now consider these in more detail.

Cravings, aversions and somatic symptoms

Many women report cravings and aversions towards particular foods during pregnancy; the reported occurrence in the literature ranges from 66 to 85 per cent. Cravings and aversions are undoubtedly at least partially interrelated with beliefs as the behaviour of consuming or avoiding particular foods during pregnancy may be directly related to cultural or social values. For example, there is a strong belief system within certain cultures to support pica, which is the consumption of non-food substances such as clay and earth. Food cravings may also be experienced as a somatic symptom though these are also likely to be influenced by cultural beliefs (Bayley et al., 2002).

The medical model of pregnancy suggests that all experience of pregnancy is related to physiological and endocrinal change, thus much early research on cravings and aversions assumed that the root of these desires is a mechanism to protect the foetus. Therefore, cravings are seen as a way of making up for dietary inadequacies and aversions, and nausea and vomiting are seen as a way of protecting the foetus from noxious substances. Traditional beliefs about food restrictions have also been investigated in this way. Fessler (2002), for example, suggests that maternal immunosuppression, which is necessary for tolerance of the foetus, results in vulnerability to pathogens. Symptoms could be a 'behavioural prophylaxis' against infection, with nausea and aversions leading to the avoidance of foods likely to carry pathogens, and cravings leading to foods which boost the immune system. A similar conclusion is reached in a review by Flaxman and Sherman (2000) of morning sickness and pregnancy outcome. This was particularly assumed in the case of pica, the most extreme and unusual of cravings. These assumptions are also found in the explanations women themselves give for what they are experiencing. Several studies carried out in the US by Carruth and Skinner on pregnant adolescents identified beliefs which gave a 'physiological basis' for cravings. For example 'I should give in to my cravings or I will harm my baby' and 'foods that make me feel sick must be bad for my baby' (Pope et al. 1992).

Several other studies which have looked at the impact of pica on pregnancy outcome appear to refute the dietary deficiency theory. In certain societies pica is common. Luoba et al. (2004) found that 378 of the 827 women they studied in western Kenya were eating earth. Horner et al. (1991), in a review of pica in the US, showed that the prevalence of pica among pregnant women from poor, rural and predominantly black areas declined between the 1950s and the 1970s but then remained constant. They conclude that the evidence suggests that pica during pregnancy is associated with anaemia and with maternal and perinatal mortality. Lopez et al. (2004) found a prevalence of 23 to 44 per cent in Latin America. Rainville (1998) investigated the association of pica with two adverse pregnancy outcomes: low birthweight and preterm birth in a group of women from Texas, US. This study found a wide range and a high prevalence of pica if it was more broadly defined than usual; normally pica is used to refer to the craving for and practice of eating soil, clay or dirt. In particular, the pica sample comprised those eating: ice, 53.7 per cent of their sample; ice and freezer frost, 14.6 per cent; other substances such as baking soda, baking powder, cornstarch, laundry starch, baby powder, clay or dirt, 8.2 per cent. Those reporting no pica as defined in this way only amounted to 23.5 per cent of the sample. Women in all three pica groups had lower iron levels at delivery but there were no differences in mean birthweight. In the UK, pica is rarer; our study (Pattison and Bhagrath, 2003) found only three women who experienced craving for non-food substances, all of whom came from non-European ethnic groups and none of whom actually ate the substances they craved.

So there is little evidence that pica attenuates dietary deficiencies, though this may be the belief of women who practice it (Ukaonu et al., 2003); in fact it probably increases them. A meta-analysis of pica research found that ethnicity was the most important predictive variable (Simpson et al., 2000). Geissler et al. (1999) showed a strong associated between pica and anaemia and iron depletion in women from Kenya. The women themselves described soil-eating as a predominantly female practice with strong relations to fertility and reproduction. They made associations between soil-eating, the condition of the blood and certain bodily states. The beliefs women held about eating soil reflect both a kind of dietary deficiency thesis and the protection against illness thesis explored below. Geissler et al. emphasise the importance of social and cultural contexts for how women interpret the experience of pregnancy. They conclude that pica is not simply a behavioural response to physiological need but rather that it is a rich cultural practice. Most western cultures regard pica as deviant and repulsive; Lopez et al. (2004) describe pica as a 'disorder'. Its practice is therefore secret and hidden and Henry and Kwong (2003) argue that pica is stigmatised in American society because of the meaning of dirt in that culture. However, they also argue that the consumption of vitamins and dietary supplements constitutes a similar type of behaviour, done for similar reasons, albeit that it is regarded differently in health terms.

In contrast to pica, nausea is experienced by pregnant women of many cultures. In studies in the developed world, the majority of women report experiencing some nausea. A cross-cultural analysis by Flaxman and Sherman (2000) revealed 20 'traditional' societies in which morning sickness has been observed and seven in which it has never been observed. As we discuss below, there is evidence that nausea affects food choice and is related to food aversions. However, the theory or belief that nausea and vomiting in pregnancy protect women from ingesting certain vegetables or foods that cause congenital abnormalities and other adverse outcomes of pregnancy is questionable. There have been a number of studies exploring the links between nausea, dietary intake and pregnancy outcome in terms of miscarriage or birthweight. Several of these have found no significant association between them (Brown et al., 1997; Hook, 1978; Walker et al.,

1985; Wijwardene *et al.*, 1994) but Lee *et al.* (2004) found an association between even mild morning sickness and birthweight, and concluded that this was because it reduces dietary diversity and nutrient intakes. A study carried out in the US suggested that the women with the most extreme condition (hyperemesis gravidarum) had babies of lower gestational age and had longer antenatal hospital stays (Paauw *et al.*, 2005).

In our own work (Pattison and Bhagrath, 2003, 2004), nausea and vomiting were the most common symptoms affecting food choice; most women responded by avoiding altogether foods they associated with nausea. Reasons that were cited for aversions in a study among Saudi women were smell (9.4 per cent), vomiting (28 per cent), diarrhoea (2.5 per cent), undesirable effect on foetus (7.8 per cent) and heartburn (18.7 per cent) (Al-Kanhal and Bani, 1995).

Dietary aversions usually occur earlier in pregnancy than do cravings and are frequently reported as being more severe. The most common aversions in US samples appear to be towards alcohol, coffee, meat and foods which have a distinct flavour or smell, for example spicy foods or Italian foods (Hook, 1978; Pope *et al.*, 1992). Pope *et al.* (1997) found that many of the adolescents they studied (66 per cent) experienced aversions during pregnancy towards previously liked foods. The most common aversions were to meats, eggs and pizza and led to decreased consumption of these foods. In our study too (Pattison and Bhagrath, 2003), 72 per cent of women developed aversions to food. The most commonly reported aversions were to meat (20 per cent) and spicy foods (20 per cent), though a small number (3 per cent) had developed an aversion to fruit and vegetables. Aversions were usually linked to nausea, with the smell or taste of these foods inducing nausea and/or being associated with an incidence of vomiting.

This pattern of aversion suggests that rather than being a specific characteristic of pregnancy, aversions could reflect a way in which women respond generally to foods that they associate with nausea. It is well known that people generally can develop aversions to foods through a process of associative learning. Whether or not the food was the cause of the nausea, the coincidental association of a bout of nausea or vomiting with a food is enough to create an aversion. In other words, nausea is created by hormonal changes during pregnancy but women interpret this symptom in the same way they would at other times and develop a taste aversion. Data to support this come from a study by Bayley *et al.* (2002) who studied the temporal association between the first occurrences of nausea, vomiting, food cravings and food aversions during pregnancy. Of the women in their sample, nausea and vomiting were reported by 80 per cent and 56 per cent respectively, and food cravings and aversions by 61 per cent and 54 per cent respectively. Cravings and aversions were not related. There was a significant positive correlation between week of onset of nausea and of aversions. In 60 per cent of women reporting both nausea

83

and food aversions the first occurrence of each happened in the same week of pregnancy. No such association was found for cravings.

In the developed world, while pica is very uncommon, other cravings and aversions are common and rather prosaic. Pope *et al.* (1997) found that their US sample most frequently reported cravings for: sweets, especially chocolate; fruit and fruit juices; fast foods; pickles; ice cream; and pizza. Adolescents craving sweets during pregnancy consumed more sugar than those who did not crave sweets. Cravings generally resulted in increased intake, and aversions led to decreased food consumption. In our study (Pattison and Bhagrath, 2003), 62 per cent of women reported cravings. The most popular food craved was chocolate (32 per cent) and other foods craved were generally high carbohydrate and/or high fat foods, that is, bread, pasta, ice cream, chips, fruit, meat and what was generically termed 'McDonalds' (5 per cent of the sample). As in the study reported earlier (Pope *et al.*, 1997), the women with cravings had increased their intake of these foods, with 91 per cent having consumed the food they craved in the 24 hours before they were interviewed.

It is clear then that cravings can have a significant role in diet during pregnancy as they may increase total intake of food or change the proportion of foods eaten. However, cravings are not exclusive to pregnancy. They are frequently reported in the general population and typically tend to involve foods high in sugar and/or fat, such as chocolate (Yanovski, 2003). So, can cravings in pregnancy be regarded as an extension of a normal experience?

There are two relevant theories as to why cravings develop and why they endure (Cepeda-Benito and Gleaves, 2001). The first suggests that substances in the food supply a dietary imbalance. This imbalance may be caused in various ways, for example by dieting or by a nutritional deficiency. This is the theory that most closely links to the dietary deficiency hypothesis outlined above. So the increased need for calories in pregnancy, for example, would cause cravings for high calorie foods. The second type of craving theory is that of 'incentive hypothesis' of craving. This suggests that cravings are a result of learning what foods produce feelings of well-being. This theory suggests that people have cravings for these particular foods because they have learned that the consumption of particular foods leads them to feel good. In psychological learning theory terms, they have learned to associate the food with positive reinforcement. This reinforcement can either take the form of physiological or psychological reinforcement (Wise, 1988).

The incentive hypothesis is supported by research into chocolate craving. In both the UK and the US, chocolate is widely reported to be the most commonly craved food. Michener and Rozin (1994) refuted the suggestion that this is because of the psycho-pharmacologically active substances in chocolate (e.g. caffeine), as they found that capsules containing the same substances did not reduce cravings. It seems most likely that chocolate tastes and smells good to people. Rogers and Smit (2000) concluded that chocolate is simply a common example of the kind of food which people tend to associate with pleasant taste, smell and texture, that is, one that is high in fat and sugar. Hill and Heaton-Brown (1994) looked at food cravings in healthy, non-binge-eating women. They found that the most frequently craved food was chocolate (high fat, high carbohydrate), with cravings for savoury foods, such as pizza, being much less frequently observed. In contrast to the accounts given by pregnant women, the food cravings reported by these women were seen as positive, pleasant, hunger-reducing, mood-improving experiences rather than reflecting any biological need. So despite differences in the beliefs that pregnant and non-pregnant women have for their cravings, the cravings themselves are for similar types of food. Furthermore, Crystal *et al.* (1999) found a significant association between experiencing cravings and aversions prior to pregnancy and experiencing cravings and aversions during pregnancy.

A number of more general studies suggest that women's diet during pregnancy is strongly influenced by their tastes and eating habits before pregnancy. Mathews and Neil (1998) studied 774 women in the early stages of pregnancy and found that their dietary intake was very similar to that of non-pregnant women and accordingly they were short of some nutrients thought to be important for foetal health. Perhaps the most striking results in this regard come from a qualitative study of the diets of pregnant teenagers for the Maternity Alliance and the Food Commission in the UK (Burchett and Seeley, 2003). They gave detailed accounts of the reasons why they did not eat foods that they regarded as healthy, and the most common reason, given by nearly half of the teenagers, was dislike of that foodstuff. Cost was also a factor for a fifth of them and a number also said that the foods were unfamiliar or not offered in their homes. Other reasons for avoiding healthy foods were the effort required to buy them and cook them.

In summary, most of the research on aversions and cravings in pregnancy has stemmed from the assumption that the dietary behaviour of pregnant women is a direct result of pregnancy. So aversions and cravings are assumed to result from biological processes which protect women from infection and restore dietary deficiencies. Although there may be some merit in this approach, it ignores the lifetime of experience that women have had with food, particularly in relation to cravings. So is this a time when women feel less restrained in their eating?

Restrained and unrestrained eating

Unlike diet in pregnancy, the concept of dietary restraint has been widely studied by psychologists. Dietary restraint refers to the tendency to restrict food intake, usually in order to lose weight, or to maintain slimness. It is a volitional but stable behaviour. Herman and Polivy (1983) developed the 'boundary' model of eating behaviour, which suggests that two physiological boundaries determine when people start and stop eating: hunger and satiation. However, restrained eaters have another self-imposed boundary, which overrides the other boundaries – the diet boundary, that is, the amount of food (or calories) that restrained eaters believe they should consume. This diet boundary overrides the normal hunger and satiation boundaries. Dietary restraint is common in women in western cultures as evidenced by the high proportion of women who report dieting at any one time. It is beyond the scope of this book to give a detailed account of the impact of pregnancy on severe eating disorders. Here we will look at the evidence that what might be termed 'normal' dieting behaviour before pregnancy has an impact on what and how much women eat during pregnancy. Pregnancy might be a time when social pressures for slimness could be expected to be relaxed, thus resulting in reduced weight concern despite an increase in body size. Women may therefore be less restrained in terms of what and how much they choose to eat, causing weight gain to be higher. On the other hand, restrained eaters may remain subject to the cultural pressure to be slim and continue or even increase their dieting behaviour. Similarly, restrained eaters may be happy with their pregnancy shape, as it is something apart from their normal experience, or restrained eaters may see the weight and size gained in pregnancy as distasteful. The evidence on both these issues is contradictory.

Davies and Wardle (1994) evaluated body image, body satisfaction and dieting behaviour in pregnancy, expecting women to feel less social pressure to be slim. Pregnant women certainly had a lower 'drive for thinness', had lower body dissatisfaction and rated themselves as less overweight than non-pregnant comparisons. However, they showed similar preference for size of figure to non-pregnant women. These findings suggest that pregnancy is a time of relaxation in concerns about weight, but that this change is temporary and does not override women's general beliefs about their ideal weight and body shape. Davies and Wardle's findings chime with our study (Pattison and Bhagrath, 2003). We did not measure dietary restraint directly; however, the women we interviewed were significantly more likely to be satisfied with their pre-pregnancy shape than current shape. And those who were more satisfied with their pre-pregnancy shape were more confident they could regain it. This suggests that the women who had experience of successful weight control before pregnancy were confident in their ability to exercise such control again.

Clark and Ogden (1999) investigated the role of dietary restraint in mediating changes in eating behaviour and weight concern in pregnancy. They also compared pregnant and non-pregnant women. The pregnant women reported eating more, showed lower levels of dietary restraint and were less dissatisfied with their body shape than the non-pregnant group. They also showed higher eating self-efficacy, that is, the belief that one can control one's own eating. The pregnant women rated themselves as less restrained in their eating behaviour than they had been immediately before their pregnancy and nearly half reported eating more. Clark and Ogden also found that the previously restrained eaters, when pregnant, rated themselves as significantly less hungry and having greater eating self-efficacy than the non-pregnant restrained eaters. They were comparable in these regards to non-restrained eaters. The results showed no effect of restrained eating on weight change. Clark and Ogden concluded that for women who normally restrain their eating, pregnancy both legitimises an increased food intake and removes previous intentions to eat less.

But other studies contradict these findings. For instance, Conway *et al.* (1999) studied dietary intake and weight gain during pregnancy in relation to dietary restraint in a longitudinal study of women from early to late pregnancy. In their study, current dietary restraint was measured (i.e. restraint employed during pregnancy). They found that restrained eaters were less likely to experience weight gains within the recommended range for their pre-pregnancy body mass index (a ratio of height to weight). This went either way such that some gained more weight and some less weight than recommended. DiPietro *et al.* (2003) studied pregnant women's weight-related attitudes and behaviours in relation to several psychological and social characteristics. This was not a longitudinal study, rather women's attitudes about weight gain were assessed once at 36 weeks of pregnancy Several variables had been assessed prior to this, namely anxiety, depression, social support, emotionality and perceived stress (pregnancy-specific and non-specific). Twenty-one per cent of the women were restricting their food intake in some way during pregnancy. The women who reported more restrictive behaviours were more anxious, depressed, angry, stressed and felt less uplifted about their pregnancies in general. Those women who were more positive about their bodies during pregnancy felt better about their pregnancies in general. They also were less depressed and felt less angry. On the other hand, women who were self-conscious about their pregnancy weight gain felt more hassled by their pregnancies and felt greater anger, though they also reported more support from their partners. Women's feelings about their weight gain were not related to their body mass index before their pregnancy. The authors noted that negative attitudes about weight gain existed among women who gained weight within the recommended ranges. All this suggests that women's attitudes to weight gain during pregnancy are related to their general feelings about their pregnancy and psychological health rather than to their general feelings about their weight and their eating habits during pregnancy. A number of other studies have also found that women with a history of dieting are less satisfied with their bodies during pregnancy than those who do not normally diet (Abraham *et al.*, 1994; Fairburn and Welch, 1990; Wood Baker *et al.*, 1999).

So why do different studies have contradictory findings on the influence of women's dietary restraint before pregnancy? One obvious difference between studies is whether they involve women who restrained their eating before pregnancy (e.g. Clark and Ogden, 1999) or refer only to women who restrained their eating during pregnancy (e.g. Conway *et al.*, 1999). These may well represent different groups of women, or the latter may be a subset of the former. However, other reasons for contradictory findings may lie in more recent theories of dietary restraint.

Recent work has established that dietary restraint itself is not a unitary phenomenon and can be applied in different ways. Joachim Westenhoefer proposes that there are two types of restraint: *flexible* and *rigid*. These two styles may lead to different strategies for dietary change during pregnancy. Flexible restraint involves adaptation to the current circumstances, so while food intake is carefully controlled overall, if large amounts of food, or high calorie foods, are eaten on one occasion, this is compensated for by eating less on a later occasion. Rigid restraint on the other hand is an 'all or nothing' approach. Rigidly restrained eaters tend to diet frequently, but if they do eat foods that they feel they should avoid, then they do not compensate by eating less. These are the classic type of restrainers classified by Herman and Polivy (1983) as exhibiting the 'what the hell' effect. One implication of this for diet during pregnancy is that rigidly restrained women, once they have veered away from a weight control diet, may be expected to give up weight control entirely. The main reasons why rigid restrainers may stop restraining what they eat are the lack of social pressure to be slim and the sanction of eating forbidden foods because of cravings. Herman and Mack (1975) discovered that an important characteristic of restrained eaters is that they can be induced to eat more than non-restrained eaters if they first consume a 'preload' – usually a sweet high calorie drink. However, Westenhoefer *et al.* (1994) found that flexible restrained eaters ate less following eating the preload than did rigid restrained eaters. Presumably this mimics their normal eating patterns. So flexible eaters make up for eating a high calorie food by eating less or low calorie foods, whereas once rigid eaters breach their 'diet boundary' they do not seem able to control their eating. It is noteworthy that most craved foods during pregnancy have high sugar content and are high in calories. If rigidly restrained eaters eat craved foods one would predict that this would act like a preload, and they would not compensate for it. Flexible restraint is associated with the absence of overeating more generally and low levels of depression and anxiety (Smith *et al.*, 1999). If the participants in different studies of eating during pregnancy involve different types of restrained eaters, or a mixture of the two, they should find different patterns of restraint and different levels of weight control. Unfortunately, studies of dietary change in pregnancy have not provided conclusive evidence on this yet.

Advice, recommendations and food scares

During the last century the majority of medical authorities recommended that weight gain during pregnancy should not exceed 9.1kg, primarily to prevent the development of maternal toxaemia, foetal macrosomia and caesarean deliveries. These recommendations increased to 11.4kg in the 1970s because it was felt that insufficient weight gain could contribute to premature births and to low birthweight babies born at the expected date. However, in 1990, an influential report from the Institute of Medicine in the US (U.S. Institute of Medicine, 1990) recommended weight gain ranges of 11.4–15.9kg with the primary goals of improving infant birthweight and ensuring the best outcome for the mother. These weight gain recommendations vary according to the pre-pregnancy weight to height ratio as measured by body mass index (BMI). However, a significant number of normal weight women and an even greater proportion of overweight women in the US exceed these guidelines (Abrams *et al.*, 2000). In fact, published studies suggest that only 30–40 per cent of women have weight gains within the Institute of Medicine's recommended ranges, with some gaining less weight than recommended but most gaining more weight than the guidelines suggest they should (International Federation of Gynaecology and Obstetrics, 1993).

In countries such as the US and UK, midwives and other health professionals see it as part of their role to offer advice on diet and weight gain, so why is this advice apparently not acted on? Is it so difficult to follow? As we have discussed above, there are various factors which influence dietary behaviour which may lead to weight gain above or below guidelines, such as dietary beliefs, cravings and aversions. However, the nature of the advice that women receive and their interpretation of that advice may also influence behaviour. As we also discuss in relation to physical activity in the next chapter, advice given by midwives and publications for pregnant women is often vague, recommending a 'healthy diet'. Here, as in the general population, if health education messages do not fit lay health models, they are less likely to be taken up (Ikeda, 1999; Lupton and Chapman, 1995). In other words, the form and content of the advice, the language used and directions for how to act on the advice have to be understood and integrated into what the woman knows and believes. For example, American adolescents interviewed by Skinner *et al.* (1996) said they would prefer to watch a video with a 'talking baby' or teenage actresses presenting the information than read a leaflet or book. They also wanted more information about food than nutrients.

It should also be remembered that health professionals are not the only sources of advice; women have access, to varying degrees, to information from family, friends, magazines, books, television and other media and increasingly to the internet. For example, Lewallen (2004) found that family members were a common source of advice for low-income pregnant women in the US, and in our study of a varied group of women in the UK (Pattison and Bhagrath, 2003), less highly educated women and women from minority ethnic groups were less likely to use books, magazines and the internet. These variations are important because the type and content of advice from different sources vary and may conflict.

The majority of women in Norman and Adams' (1970) study reported that they had made changes in their diet because of dietary advice from health professionals. Orr and Simmons (1979) assessed patients' satisfaction with dietary advice received and found that the majority of patients expressed satisfaction with the amount of information received. A study by Cogswell et al. (1999) revealed that reported advice during pregnancy is strongly associated with actual weight gain. However, about half of the women in their study reported having received no advice, or inappropriate advice from healthcare professionals about weight gain during pregnancy: Overweight women were more likely to report having received advice to gain weight greater than the recommended amount during pregnancy. What these studies have in common is that the reported behaviour fits in with the reported advice. Thus, women have created a narrative which is internally consistent, sanctioning behaviour by providing an account of official advice.

In our study (Pattison and Bhagrath, 2003) 30 per cent reported having received no advice from their midwife or general practitioner, something we return to in the discussion of advice on activity in Chapter 6. The majority of women who remembered receiving advice said they would have liked more than simply being advised to 'eat healthily' and explanations of why certain foods should be avoided. Women who were more highly educated and expecting their first child were most likely to seek out alternative sources of information, particularly books, magazines and the internet. Often, nutritional advice is given in antenatal clinics, however not all women actually attend these clinics and the women who do are usually found to be of higher than average socioeconomic, educational and occupational status, characteristics which are also found to be associated with already better than average nutritional knowledge and dietary practices (Fowles, 2002). This implies that populations that are more in need of additional advice and information are less likely to receive it.

Midwives in the UK no longer specify optimum levels of weight gain for most women, and for several years women were not weighed. Fowles (2002) found that most women had inadequate general nutritional knowledge and therefore, hardly surprisingly, their dietary intake did not meet all the nutritional requirements of pregnancy. Women are usually encouraged to improve their diet during pregnancy but information on how to improve diet is vague. Most advice mentions fresh fruit and vegetables or eating a 'balanced diet'. However, this kind of advice, to simply eat 'more healthily' throughout pregnancy, is not sufficient if women do not have the knowledge for it to act as a prompt to particular behaviours. Furthermore, as we have discussed above, traditional beliefs about what constitutes a healthy diet during pregnancy are likely to be at odds with current nutritional theories.

The vagueness of advice on positively improving diet during pregnancy is in stark contrast to advice on what should be avoided. Often starting as food scares in newspapers, or on television and radio news programmes, advice about avoiding hazardous foodstuffs is often extremely specific. As we said in the introduction to this chapter, pregnant women often find themselves the focus of food scares. They may be a specific focus of information because a link has been made between a food and foetal or, more rarely, maternal health. They may also be targeted because they are perceived as vulnerable to health hazards. Women are more vulnerable, of course, during pregnancy because of their suppressed immune system (necessary so their body does not reject the foreign tissue of their baby). However, in this instance the person perceived to be vulnerable is more likely to be the baby; the targeting of the mother stems from their custodianship of their baby's health.

During the period of our study (Pattison and Bhagrath, 2003) there were two main food scares directed at pregnant women. One concerned coffee, which was linked to stillbirth and early infant death in an epidemiological study published in the *British Medical Journal* (Wisborg *et al.*, 2003). This finding was taken up by various newspapers and other media in the UK. The second concerned tuna fish, and followed on from previous studies on the mercury content of oily sea fish such as marlin and shark. These other fish do not form a major part of British women's diets. However, when it was found that tuna may also contain high levels of mercury, this information was quickly spread in the media and incorporated into The Food Standard Agency guidelines. Of the women we interviewed only about a third had heard either or both the coffee and tuna stories. However, 72 per cent of those who had heard responded by eliminating or drastically reducing their intake of the food, but the others did not change their consumption at all. This emphasises one of the harmful effects of food scares. While reducing coffee intake is unlikely to harm women, it may make them feel uncomfortable. However, tuna is generally regarded as a healthy food, so the elimination of it is not likely to improve women's diets.

In a survey commissioned by SMA (a baby milk producer) in 2003, 558 mothers with children aged between 12 months and two years in the UK and the Republic of Ireland were questioned about their diet during pregnancy and what they believed about foods that constituted a healthy diet. The results showed that while they were aware of food scares, they did not always know or understand the research findings which formed their basis. Some foods were regarded as unsafe through a generalisation from another food. So 60 per cent of women believed that cottage cheese, which is a safe, low-fat source of protein, was unsafe because they failed to make a distinction between this and soft cheeses which may carry listeria. However, in other cases women failed to generalise from one food to others which were similarly hazardous. For example, most avoided or reduced their intake of coffee, because of the risk of caffeine, yet 70 per cent believed that diet cola drinks, which also contain caffeine, were safe. In one of our studies we also found that women reduced their intake of coffee in an attempt to avoid caffeine, but increased their intake of other caffeine-containing drinks such as tea and cola drinks (Gross and Pattison, 1995).

Research that underpins dietary advice is often presented in a way which makes it very difficult to interpret. Take the following extract from the Babyworld website:

> Research published in 1999 suggested that high doses of vitamin C and vitamin E may help reduce the incidence of pre-eclampsia in women at high risk of developing the illness. Although this seems encouraging news, most experts remain unconvinced. First, the study was very small (only 160 women completed the study) so the results may not be accurate (a larger trial is being planned). Secondly, there is some doubt over the safety of the massive doses required of the two vitamins.
>
> (Hulme Hunter, 2005)

Women who are concerned about pre-eclampsia are advised to talk this study over with their obstetrician. However, the study is unattributed and is so heavily criticised that it would be difficult to imagine any woman feeling comfortable raising these findings if she does not have knowledge of scientific procedures, or access to medical journals to look up the study. It seems that an attempt not to blind readers with science has led to an oversimplified version, which will only have the effect of making women feel worried.

However, attempting to produce all the caveats and exceptions to advice given is also confusing and likely to make readers worried. Take, for example, the following extract from the BBC website:

> Research indicates that mothers who eat fish once a week are less likely to give birth prematurely. Oily fish eaten in pregnancy also helps with children's eyesight. However, when you're pregnant

have no more than two portions of oily fish a week. Oily fish includes fresh tuna (not canned tuna, which does not count as oily fish), mackerel, sardines and trout. Avoid eating shark, swordfish and marlin and limit the amount of tuna to no more than two tuna steaks a week (weighing about 140g cooked or 170g raw) or four medium-size cans of tuna a week (with a drained weight of about 140g per can). This is because of the levels of mercury in these fish. At high levels, mercury can harm a baby's developing nervous system.

(Welford, 2005)

Again the research is unattributed, and even undated, making it very difficult to trace, and there is not enough information to evaluate it. What constitutes oily fish here is unclear; the passage seems to suggest both that women should and should not eat tuna, fresh or canned. In an attempt to be accurate and all encompassing, the advice becomes controlling.

While information from research that is incorporated into professional leaflets and websites may be balanced, much of what appears in the media is not. For example, the research paper referred to above on coffee actually indicated that this was not really a problem for women who were drinking less than eight cups of coffee a day (Wisborg et al., 2003). Similarly, a later report by Bech et al. (2005) suggested that the risk of foetal death was only significantly higher if women drank more than four cups of coffee a day. However, as we have shown in Chapter 2, people tend to classify things as either safe or unsafe, so the media portrays foods in this way and the likelihood is that, if women act on food scares at all, they will avoid the apparently hazardous foods completely. The distinction between safe and unsafe foods also tends to vary across cultures and be embedded in more general eating habits. So people from European countries tend to regard wine as safe in moderation, whereas it is definitely on the list of things to avoid completely in the US, even though the research evidence on which advice is based is the same.

A final aspect of food scares to consider is that they nearly always come too late for pregnant women to act on them. Finding out that tuna contains mercury when you are several weeks into pregnancy, and you have already consumed large quantities of this formerly healthy food, is only likely to induce guilt and anxiety. Neither of these emotions are likely to increase the health of women or their babies. The BUPA website even gives a list of foods that women should have avoided before pregnancy:

There are also certain foods that women should avoid pre-pregnancy. These include:

- liver and large quantities of vitamin A in supplements,
- unpasteurized dairy products,

- raw eggs,
- pâtés,
- soft cheese.

(BUPA, 2005)

There is little evidence to support this draconian advice and since so many pregnancies are not planned with the precision required by this, many women will not have been able to act on it anyway.

Concluding remarks

Research on diet and dietary change during pregnancy is unusual in several respects. One important characteristic is the amount of research which has been carried out in countries other than those in the developed world. While little of this work could be said to be cross-cultural, it does at least give us some insight into how pregnancy is experienced by the women outside the mainstream focus. The differences and similarities between women of different cultures are illuminating in that they show how important it is to consider the context and cultural underpinnings of women's lives.

We have reiterated several times in this chapter that women's eating behaviour during pregnancy is studied out of the context of their everyday lives and history. In particular, little account is taken of dietary restraint and dieting behaviour before pregnancy. Yet at the same time the exception to this is a fascination with the dietary habits of what to most researchers is 'the other', notably pica.

A further unusual feature of research on diet is the direct impact that research has on sanctioning women's behaviour during pregnancy. Epidemiological studies which show some association between what women have eaten during pregnancy and subsequent pregnancy outcomes make almost daily appearances in the media. The risks associated with food types are amplified through newspapers, magazines and television, and, perhaps most pervasively, through the internet. Often these studies are later refuted, dealing as they often do with statistically very small increases in risk. However, few women in the developed world can be unaware of the food scares and risk messages directed at them. Yet, what use they make of this information, or the effect of receiving risk messages, often too late to act, on psychological health still goes largely unexplored.

6

KEEPING ACTIVE

Daily activity and exercise in pregnancy

I've slowed down. Its common sense really isn't it?
(Gross and Clarke, 2004b: 167)

The 2003 guidelines published by the American College of Obstetricians and Gynecologists (ACOG) on Exercise in Pregnancy and the Postnatal Period state that: 'pregnant women with uncomplicated pregnancies should be encouraged to continue and engage in physical activities . . . exercise has minimal risks and confirmed benefits for most women' (ACOG, 2003, cited in Artal and O'Toole, 2003: 8).

This advice, which comes from an established medical authority, is derived from a plethora of research on the potential effects of strenuous exercise on pregnancy outcome and maternal wellbeing. It is such guidelines as these which inform professional advice around the world. The expectations behind such guidelines are that with appropriate medical input, women's health and that of their baby – the pregnancy outcome – can be assured. But how relevant is this advice beyond extreme cases, either of high-risk pregnancies, since the guidelines provide many details of contraindications for continuing with exercise, or of a very few high-level athletes. What is the link between such advice and most women's experience?

The research on physical exercise has taken place within a context where the various discourses of pregnancy, both lay and medical, have presented it as a time of moderation and the emphasis has been on the giving up of activities that might put the baby at risk. As we discussed in Chapter 4, there is plenty of advice on how to behave during pregnancy in order to ensure the safety of the pregnancy and to maintain maternal health. By contrast with some of the domains of research we have already discussed (for example paid work, diet), research on physical exercise in pregnancy has instead provided confirmation that physical stresses arising from recreational exercise do not appear to increase the incidence of poor outcomes and in fact may significantly reduce the risks. The current advice from ACOG and similar authorities is thus a commonsense position that we should be able to endorse and to act upon.

However, first, these current guidelines represent quite a shift in the medical literature from previous recommendations of moderation to the present maintenance recommendations, and these still require consultation with professionals. Second, the focus of the guidelines is more on exercise than physical activity more generally and the apparently straightforward statement of encouragement is less easy to translate when all forms of activity are considered. Clearly, women habitually participate in a combination of occupational, domestic and recreational activities and their experience of pregnancy is effectively a process of negotiating being pregnant within the multiple demands of their daily lives. In this context, therefore, physical exercise programmes may be a very small part of their physical activity. How women with ordinary lives respond to advice to sustain physical activity at the same time as moderating other of their behaviours is more complex than the guidelines alone might suggest.

In this chapter, we look at some of the research evidence that has informed, and continues to inform and update, such guidelines and advice on exercise and activity with a view to identifying the kinds of activity referred to and the nature of the advice that they have produced. Then, through material from our own work on women's activity during pregnancy, we explore how women manage the competing expectations of their behaviour in pregnancy.

Exercise activity and outcomes: infant and mother

When investigating the topic of physical activity in pregnancy, there is a wide-ranging literature reporting research on exercise, including work on animals, undertaken from a primarily biomedical perspective, which makes some reference to psychological effects. The research seeks to examine the physiological response of the body in order to identify where risks may or may not occur and the extent to which changes taking place in pregnancy may extend or reduce such risks. For example, a book edited by Artal and his colleagues on *Exercise in Pregnancy* (Artal *et al.*, 1991) draws on a range of existing expertise to address not only the physiological adaptations to pregnancy, but also the physiology of exercise during pregnancy and, significantly, the practical applications of this research in terms of advice. The appendix to the book contains what were the current ACOG guidelines at the time the first edition of the book was produced (1986), which were more cautious in their advice than those cited above. The editors indicate that one of the reasons for caution in both the earlier guidelines and their own conclusions, that they 'no longer have to claim that there is lack of data to *allow* sage, moderate exercise prescription in pregnancy' (Artal *et al.*, 1991: ix, emphasis added), is the lack of statistical power in some of the studies on strenuous exercise in particular. We shall examine further the concept of permission for women to exercise represented in this statement, once we have looked at the nature of the evidence to which they refer. The historical development of the exercise guidelines is interesting in itself, reflecting as it does the available evidence base; the 1994 revision of the ACOG guidelines (ACOG, 1994), though still cautious, by incorporating phrases such as 'should be able to' was more relaxed in tone and even somewhat prescriptive about the value of exercise.

Typically, in research terms, exercise has been used to refer to structured programmes or practices of physical activity, such as those of competitive and recreational athletes and participants in organised sporting activities, which can include gym attendance. The increased attention to the value of exercise is reflected both in health promotion literature which appears in a variety of media and in the research that has gone on to examine its impact. The benefits of physical activity and its relation to physical and psychological health have been increasingly emphasised for all groups (Hagger and Chatzisarantis, 2005). Even in 1991, Artal and Gardin were able to state, albeit rather patronisingly, that 'the exercise spirit has enraptured women of all ages, including women in their childbearing years' (Artal and Gardin, 1991: 1).

The discussion now turns to research on the extent to which physical activity may impact on pregnancy and pregnancy outcome and examines whether or not the traditional consensus of discouraging physical activity can be scientifically supported. Coming from very different perspectives, physiologists like Artal, sociologists (e.g. Barker, 1998) and literary analysts (e.g. Hanson, 2004) take the position that, throughout history, recommendations for physical activity in pregnancy have typically been based more on social and cultural expectations than they have on any definitive evidence. Nonetheless, there has been an accumulation of literature that suggests there may once have been a genuine theoretical basis for reducing exertion.

The central concern is the body and the physiological response to pregnancy since it is clearly the case, as Sternfeld (1997: 34) indicates, that: 'Pregnancy stresses the body more than any other physiological event in a healthy woman's life and requires considerable cardiovascular, metabolic, hormonal, respiratory and musculo-skeletal adaptations'.

The adaptations occur whether or not women are participating in exercise regimes; the issue is whether the addition of exercise pushes the systems beyond their capacity and thus causes harm, either directly to the foetus or via the impact on maternal functioning. Thus, the medical and safety issues regarding physical activity in pregnancy have been based upon the concern that certain aspects of cardiovascular, metabolic, thermal and mechanical stress could act to threaten outcome.

The essential and routine changes in the human circulatory system are quite dramatic in nature and may manifest in many of the unpleasant symptoms of pregnancy including dizziness, nausea and waves of sudden fatigue, but they are not necessarily damaging. As the vascular network expands, increased dilation particularly occurs in the blood vessels supplying the skin, kidneys and reproductive tissues. In many ways, the circulatory adaptations induced by pregnancy appear to complement those produced by regular weight-bearing activity in the non-pregnant state; studies of the circulatory effects of regular exercise have demonstrated that vigorous training will increase blood volume and increase the maximum cardiac output that an individual can achieve. It will also increase the density and growth of blood vessels and improve an individual's ability to dissipate heat. Moreover, research evidence suggests that when an adequate exercise regime is maintained during pregnancy, the results of the interaction between these two sources of cardiovascular adaptation are at least additive (Clapp, 1998). Benefits for the prospective mother have also been postulated and include what are regarded as signs of fitness in non-pregnant individuals: reduced heart rate and reduced blood pressure (Simpson, 1993).

Despite the positive effects of the physiological vascular changes, there nonetheless remained some concerns regarding the capabilities of the human cardiovascular system to meet the dual demands of exercise and pregnancy. As with the investigations of the impact of paid work in pregnancy on outcomes, it could be convincingly argued that this concern and the ensuing research was particularly eurocentric (or Western-centric); many women in the developing world almost certainly continue to undertake strenuous activities that give rise to the same physiological changes as exercise and have little opportunity to choose to moderate such activity. The main rationale for considering physical stress as a risk factor for poor pregnancy outcome lies in the assumption that heavy physical effort during pregnancy may divert blood flow from the uterus and, by doing so, reduce oxygen and nutrient delivery to the foetus, or that increase in muscle action will divert effort to the skeletal muscles (McMurray et al., 1993; Stein et al., 1986). Compounding this response further is the proposition that foetal oxygen requirements may increase with strenuous physical work, primarily as a consequence of concurrent increases in temperature and metabolic activity (Lotgering et al., 1985). If this were the case then any reduction in uterine blood flow initiated by physical exertion might be associated with a more severe foetal hypoxia than a similar reduction occurring at rest (Bell and O'Neill, 1994), raising alarm bells for the pursuance of maternal exercise at high levels.

However, reassuringly, investigations suggest that the biological system appears to be robust, since several mechanisms have been identified which may act to ensure that foetal oxygen consumption is not easily compromised and the cardiovascular adaptations that occur during pregnancy appear sufficient to maintain adequate blood flow and oxygen delivery to both the exercising muscles and the developing foetus (Clapp, 1980; Rauramo and Forss, 1988). Recent research by Larsson and Lindqvuist (2005) suggests that low-impact aerobics has little or no effect on maternal hyperthermia. From this perspective at least, therefore, it seems that physical activity in pregnancy need not be discouraged. The evidence would, therefore, seem to be at odds with the advice appearing at the time. The basis for such guidelines, to stringently limit exercise during pregnancy, must therefore have arisen from other evidence. This evidence was likely to be that derived from the results of clinical investigations which concentrated directly on the strength of association between activity participation and pregnancy outcome. In this research, the variables that were considered are those that suggested the greatest foetal risk or poorer foetal outcome and include the standard obstetric parameters of foetal growth, length of gestation and type of delivery. Maternal wellbeing has been addressed, though this received less attention in the first instance.

In one of the earliest epidemiological studies of recreational activities, Clapp and Dickstein (1984) observed an adverse pregnancy outcome among women continuing vigorous exercising late into their pregnancy. Comparisons were made between pregnant women who maintained their exercise until late into the third trimester and those who either reduced their activity or remained sedentary. Women who continued to exercise at an intensity greater than 50 per cent of their age-predicted maximum heart rate for 30 minutes or more, three times a week, were found to exhibit significantly less pregnancy weight gain and a shorter pregnancy. The same women also demonstrated a higher incidence of small for gestational age (SGA) babies and a mean birthweight 500g less than either women who were sedentary or women who had stopped exercising prior to the 28th week of their pregnancy. In a similar manner, Clapp and Capeless (1990) later reported that babies born to women who continued to exercise at or above 50 per cent of their pre-pregnancy level were found to weigh an average of 310g less than those who did not. These authors concluded that approximately 70 per cent of the observed variance in infant birthweight could be directly attributed to differences in infant body fat. Typically, infant body fat develops in the last trimester, thus exercise at this time would have appeared to reduce both maternal and infant body fat.

Nonetheless, this work is by no means conclusive since subsequent and already existing research studies found no effects. Rose et al. (1991) did not find the same rates of lowered birthweight in the babies of women undertaking vigorous physical activity and other studies have reported that physical stress arising from recreational exercise activity does not increase the incidence of either SGA infants or premature labour, and may even decrease the incidence of both (Berkowitz *et al.*, 1983; Klebanoff *et al.*, 1990; Rabkin *et al.*, 1990). Furthermore, case studies of athletes found that they delivered normal birthweight infants despite running regularly throughout their pregnancies (Korcok, 1981). These studies are complemented by laboratory studies which found a similar absence of relationship between work effort or fitness on birthweight (Dibblee and Graham, 1983; Wong and McKenzie, 1987).

While the results of such biologically focused research may be criticised for their small sample sizes and insufficient statistical power to detect a true association, as Artal and his colleagues (1991) conclude, nevertheless, the available larger studies have only served to substantiate their findings. Hall and Kaufmann (1987) recruited 845 pregnant women, each given the option of participating in an individually prescribed prenatal exercise programme. Foetal heart rates were monitored throughout the exercise sessions and no abnormalities were observed. Participants were later categorised on the basis of the total number of exercise sessions they completed during their pregnancy and no adverse effect of exercise programme on gestational age or birthweight was reported. In fact, the authors observed a trend for birthweight to be higher in the exercise group. Moreover, greater amounts of exercise were revealed to be associated with a reduced incidence of caesarean section, higher infant Apgar scores (a composite rating of colour, breathing, heart rate, movements and reflexes normally assigned one and five minutes after birth) and shorter hospitalisation. In this instance, therefore, higher levels of physical activity actually appeared to be of benefit. Research has confirmed that labour and delivery appear to be shorter in women who exercise regularly (Clapp, 1990), although the contradictory nature of these findings also shows that in a cohort of runners there was a higher likelihood of caesarean delivery (Dale *et al.*, 1982). However, in an Australian study of perinatal outcome in a low-risk obstetric population, referred to in Chapter 4, Magann and colleagues (2002) contribute to the confusion by finding that exercise in working women was associated with smaller babies, increased incidence of induction of labour and longer labours.

Nevertheless, the cumulative result of this research provides little indication of a negative relationship between higher levels of physical activity and adverse pregnancy outcome. Most studies demonstrate neutral if not favourable associations between maternal fitness and length or type of delivery and although there are clearly studies which do give cause for concerns about pregnancy outcome it may be that the differences are small despite their statistical significance. Of course, if there are other risk factors present, a small difference arising from exercise may be compounded and the medical concerns would be legitimate as there could be serious repercussions for both mother and baby. But, what about the possible impact on maternal health and wellbeing?

As the findings from the studies indicate, physical exercise may well be beneficial in terms of labour and delivery. More than this, it may also be of direct physiological benefit, in terms of aerobic capacity (Sternfeld, 1997). Support for this view has been provided both by competitive athletes, who anecdotally reported improved performance following delivery (Sady and Carpenter, 1989), and by case studies of recreational athletes (Hutchinson, 1981). Additionally, physical activity during pregnancy has also been linked with the promotion of good maternal posture, prevention of excess maternal weight gain and the prevention of lower back pain (Dewey and McRory, 1994) as well as reduced risk of gestational diabetes (Dye *et al.*, 1997). Evidence for the value of exercise for women's physical health in general is reported by Haas *et al.* (2005) who find that a lack of exercise is associated with poorer health status pre-pregnancy, during pregnancy and after pregnancy.

There is also literature considering the potential impact of exercise on maternal perceptions of their physical and psychological wellbeing during pregnancy. For some time, there have been studies showing that women who exercise during pregnancy typically report fewer pregnancy-associated symptoms than those who are sedentary (Hall and Kaufmann, 1987; Sternfeld, 1997; Wallace *et al.*, 1986). This applied to symptoms of nausea, fatigue, leg cramps, ligament pain and lower back pain. In addition, work by Sternfeld *et al.* (1995) appeared to identify a temporal association between exercise and wellbeing such that increases in symptom reporting were preceded by a decrease in exercise, leading to the conclusion that women were feeling better because they were exercising. This kind of relationship needs to be viewed with caution, first because of the social pressure to conform to the positive messages about exercise and second since it could be used to put women in a position where exercise was in fact prescribed as a solution to some of the physical symptoms of pregnancy. Nevertheless, such findings would have been instrumental in the revisions of the ACOG guidelines.

As far as psychological wellbeing is concerned, research conducted within the general population over the past 20 years has also pointed to the benefits of exercise and physical activity. There is an extensive literature on this topic, much of which also attempts to take account of reservations about confounding variables. For example, people do not choose to exercise at random. There may be significant other differences between active and inactive people that are responsible for differences in mental health (as measured in the biologically oriented exercise studies) and that are more relevant than activity in terms of outcomes and benefits. Furthermore, people may have differential expectations of intervention exercise programmes, which may in themselves have an effect on psychological wellbeing.

Nevertheless, this work demonstrates unequivocally that physical activity and psychological health appear to be related in a bi-directional manner. There have been several reviews and meta-analyses (e.g. Long and van Stavel, 1995; North *et al.*, 1990) which show that exercise reduces anxiety and depression and increases self-concept, self-esteem, aspects of cognitive functioning and mood. Longitudinal studies have been carried out investigating the effects of exercise training on psychological wellbeing with a range of populations, including students, groups of older people, people with psychiatric or medical disorders and members of specific groups like the police or the military. Virtually none of these have shown aerobic exercise to have a deleterious effect on psychological health and studies involving comparisons of intervention and control groups demonstrate that the active group show greater psychological improvement even when the control group undertakes another group activity apart from exercise (Steptoe, 1992). The overwhelming conclusion is that physical exercise can exert a positive effect on psychological wellbeing over and above that which might be attributed to other factors.

The findings of studies investigating the impact of exercise on maternal wellbeing in pregnancy produce the same conclusions: in 1981 Sibley and colleagues found that women who participated in swimming activity during the second trimester of pregnancy did not improve their fitness but did have improved appetite and a more restful sleep pattern; Wallace *et al.* (1986) found higher levels of self-esteem and Dewey and McCrory (1994) reported fewer depressive symptoms in women who exercised. These findings are endorsed by recent studies and reviews, for example Da Costa *et al.* (2003) and Morris and Johnson (2005), which have shown that exercise in pregnancy improves maternal wellbeing.

The initial focus of medical concern about the potential risks of exercise in pregnancy was driven by the historic need to reduce infant mortality and was centred around the need to reduce or moderate physical activity. The positive benefits of exercise, which have been demonstrated through these mainly physiological studies over time, have undoubtedly contributed to the change in the tenor of advice from official sources such as the contemporary advice on exercise in pregnancy issued by the ACOG. As the 1994 guidelines suggested, women have now been granted permission, on the basis of what might be considered as suitably founded research, to continue with moderate, and even some strenuous, exercise in pregnancy, with the caveat that the pregnancy itself is designated as medically low risk. In fact, there is almost a suggestion that women should now participate in exercise in order to ensure a healthy outcome for themselves and their baby. This may be a reflection of what is acknowledged to be a highly body-conscious society as much as a concern for women's health and wellbeing. (See also below 'Body image as a barrier'.) As with diet, women's behaviour in pregnancy would seem to be determined by the exhortations of official admonitions rather than solely by personal choice.

Daily activities, health and outcomes

Current figures on participation in physical exercise, based on the UK General Household Survey, suggest that nearly 60 per cent of adults take part in sport or physical activity on a regular basis and around a quarter of the population report participating in an active sport at least three times a week, the most popular activity being walking (Sport England, 2006). However, the figures are lower than this for women, for those from minority ethnic groups and those with limited incomes. The figures suggest that around 50 per cent of women participate in at least one type of active sport once a month. This does not necessarily equate to regular partici-pation in strenuous exercise activity. As for women during pregnancy, the figures do not relate. In fact, it is probably the case that for most women who become pregnant, physical activity is likely to centre around the regular routines of their daily lives, together with recreational activities involving some physical exertion such as swimming, dancing, weekly aerobics classes, walking, gardening and so on. The competing demands of employment, relationships and the household mean that these recreational activities may in themselves be limited. What does research have to say about daily activity, which may be less amenable to moderation or change?

Studies of the general population are more limited in this area, apart that is from studies of older people, who are considered to be at risk from inactivity in two ways (Milligan *et al.*, 2004; Shepard and Montelpare, 1988). One of these is that the restriction of physical mobility reduces wellbeing through loss of independence and control. The other is the potential reduction in social participation as a result of physical inactivity, also leading to reduced psychological wellbeing. Aside from studies of older people, Fallowfield (1990) and Maloni (1996) point to the import-ance of job role in self-esteem in the general population, and of course jobs usually entail some kind of activity outside the home. Thus, the positive benefits of routine activity are assumed to flow from the elements of independence and control. However, these types of studies are looking at either very specific elements of activity, such as physical mobility, or at what might be called components of a person's lifestyle. The significance of levels of physical activity aside from formal exercise programmes is not as easily discovered in the research, although the increase in rates of obesity in Western cultures has led to concern that people's lives are too inactive for long-term health (Lees and Booth, 2004). Morris and Hardman (1997), for example, suggested that although the pleasurable, therapeutic/health, psychological and social dimensions of walking are evident, they had rarely been studied within the context of an occupational or domestic routine. Outside specifically physical activities, there is some interesting work by Ehlers *et al.* (1988) and others (Hofer, 1984; Wever, 1985) that emphasises the importance of social activities in stabilising biological rhythms which may affect feelings of depression and reported somatic symptoms. It is possible therefore that the maintenance of a daily routine may serve to sustain social cues and protect against the impact of disruptions to regulating mechanisms, whether these are socially or biologically determined.

There is very little work looking at pregnant groups and daily activity in terms of pregnancy outcome or maternal wellbeing in the way that exercise has been examined. Launer *et al.* (1990), in a study looking at both employment- and non-employment-related physical activity in Western women, found that women who had three or more children and received no household help were at increased risk of delivering a small for dates baby, although not of having preterm delivery. Woo (1997) attributes the higher rates of small for dates babies in women with other children to the strenuous activities associated with caring for young children – something it was perhaps not necessary to carry out a study to discover! However, once again the research is not conclusive, with several other studies failing to find an association between domestic activity and pregnancy outcome (Rabkin *et al.*, 1990; Schramm *et al.*, 1996). The difficulty is, as before, of defining what is meant by strenuous activity. The impact of performing household chores may depend on the population being studied. Even the fundamental aspects of daily living may be a risk for some low-income women during pregnancy, for example climbing stairs and walking are particularly demanding. There may also be cultural differences: Hickey and colleagues (1995) report that carrying loads may be associated with an elevated risk of premature birth in white women while strenuous home-based chores may heighten the risk in black women.

In terms of psychological wellbeing and activity, what research there is comes from studies of women whose pregnancies are deemed at risk and who are ordered bed rest, something they find surprisingly unwelcome especially since they feel well (Curtis, 1986; Mackey and Coster-Schultz, 1992). This reduction in psychological wellbeing, which includes anxiety and depression beyond that related directly to the pregnancy risk, is attributed to restriction of activity, as with older people. Monaham and De Joseph (1991) have suggested that this is because of loss of control; bed rest at home still involves the competing demands from relationships, households and careers which may be hard to manage and meant that women 'cheated' so that they could accomplish what they saw as necessary for the smooth functioning of their home life. Of course, women with low-risk pregnancies will not be required by medical practitioners to undergo total restriction on their activity, but they may find that their routine is affected by the various discomforts of pregnancy itself, such as tiredness, nausea and increasing weight. Furthermore, women's own concerns or the reactions of others, arising perhaps from information they have received, may deter them from participating in certain activities or discourage them from public outings (Unger and Crawford, 1996). Anderson *et al.* (1994)

found that pregnant women who reported more depressed mood also said that they were bored and that they wished they could socialise more.

Notwithstanding the very small amount of research on daily activity, the benefits would appear to be very similar to that of exercise, for both the general population and for women during pregnancy. In particular, these refer to the sense of control and self-esteem associated with being active and making choices about what activities to pursue, whether in the public or in the private domain. Having reviewed the larger literature on exercise we can clearly see that the emphasis is on taking responsibility for health through appropriate physical activities, something that is extremely familiar in the context of women's experiences during pregnancy in particular. We turn now to some examples of the kinds of advice that women receive, where they find this advice and how they feel about it. In doing so, we have to consider the various sources of advice and nature of those sources. It is likely that the sources themselves have particular expectations about women's continuing participation in activity during their pregnancy and that these will impact on women's own responses.

Activity advice

Like advice on other areas of pregnancy, we can look at a variety of types of available advice that is available to women. Others have reviewed some of these types of literature in particular (e.g. Barker, 1998; Woollett and Marshall, 1997) and highlighted the typically biomedical discourses they represent. We have also discussed in Chapter 4 how published advice sustains a series of discourses of responsibility. A further discourse is that of moderation and self-management, something integral to the advice we have already mentioned in this chapter. Interestingly, while the ACOG guidelines quoted and discussed in the sections above may inform medical advice or official literature, they are not directly available to women themselves. Advice on exercise activity is commonly included in general health advice during pregnancy, alongside advice on smoking, diet (see Chapter 5), alcohol and so on. Publications on pregnancy and birth may also refer directly to research data on such issues. For example, work by Kelly (2005) indicates that 15 minutes of exercise three times a week is acceptable, and Kardel (2005) suggests that it is acceptable for top athletes to continue vigorous exercise; such general statements may emerge in the print and electronic media. However, Lumbers (2002) points out that there is no simple exercise prescription and that generally the approach to advice is to encourage women to maintain existing exercise regimes but not to take up new ones. Kagan and Kuhn (2004) highlight the benefits of moderate exercise, though of course the term moderate is notoriously unhelpful in terms of actual activity and will depend on the current or previous levels of exercise activity. If information on exercise is difficult to interpret, then what about information on daily activity?

As we have pointed out already, there are plenty of sources of material available to women about pregnancy. Any search, real or virtual, will provide a list of hundreds of titles concerning pregnancy and childcare. These are written by experts of various kinds: family doctors, obstetricians, celebrity mothers, midwives, childcare experts and so on. Taking only the pregnancy aspect of these publications, all of them provide at least some information and practical advice on the changes accompanying pregnancy, the common symptoms, antenatal testing, health concerns and anxieties, diet, childbirth choices, preparing for baby and so on. There are also monthly magazines available on the newsstands that deal with the same topics. The style of such publications and the prescriptiveness of advice vary according to the author but are universally concerned to give the same message – how to ensure a safe and normal pregnancy and pregnancy outcome.

There are also publications specifically on fitness in pregnancy, many of which are published in America. For example, in Joan Butler's (1996) book *Fit and Pregnant: The Pregnant Woman's Guide to Exercise* (in its 10th edition), which is described in the publisher's catalogue as a 'terrific book for active women who want to keep up their workouts', readers can learn, among other things, how the baby is affected by the exercise they do, and how to modify their exercise. Joan Butler is a nurse. Another title, also written by experts in exercise and maternal health, is *Fit Pregnancy for Dummies* (Cram and Stouffer Drenth, 2004), which indicates that it helps women to understand how a fit pregnancy helps with delivery and postpartum shape-up. There is also specialist material, for example the *Runners World Guide to Running and Pregnancy*, subtitled *How to Stay Fit, Keep Safe and Have a Healthy Baby* (Lundgren, 2003). Publicity material for this book makes explicit reference to the differing messages women may encounter on exercise in the phrase 'never be puzzled by conflicting advice again', something we discuss further below. There is clearly a wide range of potentially helpful material for all kinds of women, which makes reference to the benefits of exercise and physical activity as well as to the need to moderate such activity. Such material is fascinating in itself but it is not the subject of this current chapter or book. If the health messages about exercise are to be understood they need to be easily available to everybody.

Aside from these books on pregnancy and childbirth, which women would have to purchase or borrow through the public library system or from friends, women in the UK are routinely given *The Pregnancy Book* (Department of Health, 2006) via their antenatal clinics. The advice and information it contains cover all aspects of pregnancy, childbirth and the first few weeks with a new baby. In the first chapter 'Your health in pregnancy', there is one full page on physical activity, which suggests that the more active women remain the easier it will be to adapt to the physical changes of pregnancy. As far as daily activity is concerned its recommendation is that women should 'keep up [their] normal daily physical activity or exercise' (Department of Health, 2006: 15) whether this is a sport or just walking to the shops, for as long as they feel comfortable. The same section also says that women should not exhaust themselves and that they may need to slow down as pregnancy progresses. With a recommendation to keep active on a daily basis, for example by walking, the text says that any amount of activity is better than nothing. Finally, swimming is recommended as a suitable form of exercise. These recommendations therefore chime with the types of exercise that most women do – in fact the accompanying pictures are of women swimming, on a bicycle and gardening – and with the research findings, emphasising again the benefits of exercise and activity. It is clearly making reference to the nature of daily lives by including routine activity such as shopping. However, the advice does also represent a message of moderation and slowing down, allowing women to act on such advice if it corresponds with other information they may have been given. On a following page, the emphasis is on exercise in pregnancy. As we indicated earlier, this refers to specific exercises that will benefit both labour and postnatal recovery rather than how to continue existing exercise programmes. It therefore describes particular exercises that women might undertake, such as pelvic floor exercises, to generally improve their health.

Another major source of information is via the world wide web. In the UK, the BBC website is both popular and respected (www.bbc.co.uk). As well as providing news and current affairs coverage, the website provides information about the range of much of the BBC's output as well as background material to BBC television programmes and issues that are considered of interest or relevance to the general public. It has a magazine-type format with links to many external sites and also hosts interactive notice boards and discussion groups. One major area of the site is the Health Website, which has a heading of 'Women's health', under which a range of topics are addressed, including 'Parenting' (BBC, 2006). Parenting concerns include, for example, having a baby, which in turn has pages dealing with pregnancy, sleep, skin, hair and clothes as well as coping with advice, exercise and fitness, diet and health, and antenatal care. The web pages on this area of the site are written by Heather Welford, a freelance health writer, and offer advice about the process and progress of pregnancy. Like *The Pregnancy Book*, suggested exercises to enjoy are walking, swimming and toning and stretching classes: a further reference to both the actual participation in activities and thus women's real lives. It would seem, therefore, that advice that is available to women in the UK, at least some of it, does provide limited information about how to continue with an active lifestyle. Whether this advice is perceived as such is open to debate, given the continuing and parallel references to taking it easy. As far as exercise is concerned, available advice is in line with research and guidelines but how does it actually impact on women's lives when they are pregnant?

Changing behaviour?

One of our major concerns in this book has been to reflect how the changes associated with pregnancy, aside from those physiological changes which are largely outside women's control, are the result of a complex interaction between women's own experiences, their understanding and expectations of their physical state and those of others, both generally and personally in terms of family or work colleagues.

Typically, investigation of women's participation in exercise and activity outside the physiological has tended to take a health psychology approach, where the emphasis has been on identifying the factors which will determine appropriate changes in health behaviour in line with available evidence for positive outcomes (in terms of maternal and foetal health). The popular models of health behaviour (such as the Health Belief Model or the Theory of Planned Behaviour) incorporate the role of attitudes and beliefs in determining health behaviours. In our view, while such an approach has provided some useful information that we have already referred to on predictors of exercise activity for example, in our view this has not generally taken account of the complexity of women's daily activities and the complexity of the differing and simultaneous demands for changes that occur during pregnancy. Thus, women may be expected to change their behaviour in line with cultural expectations mediated through professional advice, friends and family, as well as to manage the activities of their daily lives and to respond to the changes taking place in their bodies, within a relatively short time period. While the obvious benefits of reducing smoking or alcohol or increasing exercise may be solved by one relatively simple process, this is not so for the various different activities that make up women's lives.

In our longitudinal study of daily activity in 57 pregnant women (Rousham et al., 2006) we found that as a whole, and perhaps not surprisingly, women's routine daily activity declined over the period of their pregnancy. This measured and reported change allowed for changes in weight, thus the reduction in activity over the course of pregnancy could not be attributed solely to the weight gains associated with the pregnancy. The reduction in activity occurred significantly in domestic activity and leisure activity, sometimes including physical exercise activity, and included some elements of occupational activity. We have discussed some of the changes that women made at work in Chapter 4. Of particular interest here is that although several of the women in the study had participated in regular physical exercise activity prior to pregnancy, most of them had given this up during their pregnancy and their daily lives were therefore relatively inactive. Furthermore, most of them had essentially sedentary jobs. In discussing changes in physical activity, therefore, we are really looking at routine activity that is undertaken in order to perform the basic functions of living, rather than the limiting of physical exercise activity as recommended by the research.

In the context of the current chapter our focus is on how women described and explained their changes in behaviour and on whether the changes reflected the advice they had received. We identified several 'barriers' to maintaining their habitual activities. These barriers include the physical symptoms of pregnancy, maternal perceptions of risk, poor maternal body image, reduced motivation, social and cultural discouragement and a lack of appropriate facilities. The relative impact of each of these barriers varied according to the point of pregnancy at which women were interviewed. We shall discuss some of these barriers briefly here in the context of physical activity and exercise and then go on to examine what coping strategies they were able to negotiate to overcome these barriers and deal with advice.

The findings from the study suggest that the perceived responsibilities of pregnancy begin early in pregnancy. Up to 25 weeks, the most common reason women gave for reducing their activity was physical limitations, and this was mostly nausea and vomiting and maternal fatigue; interestingly Downs and Hausenblas (2004) found that women's beliefs about exercise were that it improves mood but that physical limitations restrict exercise. Thus, physical limitations may operate both at the level of beliefs about appropriate behaviours as well as making it actually difficult to persist with physical exercise or activity. If women suffered from physical symptoms, their strategy was to try to use their available energy to sustain their working week, often at the expense of their routine home and leisure activities: 'I'm less active, I'm too tired. I can't go out at weekends – sometimes I struggle to get dressed in the morning I'm so tired'. However, as well as the limitations induced by their physical symptoms, the women had clearly also made a conscious decision to reduce their general activity level. The rationale for both avoiding specific tasks and modifying more general activity was similar: 'I'm not socialising so much. I've slowed down. It's common sense really, isn't it'.

The physical symptoms of pregnancy, in particular the profound tiredness of early pregnancy, also appear to provide women with a legitimate justification for changing behaviour or at least avoiding activities later in pregnancy. This is facilitated by the identification of tiredness as a symptom of pregnancy and one that can be avoided or reduced by resting, as we highlighted in the section on advice above. Women are therefore able to recruit tiredness as an explanation for their behaviour or lack of behaviour in describing the changes to us and to others, without having recourse to any other justification: a commonly recurring response was that they would have liked to do more 'but have been too tired'. It is also irrefutable, since it is the case that simply being pregnant can make women tired, without even the extra weight of effort of exercising. Thus, women are free from blame and permitted to be inactive, at the same time as fulfilling their responsibility as carer/container in the maternal role.

Moreover, the importance that women in the study attributed to rest during pregnancy was found to be comparable to the importance that they attributed to other well-established health behaviours, such as not smoking or abstaining from alcohol, and to be significantly higher than the importance accorded to regular exercise or an active lifestyle. Whereas advice to cut down on cigarettes or alcohol (or other substances) highlights the potential and invisible risks of continuing, rest and sleep tend to be seen only as beneficial to both mother and baby, whatever else might be happening. Once at home, it is also easy to accomplish, especially in an environment where others are concerned for your wellbeing. As far as the importance of sleep and rest during pregnancy is concerned, this may partially reflect an expectation of a disrupted sleep pattern after the birth but also the prevalence of advice on resting, which is endorsed by friends and family. The visibility of some areas of advice and information is high, certainly in the early stages of pregnancy. The lower importance assigned to exercise and activity may be in part a feature of its lower visibility compared to rest or relaxation.

In addition to tiredness and physical limitations, another 'legitimate' barrier was the direct or indirect risks arising from activity. Women described how they believed that there was an unnecessary degree of risk associated with many of the activities that they had routinely undertaken prior to becoming pregnant and the advice on exercise to avoid makes clear that they are right. Direct risks arose from various aspects of occupational, domestic and recreational activity and usually occurred wherever a particular task was assumed to be too strenuous or too dangerous to perform. Many women, however, left the precise nature of the perceived risk unspecified although almost all of the women in the study believed that an aspect of their former behaviour could directly jeopardise the progress of the pregnancy: 'I haven't done any DIY, I won't lift the heavy toolbox. I just don't want to overdo it'.

It should be mentioned again here that none of the women had jobs that required heavy lifting or that might be considered inherently dangerous in health and safety terms. Significantly, when asked about strenuous physical activity the women discussed the possibility of it leading to unwanted accidents, falls or muscular strain, in relation to their own welfare rather than that of the baby. In the few cases where the baby's health or development was considered to be at risk, the women described themselves as consciously tailoring their activity to place the perceived needs of their unborn child above their own. A participant, who considered herself previously as an active person, said that she did not 'rush around so much or carry heavy things or go dancing. It's my choice, something growing in me needs as much help as it can get'.

Women also felt that it was necessary to make changes in order to avoid indirect risks. Indirect risks arose from the notion that, while the performance of an activity in itself might not be dangerous, there were associated with it other potential hazards that may threaten health. The vast majority of indirect risks arose from recreational pursuits. Within this context, three specific limitations to activity were cited. These occurred in roughly equal proportion and referred to the potential harm that could be caused by activities commonly associated with passive smoking, overcrowded locations and alcohol consumption. Two of these have risks associated with them at any time, while the danger of crowds was something specific to pregnancy. The overriding effect of these concerns was to discourage women from engaging in social activities outside the home and for some this included physical activities. For example, one woman had not only limited her social activities but also had limited her swimming to times when only adults would be present: 'I always have to try to protect myself in crowded rooms, so I don't want to go out. I like swimming but I can only go when it's adults only. I went before and got kicked by the children'. Particularly in later pregnancy when they had often given up work, the women spoke of the isolation that can follow from the limiting of their social activities and not only their own limitations. The pressure from others to reduce activity contributed significantly to their feelings of boredom and social isolation. While women felt they had to fulfil their maternal role, there was also some resistance to this external pressure: 'My friends don't think I should be going out, so they don't bother phoning me. I haven't seen anyone for ages. I feel like I've given everything up, my job, my life'. Another woman explained how frustrating it could be to be prevented from doing what she wanted at home: 'I'm not allowed to do things like gardening or housework. My partner stops me so I try to rest more but then I get very frustrated. I know when to stop but he won't believe me. It's so boring just sitting'.

Alongside the perceived risks to health, a further and important issue that the women raised with us was an increased anxiety over their new body shape. This contributed to their feeling unwilling or uncertain about participating in recreational activity. The issue of body image has not been addressed elsewhere in this chapter and it is perhaps worth exploring it a little further at this point before coming back to the topic of how and what advice the women in our study had received about physical activity during pregnancy.

Body image as a barrier

Even quite early in pregnancy, women often described themselves as 'feeling fat', 'feeling heavy' and 'feeling awkward' and this affected their behaviour: 'I'm going out less. I feel fat, very body-conscious . . . I feel like people are looking at me a lot. Maybe I'm just paranoid'. This is not unusual in the sense that women's bodies do undergo significant changes in a short period of time and within a few months they may have changed shape dramatically. Earle (2003) argues that concerns with fatness and physical appearance are significant factors in women's lives during pregnancy. The experience of embodiment clearly represented by pregnancy can be a frightening one. It is thus not surprising that even in the earliest stages of pregnancy concerns over body image may influence women's activity levels, in part because of their ambivalence towards the physical changes that accompany pregnancy. It has been suggested that anxiety over physique or bodily appearance may be responsible for a lower rate of participation in recreational and social activities by women, especially those who perceive themselves to be overweight (Spink, 1992; Wiles, 1994). One of the reasons given for taking exercise is to keep fit; another is to improve body image (e.g. Choi, 2000; Grogan, 2000). Women in industrialised societies are immersed in issues of weight control and appearance, neither of which may be acceptable to them during pregnancy and there is increasing pressure on women to return quickly to their pre-pregnancy appearance, often prompted by the coverage of celebrity pregnancies (see Chapters 5 and 7). One study of pregnant women found that only a small minority responded positively to their new figure (Zajicek, 1979) and there is earlier research evidence of dissatisfaction with body during later pregnancy in particular (Harris, 1979; McConnell and Datson, 1961; Mercer, 1986). It is also possible that women who are less positive about being pregnant or who are anxious in the first instance may also respond more negatively to their bodily changes and pregnancy more generally.

However, the response is by no means universal. For some women pregnancy can represent a welcome period during which they feel temporarily free from cultural demands to be slim (Unger and Crawford, 1996; Wiles, 1994). Baker *et al.* (1999) found that weight and shape satisfaction were higher in pregnancy than at four months post partum. Similarly, Clark and Ogden (1999) found that the pregnant women in their study of health behaviours were less dissatisfied with their body shape than non-pregnant women. Boscaglia *et al.* (2003) reported that women who exercised regularly were happier with their changed body image when they became pregnant. Clearly, women will differ in their responses to exercise or activity during pregnancy itself and to some extent this may be determined by their pre-pregnancy attitudes both to exercise and to their body image (Devine *et al.*, 2000; Downs and Hausenblas, 2003).

The women's various concerns and experiences, which contributed to what we have described as barriers to activity, may not only affect women's willingness to participate in the recommended exercise activities but also in routine activities and therefore contribute to the changes in behaviour we identified in the study. The physical symptoms of pregnancy and the concept of risky activities provide women with a form of control over their choices of behaviours. However, concerns over body image may in part reflect women's feelings of being out of control, which they do not wish to be visible to others. Although recourse to physical limitations and risk may offer women control over their activity, these concepts also allow others to comment on and determine how women should behave. The balancing and negotiation of their own needs and requirements in respect of activity have to take account of what others may expect.

Taking advice?

In the longitudinal study we asked the women participating whether they had received any advice regarding their physical activity behaviour in the four weeks prior to each of the five interview points. Nearly all of the women indicated that they had received advice or information at least once during the course of their pregnancy about exercise and activity more generally. The primary sources of information changed over pregnancy, with books or magazines being the main source at the start and least used towards the end. A consistent source of advice across pregnancy was that from friends and family.

Written sources of advice that were mentioned included a variety of the professional and lay self-care books, pregnancy and parenting magazines and *The Pregnancy Book* that we referred to above. They also mentioned leaflets and newspapers. The inclusion of newspaper items may have provided them with up-to-date information, but as we have already seen in regard to dietary advice, the information can be misleading or confusing about which changes should be made on a personal basis. Those who did seek or read information did not necessarily find it helpful: 'The books I've read have been very vague. They recommend swimming and yoga but little else. There's no black and white about what you should and shouldn't do so I don't, I can't follow it at all'.

Health professionals, who included midwives and doctors, appeared to play a substantial role in disseminating advice in the early weeks of pregnancy but less so thereafter. A small number of participants received additional advice from other 'expert' sources. In all cases the nature of the advice that was read or received centred on two main aspects of structured recreational activity. The first was concerned with informing women about the specific benefits and risks of different leisure time pursuits. The second focused on the importance of prenatal exercise and home stretching routines, as the publications also suggest. In neither case was advice on routine daily activity specifically recalled, and once again the information that they did recall was often conflicting or negative: 'I asked various people if it was OK to carry on running. My GP advised me to do my normal level, but my midwife told me to take it easy, to listen to my body. The practice nurse told me not to do it at all'.

The most constant source of advice and support across pregnancy that the women talked about proved to be that of family, friends and work colleagues and by 25 weeks into pregnancy family and friends had become the principal source of information. It is worth pointing out, however, that the types of advice received and recalled did vary according to the women's backgrounds. For example, participants who reported receiving advice from family and friends were likely to be significantly older, more likely to have been educated beyond the age of 16 and to have had a higher pre-pregnancy activity level than other members of the group in the study. This may reflect not only genuine individual differences but also differential perceptions of the expected response to this question.

The nature of the advice given by participants' family, friends and colleagues was much more generic than that provided elsewhere, with study participants frequently responding that they had been told to 'take it easy' or to 'slow down'. At four out of five stages of pregnancy, family discouragement of activity outweighed family encouragement. Downs and Hausenblas (2004) also point to the significance of family in determining whether or not women exercised during pregnancy. So, although the details of activity recommendations were found to vary between different individuals and different stages of pregnancy, the general lay consensus was that physical activity should be limited, whatever the professional advice or research evidence might suggest.

It is one thing to be given advice and another to act on it. As we have seen, there has been considerable effort put into the development of guidelines, arising from research, which may form the basis of professional advice. Our evidence would appear to suggest that women may receive advice on physical exercise and activity as only one element in a whole array of advice, and, especially where the advice may be conflicting or is irrelevant to their lifestyle, such information may slip down the hierarchy of activity. Irrespective of whether they had been seeking information on a specific activity or had simply recalled seeing activity-orientated advice, many reported that they had often been met with a confusing and contradictory array of responses and recommendations. The evidence also suggests that whatever the nature of the advice, it is perhaps the cultural pressure to conform to the maternal role that informs much of the motivation for change. While women reported changing their behaviour, this may not have been directly related to the advice they received and certainly varied across the course of pregnancy. The extent to which specific advice was followed may not have depended so much on the women themselves as on the clarity and applicability of the information they were given. Where women wanted to carry on with their existing activity they also found difficulties, because of either unavailability or reluctance by providers. For example, when asked if she was happy with her current activity level, one woman replied that she would have preferred to do more but that there was nothing available in her area. Whether it was formal advice emanating from professionals or informal advice from family and friends, many women held other people responsible for a decline in their daily activity level at least once during the course of their pregnancy. These enforced changes occurred across their regular routines and could have been in their occupational, domestic or recreational activity.

Of course, it is always possible that women were reporting advice and information from health professionals and family or friends that was in line with their own preferred behaviour. There have been suggestions at various times that pregnancy may afford women the opportunity to avoid other life tasks (Artal and Gardin, 1991; Harris and Campbell, 1999). However, our examination of women's responses to advice does not suggest this and nor does work by Rodriguez *et al.* (2000) on psychosocial predictors of smoking and exercise, which suggests that the same factors predict exercise in pregnancy as predict health behaviours in general. Nevertheless, when we are discussing daily domestic and recreational activity rather than exercise, the women in the study certainly suggested that they were taking the opportunity to avoid doing things they had never liked very much, such as less housework, not going down into the cellar: 'It's a good excuse really'. Pregnancy can clearly be a time when various forms of advice give legitimacy to particular types of behaviour and pregnancy itself provides a buffer to unwanted activity. It remains to be seen whether the increasing emphasis on fitness and exercise will filter through into the context of lay advice on pregnancy, given that existing research which sanctions activity and exercise would seem to make little difference to the cultural stereotypes of maternal responsibility and preparation.

It would be unfair on the women involved to give the impression that they all reduced their activity wherever they could. Although it was certainly the case that some of the women we talked to did relinquish activities, others continued to be active and took the opportunity of finishing paid work to do household jobs, such as preparing the home for the new baby, and tried to retain their social lives at the same time as taking care of themselves. Effectively we are talking about the way that different individual women negotiated the information and advice they received and the pressure they felt to conform to other people's expectations. In some cases, such negotiation involved adopting the behaviour that was expected of them, such as resting or doing less, while at the same time developing various coping strategies that allowed them to continue to participate, through, for example: carefully monitoring the consequences of their activities and giving them up if they did not feel comfortable; pacing themselves, by which they meant finding ways to complete a comparable level of activity to that prior to pregnancy, such as dividing it into shorter and shorter episodes (as discussed in Chapter 4); and by forward planning whereby the women considered what they were hoping to do, the context in which it would occur and the implications it might have either physically or socially. Then they would make a conscious decision whether or not to participate. In this way the women we talked to were able throughout their pregnancy to do most of the things that they wanted to do but with some changes in the speed or location of these activities. In addition, for some other women, pregnancy did give them a licence to leave things to others.

It must also be acknowledged that numerous other factors may discourage women from maintaining their habitual daily activity pattern during pregnancy. Although outside influences, including family and friends, often served to discourage physical activity in pregnancy, these women indicated that they themselves considered their behaviour to be appropriate during pregnancy – 'it's obvious isn't it' – and stated that at least part of their decision to change their activity, either at work or at home, had been their own choice, as much a result of their own personal preferences as it was a response to external expectation or information, activity advice or attitude to healthy behaviours. Thus, for example, a high level of importance was attributed to rest and relaxation and a lower level of importance to physical activity. If a woman also believes that she rather than professionals or chance will determine the outcome, that is, a healthy baby, then the predominance of the highly visible recommendations of rest and the reduction of tiredness may also be regarded as a legitimate priority, whatever the apparent benefits of exercise for good health in the longer term.

Concluding remarks

There is no doubt, as the ACOG guidelines and all the evidence we have discussed confirm, that a certain amount and level of exercise is 'a good thing' in pregnancy – for women, for labour and delivery and for a healthy baby. In addition, it has longer-term health benefits. For the same reasons, maintaining an active lifestyle is also a good thing; even if it does not carry quite the same level of positive benefits, it may be much easier to sustain over time. Advice is quite clear on the matter, wherever it is found, and it does address some aspects of daily lives as well as strenuous physical exercise. But, ironically, within the framework of supervision that surrounds pregnancy in the early twenty-first century (Lupton, 1999), understanding how to behave in response to advice may actually become increasingly difficult. There are competing demands to be met and negotiated by each pregnant woman. The biomedical discourses of pregnancy, in the ascendant with the advent of technologies of reproduction and replete with research evidence, place women as responsible for the pregnancy outcome. Thus, professional health advice, arising from research, exhorts necessary changes in behaviour or at least maintenance of an active lifestyle. The professional advice gives permission for women to be active, as long as it is in the service of a healthy outcome. At the same time, lay discourses of pregnancy, while paying homage to the power of the professionals, have not yet taken account of the research evidence and place women within the stereotypical feminine role, lacking agency and control, unable to act on any advice but that of family and friends, who in turn have recourse to powerful cultural expectations. By this means, women are granted permission to be inactive in order to ensure healthy outcomes. Moreover, the advice itself is ambiguous. Physical activity is good but fraught with risks, thus caution needs to be exercised in order to prevent damage to themselves or the baby; by contrast, tiredness, a natural concomitant of pregnancy, has high visibility and women are given permission to take advantage of their pregnant role and moderate their behaviour.

7

PREGNANCY UNDER SURVEILLANCE

In the preceding chapters we have explored how women may or may not change their behaviour during pregnancy. In some cases the changes are founded on information from research. The need to take action in accordance with advice can be seen as reasonable. However, it has been our contention that this message to change behaviour reflects a number of assumptions about women's behaviour, their role as mothers and their responsibility to others. We would argue that this apparently reasonable set of requirements actually subjects women to a degree of oversight that could be described as a form of surveillance. In many ways this is integral to much of women's experience inasmuch as their appearance and behaviour are frequently subject to public scrutiny and criticism. This is particularly the case for women who are, for one reason or another, in the public eye. In this chapter we look at the way that pregnancy has been represented in the media and we focus on the images and representations of pregnancy and the pregnancy of public figures, in order to examine how the public sanctioning of behaviour is enacted.

Pregnancy in the public eye

Pregnancy is highly visible. This visibility reflects the ongoing public interest, is amply demonstrated by the comments made to women once their pregnancy is announced and includes extensive coverage of celebrity pregnancies in what is now a global media. Leaving aside the issue of celebrity for a moment, this visibility can partly be explained as inherent in the accompanying physical changes that occur over the nine months of pregnancy. However, in part and more recently, it is also because fashions for maternity clothing have made this change much more obvious, as Robyn Longhurst (2005: 438) points out in her paper on this topic: 'maternity wear has become maternity fashion' – so-called 'bump chic'. A Danish anthropologist, Tove Engelhardt Matthiassen, illustrates this shift by highlighting the way that clothing has moved from veiling or hiding pregnancy, by the loose and shapeless garments worn by women in the twentieth century up to the mid-1960s, to the current point where maternity fashion has become chic, through the use of stretch fabrics and the prevalence of fitted women's clothing. Matthiassen suggests that this is because 'In an era of sports and well-trained bodies you have to survive the bodily changes of pregnancies by being fashionable' (Matthiassen, 2005: 5).

In addition to the visibility created by changes in fashion, we can think in terms of different kinds of visibility, since most women who become pregnant do not attract media attention. The first type of visibility is that which arises from pregnancies that are considered atypical or abnormal because of their non-adherence to the standard images of pregnancy available to us. As discussed in Chapter 2, unusual or abnormal pregnancies which attract attention are typically associated with specific individuals, and include single motherhood, especially where a partner may have died before conception; for example in the UK in 1999 Diane Blood applied to the courts for permission to use her dead husband's sperm for IVF. Other examples are: multiple pregnancies, especially where more than three babies are expected; very young (possibly too young) or teenage pregnancy (for example girls sitting their school exams); or the pregnancy of much older women, for example women who give birth at 58 and older following IVF. Other noteworthy examples are those resulting from new assisted conception technologies and also include surrogate pregnancies. The infrequency of these occurrences is what makes them visible or newsworthy. It also opens the door to significant commentary on the women concerned and their behaviour. The commentary is then personalised and referenced with respect to the expected outcome, which is the baby. Thus, the gaze on women permits directed comment towards the pregnancy and clearly emphasises the metaphor of containment inherent within public concerns about pregnancy: 'your baby has grown since I last saw you'.

Second, pregnancy may be made visible because of some feature relating to the nature of the women themselves. In this category, we can place women in the public domain, such as celebrities, wives or partners of well-known or famous figures, such as Cherie Blair (the British Prime Minister's wife) or members of royal families, for example Princess Kiko of Japan. Thinking of visibility in this way allows us to explore the various aspects of the visibility of pregnancy in relation to the nature of the pregnancy and the nature of the individual. In both cases, we would argue, the nature of this visibility tends to prompt critical comment.

Furthermore, the increased understanding of the developmental significance of the foetal experience in utero, which ranges from genetic and chromosomal effects to the potential toxins crossing the placenta, to the potential for influencing intelligence and behaviour, has reinforced the pressure on all women to maintain a healthy lifestyle during pregnancy and preconception. The emphasis on containment provokes a plethora of advice to women on how to behave. As the previous chapters have illustrated, advice can be viewed as a means by which pregnant women are in effect held publicly accountable for their behaviour, and is recently demonstrated by the US federal guidelines asking women between the onset of menstruation and the menopause to treat themselves as 'pre-pregnant' at all times (*Washington Post*, 16 May 2006).

In the context of the medical/biological discourses of pregnancy this public accountability is perhaps hardly surprising. It has been happening for some time. Katherine Barker (Barker, 1998) illustrates how the medicalisation of pregnancy was systematically introduced through a public health campaign in the US in the early part of the nineteenth century. By examining the content of a widely distributed manual developed at the time, *Prenatal Care*, she shows how pregnancy was conceptualised as a medically problematic state. Woollett and Marshall (1997) present a similar case through examples of this process in their analysis of publications on childbirth and our study of how employment is presented in these types of publications confirms the prevalence of the discourses of personal and public responsibility within a medical discourse of pregnancy (Gross and Pattison, 2001). Once pregnancy is defined as a medical event, its management is devolved to external and expert sources, which simultaneously draw women into the need to participate in specialised procedures that assist in ensuring a healthy outcome. It can be argued that once it was removed from the exclusively domestic sphere of home where traditionally women were in control, pregnancy and pregnant women were accorded the increased visibility associated with presence in the public domain.

In addition to the routine screening, monitoring, check-ups and the gamut of advice which make pregnancy public, there are a number of other ways that pregnancy is made publicly visible and open to scrutiny. One way that we can conceptualise this scrutiny is to examine how the 'atypical' pregnancies we identified in Chapter 1 and Chapter 2 are presented and to explore what it is that provokes such attention.

Atypical or abnormal pregnancies

In order for a pregnancy to be newsworthy it must in some way be contrasted with what is considered to be normal pregnancy, which routinely receives little media attention although there is ongoing scrutiny in the medical domain. What is normal is obviously a statistical phenomenon. However, as the research by Linnell and Bredmar (1996) highlights and the overwhelming content of pregnancy and birth magazines regularly emphasises, what is normal as a pregnancy is as much determined by the outcome as by the process. Nevertheless, there are some ways that we can conceptualise what is generally understood as a normal pregnancy and this revolves around the notion of the Good Mother and its converse, the Bad Mother.

While motherhood is highly valued in society, the attribution of that value – being a good mother – is largely restricted to pregnancy occurring within proscribed boundaries. Outside these boundaries, pregnancy may be seen as deviant. When the criteria of the Good Mother are met, she is accorded little attention. Conversely, women who fail to meet the criteria associated with the Good Mother are accorded greater visibility, since being viewed as wanting in comparison brings with it automatic censure. Thus, the Good Mother status can be bestowed upon women who are pregnant and married, or at the very least in a stable and usually hetero-sexual relationship, who are of a certain age and who are willing to conform to the required changes in behaviour. Therefore, one potential form of bad mothering is pregnancy outside marriage, as shown by the examples of treatment at work cited in Chapter 4. Given that in 2005, figures from the UK's Office of National Statistics suggest that in Britain cohabiting couples equal or outnumber married couples, this places a large number of women who might become pregnant in a position where they will attract comment. The Eurostat (2004) figures also indicate that nearly half of births occurring in the UK are to non-married women. Outside the UK, Australia and the US also have high national rates of unmarried (rather than non-married) women, at 32 per cent and 30.6 per cent respectively (2004/05 figures). These figures in themselves contain the potential for shifting what is considered normal, though this has not typically been the response. Traditional family structures remain paramount. In addition to traditional family patterns, the legitimate childbearing years also clearly exclude girls under 16 and women over normal childbearing age (49). With the average age of first pregnancy in some European countries at nearly 30 and in Australia at 30.6, these two groups of women, which also include teenage parents more generally, are considered to be 'bad mothers' and we discuss them in more detail below.

Moreover, it is also considered to be the norm that pregnancy is a positive and even uplifting experience, followed by an organised delivery and quick return to the pre-pregnancy state and appearance. So, good mothers are those who conform to the expectation of a blooming preg-nancy, a healthy baby and a return to sexy wife. Despite Jane Ussher's (1992) discussion of the tyranny of such an expectation in imposing on women the feelings of failure if they do not find it so, only recently is it becoming acceptable to admit to not enjoying pregnancy or finding it hard. Being a good mother also means enduring all the unpleasant (and sometimes life-threatening) side-effects of pregnancy with good spirits for the sake of the baby.

There are further assumptions made as part of being a good mother and this is that women will not have to give up their children for adoption and that loss of the pregnancy or infant is a source of serious distress and grief. The possibility of terminating a pregnancy for personal preference or convenience is frowned upon, except in extreme cases of illness. By contrast, for those who are seen as bad mothers, pregnancy ending by termination, stillbirth or even neonatal death can be considered in some circumstances to be an appropriate outcome for women who fall outside the prescribed boundaries and adoption of children born to single women was the norm until very recently. As films like *The Magdalene Sisters*, a fictional account of girls incarcerated in the Magdalene Laundries[1] (directed by Peter Mullan, 2002), show us, treatment of young girls was sometimes alarmingly harsh, as their equation with the concept of the bad mother would permit.

Bad mothers are not accorded the same expectations as are extended to women identifiable as good mothers. For bad mothers pregnancy can be automatically criticised as abnormal, as pathological and as unsuitable. Thus, while pregnancy as a good mother attracts positive comment and interest, for women who fall outside the framework, pregnancy can attract criticism and worse, as the discussion in Chapter 4 of women's experiences in the workplace has shown, placing working mothers too as bad mothers in this analysis. Nevertheless, both good and bad mothers may be subject to the same judgements levelled at their appearance, status, beliefs and level of responsibility. In the following sections we examine these dimensions of good and bad mothering in more detail.

Pregnancy in older women

In 1993, commentators were suggesting from population trends that by the end of the century (i.e. by 1999) 40 per cent of all births would be to women aged 30 or over and figures quoted earlier show that this point has already been reached in some countries. Even if conception and first pregnancy are delayed until this time, women are frequently considered to be acting selfishly by putting their own gratification first, rather than acting responsibly, and certainly women who remain childless into their 30s often receive negative comments (Allen, 2005). One explanation for this disapproval may be something we raised in Chapter 1 – the low birthrate and the perceived economic dangers of too few people to support public services and finance an increasingly ageing population. Another explanation is that older women in general are viewed as a homogeneous group; typically, women having first children are aggregated with women having subsequent children, who are older simply of necessity precisely like the prediction of 1993. A further reason may be the power of stereotypes we have discussed in previous chapters. How old is too old depends of course on where the average is at any time and the prevailing expectations of women's other public roles, for example as workers or as parents. Women in contemporary society are expected to participate in the public domain as well as fulfil their domestic or private roles and their willingness to accommodate public beliefs and expectations can, as we have seen, be extremely stressful.

Contrary to expectations, however, women who have their first baby later in life are not all ruthless careerists, according to Julia Berryman and her co-authors (1995), who found that in their sample of 340 older mothers only 5 per cent of women had delayed pregnancy for career reasons. Nevertheless, women in their study reported that motherhood over 40 was often seen as inappropriate and that shock, horror and disgust were not uncommon reactions when they announced their pregnancy.

As advances in reproductive technology have enabled a small number of women, who might otherwise be expected to be going through the menopause (and beyond), to become pregnant, older women have attracted attention, almost as curiosities and as potentially bad mothers. The attention is a mixture of scientific pride and moral outrage. Coverage of very late (i.e. over 50) pregnancy is typically censorious and appears to reflect pervasive political and societal beliefs that, while pregnancy in much older women may be technologically interesting, such pregnancy is somehow unsuitable, not normal, and strong sanctions may be applied to the individual, their lifestyle and their beliefs. Older women are considered to be irresponsible in becoming pregnant, and this criticism is levelled at the doctors too, for daring to cheat nature and rob the children of their rights to parents. George Monbiot wrote in *The Guardian* newspaper (25 January 2001: 29) an article entitled 'Our strange fear of older mothers', the first line of which reads: 'No longer attractive to men, they're treated as an offence against nature'. Despite this alarming introduction, the article is in fact criticising negative coverage by other newspapers of announcements of a second pregnancy by a 61-year-old woman, and the birth of twins to another woman aged 56. In an oblique reference to the public perceptions of good and bad mothers, he goes on to say that 'to suggest that late births are unethical, we have first to say whom they have wronged'. The answer, we would suggest, is that it is public sensibility that has been wronged because of the expectation of what constitutes the age of normal motherhood.

Where women already have other children, the announcement of a late pregnancy is often a cause of mirth and speculation rather than congratulations. Certainly, the woman's age and the age of any other children is a matter for comment, especially where there may be a large gap in age between the last child and the current pregnancy. As an example, when *The Mirror* newspaper announced Cherie Blair's pregnancy in November 1999 it had, below the main front-page headline 'Cherie is pregnant', the sentence (their underlining) 'She's having her fourth child at 45', a phrasing which manages to capture both the shock and amusement of being beyond normal childbearing age and late pregnancy and the potential age gap between her existing children and the new baby. Interestingly, as the discussion on celebrities below also highlights, the images and coverage tread a fine line between defining Cherie Blair as either a good or a bad mother.

One effect of delaying first childbirth is that women may encounter problems of conception; thus, pregnancy in older women may attract further disapproval because it brings together a number of categories of what we are calling abnormal pregnancies. Though statistics indicate that there are more multiple births to women over 35, this is partly explained by the increasing availability and take-up of assisted conception in this group, particularly the use of fertility drugs and the implantation of several embryos after IVF, which increase the likelihood of having multiple pregnancies. In addition, more fundamental fears of mortality are raised by the juxtaposition of the older woman and the fragility of the unborn baby. This is emphasised through attention paid to potential risks to the woman's health and the future of the baby. Older mothers (medically those over 35 are considered elderly primigravida) may be presented as being irresponsible through the association with increased risk. There is evidence from the statistics on abnormalities that the incidence of certain defects increases with age, Down's syndrome being the most commonly known. Other risks include miscarriage and both maternal and infant mortality. Very recently, not only older mothers but older fathers have been found to increase risks of later problems in children born to older parents. Though statistics indicate that there are more multiple births to women over 35, this is partly explained by access to fertility treatments. In this way older women are visible as bad mothers not just because of their age, since they are expected to have given up on childbearing, but because of their membership of multiple categories of atypical pregnancy. Lastly, pregnancy in older women also raises interesting questions about what constitutes 'natural' in the context of pregnancy as a natural and biological event or process. Natural may be an archetypal element of the Good Mother here perhaps.

Interestingly too, there is a positive side to later parenting, which gets less coverage. At a primitive or mystical level, the appearance of new life in the context of an older parent can be rejuvenating and exciting. While it is undoubtedly true that it may be more tiring to have young children later in life, there may be other benefits of delaying first pregnancy, for example commitment to parenting, being in a better financial position to support a child and the demands of family life, as well as living a healthier lifestyle. Recent research has also suggested that having children later in life may actually benefit women's health (Grundy and Tomassini, 2005). These more positive elements tend not to feature in representations of older mothers although their absence is remarked upon repeatedly in another group of potentially bad mothers – very young women.

Younger and teenage mothers

Despite the interest generated by pregnancy in older women, not least because of its risks, the greatest opprobrium, certainly in the UK and in the US, is reserved for teenage mothers. Why is this? As Bynner *et al.* (2002) point out, it was once a common occurrence for women to be pregnant in their teens, but it is now constructed as a social problem. Part of the concern arises from the numbers. Figures suggest that the number of teenage pregnancies in the UK and the US is considerably higher than in some European countries, notably the Netherlands, and despite efforts to change behaviour it has reached an unprecedented rate. In 1997, the rate of teenage pregnancies among 15- to 19-year-olds was 30 per 1,000 in the UK and only 4 per 1,000 in the Netherlands. This discrepancy has continued to the present day. UK figures published in 2005 which relate to 2003 show that the number of teenage pregnancies in the 15–17 age group was 42.1 per 1,000 and 8 per 1,000 for those aged 13–15. The figures did go down, slowly, between 1998 and 2003 but they are certainly disturbing, particularly for the younger age group. US figures indicate the rate of births to 15- to 19-year-olds as 30 per 1,000 (US Census Bureau, 2005). However, though absolute numbers may be high, as Ann Phoenix pointed out in 1991, a distinction must be made between those adolescents who become pregnant during their school years and those who choose to become mothers during their teenage years beyond the age of compulsory schooling (in the UK this is 16 years). The subtlety of this argument is not well represented in the way that teenage pregnancy is made visible, whereby all adolescents, like all older women, are treated in the same way. Sometimes, the tag 'school girl mums' is used to emphasise the extreme youth of the girls being featured. While concern centres on the numbers and the development of strategies to prevent teenage pregnancy, the possible reasons for the high rates of pregnancy in this group are less well understood.

Despite a relatively young average age of menarche (12 years 6 months in the UK and other European countries), there is increasing pressure for young people to remain at school, or extend their education elsewhere, in order to improve their future opportunities. Thus, there is a mismatch between biological maturity and the point of economic independence, which serves to highlight pregnancy as anomalous for this group, since they are not able to support themselves or a baby, thus marking them out as bad mothers. Of major concern is the likelihood that, once pregnant, adolescents will fall into a pattern of dependency on state benefits, lowered educational expectations and reduced engagement in the labour market, all of which gives cause for public concern and grounds for public intervention in teenagers' access to contraception advice, sex education or continued participation in education or employment.

Another significant explanation for the very negative comments about young people's lives is that pregnancy is a clear representation of sexuality. Of course, this is also the case for older women who become pregnant, and it may be partly this symbolism that accounts for the very punitive attitudes expressed in relation to pregnancy which offend public morals. Pregnancy is normally associated with adulthood, though whether it is becoming a mother that leads to maturity (adulthood) or whether mother-hood is an outcome of being an adult is less clear, as Anne Woollett (1991) has pointed out. The concern surrounding teenage mothers can thus be regarded as arising from a proposition that pregnancy signals deviant childhood, particularly through the association of sexuality with childhood rather than emerging adulthood.

Pregnancy is unlikely to be the intention behind most teenage sexual relationships; rather, those who get pregnant may just be the unlucky ones. Research by the Joseph Rowntree Foundation (2006) suggests that only a quarter of teenagers who become pregnant intend to have a baby. Others have suggested that pregnancy and motherhood may provide adolescent girls with a role in life, a role that is usually highly valued. In this case, the argument goes that the girls see no reason to delay motherhood (Ineichen, 1986; Ineichen et al., 1997). This would hardly be relevant to school-age mothers, however, and in their case there is a suggestion that teenagers who get pregnant subconsciously want to do so. This would scarcely seem to be an incentive to get pregnant given that the role is devalued. It is possible, however, that, on discovering the pregnancy, teenage mothers decide to keep the baby in order to fulfil other psychological needs, to be loved. In Schofield's (1994) study, some young mothers indicated that they received lots of attention while they were pregnant. At the same time, interestingly and as Phoenix (1991) also notes, as a teenage mother, they can enjoy child and adult status simultaneously, living at home and having their own mother look after them, and being able to identify themselves as a pregnant woman with a baby.

There is also an issue of choice. Moralistic arguments, following the public view of teenage pregnancy as a problem, can emphasise the need to terminate the pregnancy, often making use of arguments of inevitability of poor outcome, such as poor educational achievement and curtailment of ambition. Indeed, it would appear that in the UK on average about half of all teenage conceptions in 13- to 17-year-olds are terminated. In 2005 further legal challenges to young people's right to privacy in medical con-sultations were once again underway in England so that young women could not terminate a pregnancy without their parent's or carer's knowl-edge. This too has attracted media attention, some of which highlights the damage that would be done by such a shift in the nature of the consul-tation process and some of which endorses the imposition of parental control as a representation of moral values. Nevertheless, the visibility of pregnancy in this age group remains as pregnancy out of place and the young women are seen as examples of bad mothers.

However, in terms of our public expectations and public representations of pregnancy, the status of adolescents as mothers is thus devalued by their entering adulthood at the wrong time. The ambiguous attitude to teenage pregnancy is reflected in the mixed responses to strategies to reduce pregnancies. Plans to improve sex education offered in schools, especially for very young age groups, and to increase contraceptive advice or the availability of contraception to young people through schools or drop-in clinics in high street shops, are seen by pro-life and some religious organisations as promoting under-age sex and encouraging the use of abortion as a contraceptive. Similarly, when an under-age mother continues in education and only stops to give birth before returning to her exams, the public response is that this is setting a bad example to other youngsters, putting education and under-age pregnancy in the same bracket (*Grantham Journal*, June 1998). Currently, plans by the UK government to make it a requirement that the police are alerted to any known under-age sexual activity scarcely make it more likely that the young people involved will be able to seek appropriate advice. Furthermore, research could be said to be looking at this issue from a limited perspective. The evidence is strong that most young women who become pregnant in their teenage years are likely to have mothers who themselves were teenagers when they became pregnant. The cultural expectations within the communities and families are therefore likely to be very different from those of health educators and those concerned to break the 'cycle of disadvantage' perceived to arise from very young motherhood.

Teenage mothers who do not marry or cohabit with their partners go on to become members of another problem group, 'single mothers', a group which also falls foul of normal expectations of pregnancy and motherhood and attracts negative or condemnatory coverage. In fact, welfare-to-work programmes are specifically designed to assist such young women in developing their skills rather than staying at home and looking after their children. This is despite an ongoing concern for the welfare of children and a decline in parenting skills; such is the contradictory nature of attitudes and expectations of women. Newspapers highlight this inconsistency in their coverage: in a deliciously ironic article in the British newspaper, the *News of the World*, incredulity is expressed that a 'single mum' could turn down an offer of marriage from the millionaire she was dating (*News of the World*, 24 January 1999). The public requirement is to take up opportunities that would reposition a single mother as a good mother at a stroke and is paramount in this case, even if in other circumstances she might be castigated for being a 'gold-digger'. Thus, teenage or under-age pregnancy, which carries the double burden of being a single mother, provides a means by which surveillance may be maintained and repeated at differing points in young women's lives; they become an object of future as well as current concern. This concern provides a rationale for continued interest and report.

The ideology whereby society defines teenage pregnancy as a problem is the means by which the private behaviour of sexual relationships, pregnancy and motherhood are brought into the public domain and sustained by cultural images. There are other ways in which pregnancy becomes visible, because it does not conform to the normal expected pattern of behaviour expected of the good mother. This lack of conformity makes it inappropriate or irresponsible. These include hidden, surrogate and multiple pregnancies.

Hidden pregnancy

In the context of the visibility of pregnancy, a hidden pregnancy would seem to be inadmissible. However, it is the visibility after the event that is of interest here, particularly in relation to concepts of good and bad mothers. Hidden pregnancy can take a number of forms. At its most extreme it can be a sign of a serious psychotic episode (Brockington, 1994); very often it involves infanticide, by killing or by neglect of the baby. It is hardly consistent with the rhetoric of good mothering. A headline which appeared in the *Mirror* newspaper in September 2005 – 'Mum nearly killed by hidden pregnancy' – indicates how a pregnancy might be hidden. The woman involved had not considered herself likely to become pregnant, due to previous physical problems, and she and her partner were not planning to have children at the time. She had shown no symptoms of pregnancy, no physical changes, until suddenly she was taken ill and rushed to hospital, where it was discovered that she had pre-eclampsia. Her premature baby was delivered safely by caesarean section and both made a good recovery. What is interesting about this particular story is that it turns the contained baby into the agent of the mother's negative experience rather than the defenceless recipient, which is how such hidden pregnancies are usually presented. For example, a *CNN* report (9 July 1998) of a case heard in the US in July 1998 concerned 'sweethearts Amy Grossberg and Brian Peterson' who received prison sentences for killing their baby son after he had been born in a motel room in 1996. In this case, the pregnancy had been disguised and kept from the young woman's parents and friends. This kind of hidden pregnancy is more common in adolescence, and may be coupled with poor understanding of the progress of pregnancy. At the same time, the pressure to deny the pregnancy because of the implications can apparently be strong enough to prevent the usual signs of pregnancy developing, so that the pregnancy is hidden not just from the public but from the woman herself. Once such cases come to court, however, their visibility is assured and the very environment in which the news comes into the public domain is likely to determine the nature of the young people's treatment, both by the media and by the legal system.

The possibility of hidden pregnancy reflecting a genuine unawareness of a physical state seems almost implausible, given the visibility of pregnancy and particularly, as we discussed in Chapter 2, at a time when the confirmation of a pregnancy can precede the typical indicators such as the first missed period. However, awareness and recognition of symptoms will depend on the individual's perspective. Both those wanting to become pregnant and those concerned specifically to avoid becoming pregnant will undoubtedly be highly alert to any changes, in the same way, we suggest, that somatic attributions are made by those reporting cognitive change for example. For those who have no reason to suspect a pregnancy or who have contra-indications for pregnancy, for example absent or irregular menstrual cycles, then identifying symptoms may be a different matter, as the mother who was rushed to hospital herself suggested. In these cases, the woman really is unaware of her changed state, and this can persist up to labour, when women are brought into emergency wards with severe pain. Unawareness in this sense is clearly not the same as keeping the pregnancy secret.

Evidence from the teenage mothers in Schofield's (1994) study suggests that girls kept their pregnancy secret in order to avoid causing problems at home. Because of the attitudes to teenage pregnancy, several girls indicated that they knew that if they told anyone, their parents for example, they would almost certainly be forced to terminate the pregnancy. However, the research evidence that teenage mothers tend to be the daughters of teenage parents suggests that pressure for termination may only be true for a subset of the girls involved. By leaving it until it was too late to safely terminate the pregnancy this option was removed, and their choice was made. Another reason given by the participants in Schofield's (1994) study to keep the pregnancy secret was to avoid admitting it to themselves and only when labour starts could they acknowledge what is happening and tell a parent. Even when it has been acknowledged at an earlier stage, treatment by health professionals is not always encouraging and rights offered to women of average childbearing age, such as being accompanied by a parent or partner during labour, were denied to the adolescents; they were effectively treated as bad mothers.

Finally, in this section, there has been a historic shift in the way that pregnancy is visible to others, alluded to above, and that is through the change in the way that maternity clothes have migrated from a form of veiling of pregnancy, to creating a pregnant silhouette as an object of desire. As Mathiassen (2005) demonstrates in her paper, these changes reflect changing times and customs in the treatment and expectations of pregnant women. However, it is a moot point whether the visibility created by the absence of disguise using smocks and loose clothing by the arrival of stretch fabrics has really allowed pregnant women more freedom.

Paradoxically, as the preceding sections have demonstrated, it remains difficult to achieve the requirements of the good mother.

Before we go on to look at how celebrity pregnancy, the ultimately visible pregnancy, is treated in terms of public attention, there are two further examples of 'bad mothers' we would like to mention. These involve the combination of assisted conception and indeed gay parenting, which together create a potent focus for public comment.

Surrogate pregnancy

Surrogacy has been portrayed in the public view as another example of bad mothering, as the following headline from 1988 attests: 'It's baby selling and it's wrong' (*New York Times*, 4 June 1988: 26). In November 2005 the *South Korea Herald* reported that the punishing of surrogate mothers had been made law. But aside from these outright condemnations, surrogacy is presented in an oddly ambivalent way. So, on the one hand, a devoted sister who offers to have a child for her childless sister may be seen as selfless and generous. On the other hand, the idea of renting out a uterus, together with the possible fertilisation process that accompanies the conception, is viewed not only with distaste when it involves a financial incentive, but also as being sordid and highly irresponsible. In 1999 there was news coverage of a British gay couple, who had just become fathers to twins born as the result of a surrogate pregnancy in the US: 'Gay couple pay for surrogate mother's twins' (*The Guardian*, 2 September 1999). The men were intending to adopt the children in order to become their legal parents and their case was ultimately successful. This was despite some very unsupportive responses provoked because they were gay, which drew, for example, on the risks of breaking the mother–child bond inherent in surrogacy and the needs of the children in terms of the natural parenting environment. This case refers explicitly to the notions of good mothers while, at the same time, surrogacy automatically invokes the metaphor of containment.

In another fascinating turn on the visibility of pregnancy, the way that surrogacy is dealt with includes commentary on the unsuitability of purchasing a womb to act as a vessel for the development of a baby that will be handed over to someone else. By referring to the concept of good mother, which includes the mother and child bond, the coverage unusually expresses concern about the wellbeing of the woman, and in particular this suggests that she will be psychologically affected by the loss of the baby. Research does not suggest that this is the case (Jadva *et al.*, 2003). Despite the negative tone of the coverage, women report their involvement as a positive experience. Although it is indeed true that the baby will go home with someone else, the process is regarded as an opportunity to help others and thus women acting as surrogates can present themselves as good mothers, even if the public view is rather different. One way to explain the concern over the surrogate mother's mental health is, of course, the reversion to female stereotypes in which emotionality and motherhood are key elements. Surrogacy, however, can be regarded as disrupting the highly charged and prescribed mother–baby emotional relationship by allocating one essential component – the antenatal experience – to another person, though it does retain the important genetic link (van den Akker, 2000). This splitting is a calculated shift in the parenting relationship compared to the straightforward adoption of somebody else's child and raises anxieties of Orwell's *1984*, clearly also undermining the concept of a natural process and of a good mother.

Multiple pregnancy

The final example of atypical or abnormal pregnancies which serve to highlight the visibility of many aspects of the experience of pregnancy and the way it is overseen is multiple pregnancy. This is where a woman is expecting more than one baby and usually more than three, which are considered rare but normal occurrences. Twins rarely attract attention and though triplets do occur without any assistive intervention negative comments are usually reserved for multiple pregnancies involving four or more babies. The Dionne quintuplets, born in 1934, were the first to survive infancy and were displayed to the public in a theme park called Quintland by the authorities (www.nomotc.org). Multiple pregnancy attracts the same combination of the fascination for the technological developments, here surrounding the creation of a pregnancy outside the accepted method of biological reproduction, and the disapproval associated with its execution, as has been discussed in relation to pregnancy in older women. An example is the case of Mandy Allwood, who in 1996 was pregnant with eight babies. Not only was this remarkable in itself, but she decided to sell her story to the newspapers, which attracted greater coverage and greater opportunities for disapproval. The phrase 'Cash for babies' appeared in a number of newspapers including the *Bolton Evening News*, which also commented that 'her relationship does not appear to be stable'. She was not married to her partner and such a reference is clearly shorthand for Mandy Allwood is a bad mother. Tragically, the pregnancy did not proceed and all the babies had died by 19 weeks. Significantly, however, coverage of the story centred more on disapproval of Mandy Allwood's apparently mercenary approach than on her personal story.

The case of Mandy Allwood and the focus on an individual and her pregnancy, which was discussed at length through the summer of 1996, brings us neatly to the topic of celebrity pregnancy, which forms the remainder of the chapter. In 1998, three well-known young women at the time were pregnant, two of the then Spice Girls band, Victoria Beckham and Melanie Brown, and Melanie Blatt of All Saints. Concern was expressed by Family and Youth Concern (a pressure group) and by the British Pregnancy Advisory Service that teenagers would be influenced by the message being given that 'it is fine to become pregnant'. The particular visibility of these women, who were in the music business – already possibly regarded as slightly unsavoury – together with the ambiguous marital status of two of them, identified them as potentially bad mothers; worse than this, they were unwittingly promoting such behaviour in others. Visibility in the public sphere, particularly for women, carries with it an unspoken expectation of good behaviour. It is interesting to explore how this requirement for good behaviour is reflected when such individuals become pregnant. In this case, because the well-known women were also young, they were tarred with the same critical comments as were their fan base – they could not get it right. The second way of addressing the issue of visibility and of surveillance is to consider the representation of pregnancy of individuals who are already visible in the public domain for something that they do (i.e. the famous) rather than those who become visible because they are pregnant.

The already visible: pregnancy and celebrity

Over the past twenty years, the press has seized on the pregnancy announcements by famous people; pictures of pregnant women abound. Images of well-known figures from the world of entertainment, sport, royalty and even politics are now routinely captured in *Hello* magazine and its worldwide equivalents. Increasingly, these images include pictures of celebrity pregnancies. Mandy Allwood appeared in one of the first year's issues of *OK* magazine; Victoria Beckham and Melanie Brown appeared on the front cover of *Now* magazine in January 1999 and it is now almost impossible to avoid news of celebrities and their pregnancies. Indeed, Tyler (2001) and Longhurst (2005) reflect on the role of celebrities in the growth of maternity fashion. It could almost be said that pregnancy itself has become something of a celebrity. The absolute visibility of the subject highlights how images of pregnancy can command public attention. In this section of the chapter, we explore how the fascination with images of pregnancy might also be seen as part of a more disturbing web of surveillance thrown over women's lives.

Images of pregnancy

In their book *Pregnant Pictures*, Sandra Matthews and Laura Wexler (2000) state that at the start of their research they were concerned to identify the pregnant subject, having been prompted to begin their search by dismay at the shortage of images of such an important life event as pregnancy in the public visual culture. However, once they had completed their research and the book was published in 2000 the situation had already changed dramatically. Since the early 1990s, when *Vanity Fair* magazine published a now famous picture of the film actress Demi Moore, heavily pregnant, on its front cover, the apparent taboo against representing pregnancy in the public visual culture has relaxed; pregnancy has now become so visible it has even reached iconic status. The pose in the photograph of Demi Moore has been used frequently since then to picture other pregnant women, more and less famous, and such images are increasingly familiar and numerous, as the cover of this book suggests. As Matthews and Wexler document in their book, the change in visibility was in type as well as frequency; in particular they point to a shift from medico-instructional texts and instrumental forms of looking to iconic forms.

Significantly, as we have discussed in relation to good and bad mothers, images that appear in the published media are not usually those of routine everyday pregnancies. Routine, normal pregnancies are usually presented in specialist publications or websites devoted to the topic, while pregnancies deemed unusual receive disproportionate and largely negatively nuanced attention. Instead, routine media images of pregnancy tend to be those of celebrities or other public figures. There are even specialist websites devoted to maintaining updated records of which celebrity is pregnant, by whom and when the baby is due.

Coverage of celebrities through both visual images and text is a major component of some publications' remit (e.g. *Heat, Hello, Now, OK* and their equivalents globally) so that individuals' visibility is high. However, given the nature of coverage of pregnancy more generally in the media, it seems simplistic to assume that widespread coverage of celebrity pregnancy is merely an extension of the media's preoccupation with celebrity. Rather, it may represent a reactionary discourse of 'family'; or it may be a response to the power of female sexuality evident in the pregnant form, making reference to representations of women as the archetypal Good Mother. Alternatively, by referring to familiar stereotypes, such coverage may be a means of repositioning women in the role of mothers as uninterested in external events, as well as being irrational or highly emotional (Lemish and Barzel, 2000; Ussher, 1992) and centred around the home. Given that these discourses also surround pregnancy for all women, it is interesting to see whether the publicly visible pregnancies of celebrities are treated differently from those of less visible women, in relation to expectations of behaviour or advice.

Coverage of celebrity pregnancies also makes reference to the other categories of atypical pregnancy that we have discussed above. Jonathan Margolis in *The Independent* newspaper (10 August 2005) draws directly on these in a piece entitled 'Natal attraction', which highlights the significance of pregnancy for celebrities: 'when cameras are trained on your belly, pregnancy can be a career maker or shaker' (*The Independent*, 10 August 2005: 35). Within the article, he identifies a series of styles or types of pregnancy and the stars associated with these. For example, the 'doctor defying' pregnancy of older actresses makes direct allusion to the issue of normal pregnancy age as well as the fertility rates discussed above: 'Normal women over 45 can consider a conception unusual. For celebrities, miracles begin at around 35 . . .' (op. cit.). He includes in this category Courteney Cox (Arquette), who was 39 when she finally became pregnant, and Holly Hunter whose first pregnancy at 47 was with twins. He also identifies the 'just a bit' pregnancy, of Britney Spears, Reese Witherspoon and others. In this case, he is talking particularly about the value of news coverage that can be gained from speculation, some of which arises from apparent changes in weight or appearance. However, as we have discussed in Chapter 2, the possibility of early confirmation of pregnancy can also drive such speculation. A final example from this collection of categories, particularly redolent of our discussions of women's behaviour in earlier chapters, is that of the 'scandalous pregnancy' (whether real or guessed at), such as that of Siena Millar or Elizabeth Hurley, where the paternity is uncertain and where behaviour such as smoking is considered unacceptable. This categorisation is clearly also drawing on the discourse of Good Mothers which we addressed in the earlier part of this chapter.

Celebrity

In order to develop our argument, it is useful to digress slightly and clarify a definition of celebrity and of the psychological relevance of the concept in relation to a discussion of pregnancy. It is significant that, as Giles (2000) points out, celebrity is essentially a media production and is largely a twentieth-century phenomenon. The distinction usually drawn between fame and celebrity is that celebrities are well known through the media for nothing in particular, whereas the truly famous are in some way deserving of individual recognition (Giles, op. cit.). Boorstin defines a celebrity as a 'person who is known for his [sic] well-known-ness' (Boorstin, 1961: 57) and fame is clearly more than celebrity. Marshall (1997: 242) identifies the celebrity as 'the public representation of individuality in contemporary culture'. Moreover, he equates the arrival of the celebrity phenomenon with the emergence of psychology as a discipline, which he criticises as reducing human activity to private personality and the inner life of the individual. What this serves to remind us is that the focus is squarely on individuals. In this context, therefore, the important issue is that the visibility is of the person and that this visibility pre-exists when an announcement of a pregnancy is reported or suspected. For celebrities and for the famous, the possibility of provoking comment is subsumed within their identity as a celebrity, whatever their avowed desire for privacy. A further point, following Marshall's concern about the role of psychology in creating a cult of the individual, is whether the dividing line between the personal and the public is so clearly drawn. As we have discussed elsewhere, for all women pregnancy offers a means by which the private is made public and there is publicly sanctioned access to the personal. Pregnancy can be regarded as a visible statement not only of women's fertility, femininity and heterosexuality but also of masculinity and potency. Thus, it comes to signify fundamental gendering of social roles rather than individual experience.

Pregnancy, the individual and the body

Unlike the often critical attention paid to atypical pregnancies discussed in the earlier part of this chapter, it might be supposed that women already visible in and through the media would attract positive comment, and at one level this is likely to be true. However, as the examples above indicate, these women are certainly not exempt from criticism. Being in the public eye itself invites and permits comment. Whether celebrities conform to the notion of good or bad mothers can be explored by looking beyond this to some other ways in which their pregnancy is represented. One possible way of exploring the phenomenon of attention to celebrity pregnancy that has already been referred to with respect to teenage pregnancies is to consider it as pregnancy 'out of place'. For celebrities, this notion of 'out of place' could be seen as a celebration of the postmodern views of motherhood arising from the many options open to women – supermodel, filmstar, mother, etc. However, as Susan Faludi pointed out in 1992, the 'having-it-all' culture has tended to result in the reinstatement of women as mothers and bearers of children as a means of reducing their visibility, rather than as extending it. The treatment of celebrity pregnancy might thus be a further example of such reduction of individuality to a more generalised 'mother'.

On what grounds might celebrity pregnancy be constructed as 'out of place'? Is it that it conflicts with the kind of activities and practices that are expected of celebrities? It is possible to think of celebrity and its attendant concerns with self-presentation as a form of work in itself, as, for example, in the following tag to an article about Julia Roberts' pregnancy with twins: 'Roberts will have to work overtime to keep up her glamorous image with the arrival of twins' (*The Guardian*, 9 June 2004: 15). If celebrity is a job, then, effectively, like other women with jobs, the expectation is that, once pregnant, women celebrities will have to work harder to prove that they are still as good as they were. Additionally, when they become pregnant, women doing this celebrity job are individually choosing to step outside the role they have previously inhabited, rather than accepting the one they are celebrated for. This is true of all women at some point: for example when women are having a second or subsequent child and they have returned to work, having ostensibly relegated their fertility to another sphere. Nevertheless, their dual role as parent and worker is made visible in a way that may otherwise be maintained as hidden (Nippert-Eng, 1996). This way of characterising pregnancy as out of place is analogous to teenage pregnancy, in that younger women have fewer competing roles until they become pregnant. It may, however, appear more instrumentally than conceptually out of place.

What is noteworthy about out-of-place pregnancies is that by disrupting routines or expectations they force a response from others, as we have seen before. The visibility of a pregnancy also determines the kinds of responses that emerge. In particular, such responses often involve the need to manage either some aspect of the pregnancy or some aspect of the pregnant person. For example, medical management is the default, whether it is a routine or a technologically novel pregnancy, and includes promotion of health education and advice; in the case of teenage pregnancies the health advice may include termination of the pregnancy. If what out-of-place pregnancy accomplishes is the positioning of women in their role as mothers, rather than as celebrities (or otherwise competent individuals), they can then be accorded additional special status that highlights stereotypically feminine attributes. In doing this, the individual is simultaneously positioned as less competent and the justification for intervention or support is in place. It can work to the women's benefit; our research on normal pregnancy (Clarke and Gross, 2004a, 2004b) suggests that women can exploit stereotypically feminine behaviours to reduce the demands on them to perform in all spheres, as discussed in Chapter 6. Harris and Campbell (1999) point to the way that pregnancy can provide a route out of employment for some women. In a similar way, pregnancy may represent an opportunity for celebrities to change other people's expectations of them (Page, 2003).

The nature of celebrity being what it is, celebrities are already subject to scrutiny and intrusion into their private lives; celebrity status involves being treated with care, if not respect. In this context, therefore, the visibility of pregnancy simply changes the focus of that expected care and may actually serve to reinforce the individual's own status and importance. A further example relating to Julia Roberts, concerning special arrangements made to accommodate her pregnancy during filming on location, serves as an illustration:

> Writers have had to rework the script to accommodate her pregnancy. . . . Another effect of her pregnancy is that she has had to frequently ask director Steven Soderbergh to halt shooting so that she can sit down and sip water during her bouts of nausea.
> (*London Evening Standard*, 17 June 2004: 23)

This example can be read as stereotyping femininity, with male acceptance of her weakened condition, as well as the according of special treatment to her at work due to her being a celebrity (not always available to other women in the workplace).

However, we can also configure celebrity pregnancy as an atypical pregnancy because it demonstrates something inconvenient or unusual which draws public attention. As we suggested in discussing non-married teenage mothers, combining different forms of atypicality also attracts media attention. Here, the example of Cherie Blair is instructive. When her fourth pregnancy was announced in 1999, she was already well known for her role of political wife, mother and as a career barrister (Page, 2003), although she had kept a low profile in the media. As discussed above, she was also 45 years old. The announcement was covered in all the daily and weekend newspapers and created a suddenly expanded personal visibility for her as an archetype of the older mother, according to the *Daily Telegraph* newspaper (20 November 1999), as well as the epitome of the successful woman. Despite the *Daily Telegraph*'s praise for her, there was also much reporting of how surprised and amazed Cherie was to find herself pregnant, implying that for someone acting as a role model she had not prepared herself at her age to have become pregnant, and that she had been irresponsible by becoming pregnant when she already had older children and other commitments. The coverage also included reference to the possible risks of a late pregnancy. The *Mirror* newspaper offered her advice on how to minimise those risks: 'take all the tests like me and you will be fine' (*Mirror*, 19 November 1999: 6).

The notion of unplanned pregnancy resonates with the label of irresponsibility applied to teenage pregnancy and conception outside the boundaries of marriage, highlighting how, in order to participate fully in the role of a good mother, celebrities also have to conform to appropriate criteria. A further example is the headline on Gwyneth Paltrow's pregnancy in an Australian gossip magazine: 'Inside: Gwyn's shock pregnancy' and a further strapline: 'Was it planned? Will Chris marry her? Will she cope?' (*NW*, 15 December 2003: 14). Speculation on the ability to cope emphasises the need to treat her carefully in her new condition and invites monitoring as a means of support. Such intrusion, we would argue, although commonplace for those in the public eye, nevertheless serves to diminish their significance and potential threat, making these especially visible pregnancies available for external interventions.

As celebrity is largely in the gift of the media, the media also has the power to downgrade it, demonstrating the power of the symbiotic relationship whereby the media accords itself the means to determine individuals' lives. One way in which this frequently occurs is through a favourite feature of such gossip magazines, the routine 'outing' of celebrities when they are looking less than glamorous – informal unscripted photo opportunities that show celebrities looking more like the rest of us. These pictures make celebrities' ordinary lives visible and have the positive effect of reassuring readers that perfection is difficult to attain. Giles (2000) suggests that being or appearing beautiful is a criterion for fame and the celebrity magazines certainly corroborate this. The effect of such 'outings' is to provide opportunities to express dissatisfaction with celebrities' perform- ance of their role whereby their accountability to the public includes permanent beauty. Although the media can be inconsistent, for example Gwyneth Paltrow was praised for her confidence in looking 'grungy' by day when this was a fashion trend, as long as she looked glamorous by night (*Evening Standard*, 7 May 2002), the obsession with appearance and looking beautiful at all times can push individuals to the limit in terms of their public appearances. In another example, the film actor Kate Hudson is described as 'being unhappy with her appearance' and the article attributes the discomfort it highlights to the actress herself. The deliberate juxtaposing of the informal photos of Kate Hudson in late pregnancy with a formally posed photograph of her pre-pregnancy can be viewed as criticism of the celebrity's refusal to play her part and maintain her image, simultaneously sanctioning her glamorous image and her contravening of it.

To conclude this section, and return to the theme of surveillance, pregnancy and celebrity pregnancy in particular would seem to offer the opportunity to comment critically about an individual making a private choice that sits uncomfortably with the public expectation of that individual or that individual's role. In this case, the pregnant individual is highly visible and their visibility provokes the comments. The next theme takes up a consistent thread appearing through this book and in much of feminist literature on pregnancy and addresses how the individual can become less visible, despite a co-existing public presence.

The pregnant body: 'pregnancy as containment'

A different but not unrelated way of thinking about the issues of celebrity pregnancy is that it is pregnancy in and of itself that forms the focus of interest. This more substantive concern reflects the literature on pregnancy and embodiment (e.g. Bordo, 1991; Young, 1990) and of pregnancy and containment (e.g. Smith, 1992; Woollett and Marshall, 1997; and others). These writers argue convincingly that contrary to what might be imagined in the light of the increased visibility of pregnancy in public images, preg- nancy has become more and more removed from women's bodies and women's control. The separation may occur directly through the new technologies of reproduction which accord greater visibility to the foetus. Maher (2002) also discusses the way such images are deployed to separate maternal and foetal interests and makes the interesting point that no attention is paid to the placenta, which inextricably links the mother and baby and which does not feature in images. Women may be made further remote from their own experiences of their pregnancies through the discourses of containment and risk. These discourses place women as responsible for the safety and health of their babies, such that they need to be proactive in ensuring that they do not behave in a way that might cause damage, as was the case with the research on diet and exercise discussed in Chapters 5 and 6. At the same time, they are expected to be passive containers, receptive to advice and comment from others. Despite a current rhetoric of maternal choice, increased awareness of potential risks prevents them from taking control.

So, through containment, embodiment (i.e. the grounding of women's experiences of their bodies) is refocused on the body contained within them. By this means, women's identity is lost or hidden (see Young, 1990) and in this regard many of the pictures collated by Matthews and Wexler (2000) are illuminating, as is a quick check on the internet for images of pregnancy (72,000 on 1 July 2004, including goats and sheep; with exponential growth in numbers over the year, up to 300,000 in October 2005). Many of the pictures are of the torso, or sometimes a silhouette only – individual women are absent from the picture. In some cases the body is naked, in others the body is clothed except for the enlarged abdomen. Such pictures remove pregnancy from the individual and reframe it as a separate embodied experience. This is accentuated by the introduction of technologies that see within the container to the contained. Such separation reprises the medico-legal discourses prevalent within the instrumental frame identified by Matthews and Wexler. Such instrumental looking is very much in keeping with the shift to the hegemonic medical model of pregnancy that accompanied the transfer of pregnancy care from women and home to hospital and doctor (Oakley, 1984). However, by contrast with many images of pregnancy, pictures of celebrity pregnancies are clearly identifiable, since without identification the pictures would be of little value. This does not mean that the individual is actually the focus of the image.

In this personalisation of pregnancy within a context of separation, we would argue that pregnancy of celebrities provides a vehicle by which pregnancy more widely can be maintained as a topic in the public domain, and also acts to separate celebrity from their pregnancy. Pregnancy thus represents one aspect of the 'cult of the feminine' that predominates in cultural images of women. This may then reprise other discourses that underpin a more reactionary positioning of women. By separating pregnancy as an embodied experience from the women involved, it is easier for such commentaries to prevail.

The discourse of containment is one that allows similar commentary on appearance, behaviour and lifestyle, as discussed in relation to the out-of-place pregnancy. Lupton (1999), in talking about risk more generally, highlights pregnancy as a means by which a public 'web of surveillance' is enacted, exhorting restrictions in diet and behaviour for the sake of their unborn child. This surveillance, she suggests, is almost courted by women themselves, particularly, as she points out, in relation to available reproductive technologies. Women demand more technological intervention to support their active responsibilities, but this intervention further removes them from their bodies and reinforces the power of others over them, or at the very least provides the opportunity for outsiders to intrude and impose their views, as the discussion of advice more generally has demonstrated (Chapters 4, 5 and 6).

Let us consider some examples of such intrusion. As we discussed in earlier chapters, the emphasis is on maintaining a healthy lifestyle and the research emanating from the strong cultural beliefs is of interference and criticism of behaviour. Coverage in the media of Britney Spears' first pregnancy in 2005 drew attention to her weight and to her diet, presenting both as in need of improvement: *Britney Spears' Pregnancy Binge*: Britney needs to work out, with up to 45 minutes of cardio six days a week and some high-intensity strength training if she is to shift the weight (www.female-first.co.uk). Elsewhere, text accompanying pictures of the pregnant star highlights that Britney was giving in to her cravings for pickled gherkins and ice cream with details of the precise calories this represented. The reference to cravings allows a mixed message to be presented. First, that she was behaving naturally but second that she was behaving irresponsibly and gaining unnecessary weight. Britney is a celebrity but she is also young and this seems to play against her in the critical comments made about her looks and behaviour and the instructions of how she should change her ways. Interestingly, Margolis' article in *The Independent* (10 August 2005) would regard Britney's preparedness to gain weight and revel in her pregnant state as an 'earth mother' pregnancy, a classification that could reposition her behaviour as indicative of good mothering. However, Britney Spears continued to attract disapproving comments for her parenting skills (e.g. *abcNews*, 17 May 2006), and maintained her position as a bad mother by posing for *Elle* magazine (*Elle* US issue, October 2005) during her first pregnancy and *Harper's* magazine when six months pregnant with her second child (*Harper's Bazaar*, August 2006).

A different type of celebrity example comes from the extensive coverage of Cherie Blair's pregnancy, which was announced in November 1999. In particular, because of her age (45), Cherie Blair's behaviour and suitability for parenthood attracted considerable comment in newspaper articles: 'She consumes little alcohol or red meat, doesn't smoke and exercises regularly' (*Mirror*, 19 November 1999: 2). Her adherence to advice on appropriate behaviour to some extent countermands her inappropriate age here. On the same page, in a further reference to sanctioned conditions for pregnancy, the article goes on to quote from an obstetrician at a Manchester hospital on the risks of pregnancy in older women: 'If *the mother* is fit and healthy, doesn't smoke and isn't overweight and has no existing conditions such as high blood pressure, there should be no problems' (our emphasis). Although the wording undoubtedly reflects standard advice on how to address the media (i.e. not commenting directly on any particular individual), it is telling in the context of this topic that the obstetrician refers to 'the mother' rather than to an individual – pregnancy and person are separate identities.

Whether celebrity pregnancy is out of place or acts to separate individuals from their embodied experience, both the themes identified here locate pregnancy squarely in the public domain, whether as a matter of personal and private choices or as a public matter for inspection and concern. Lupton's (1999) idea of the 'web of surveillance' provides a way of conceptualising both the issue of pregnancy and of celebrity and brings us back to our initial point of engagement with the issue of celebrity pregnancy. While Lupton is talking about the management and representation of risk, we can extend the notion of the web of surveillance more widely to the concept of celebrity, particularly women celebrities. By apparently being the embodiment of the range of femininity, celebrities only need pregnancy to complete the picture. Indeed, it is almost a compulsory rite of passage (Longhurst, 2005). At the same time, the legitimisation of commentary that accompanies lives lived in the public domain is analogous to the spotlighting of individuals who become pregnant, together with those who fall outside the boundaries of good motherhood.

Concluding remarks

Like all pregnant women, celebrities are not permitted to remain private, their lives are lived on the boundary of the private and the public; like women and women's appearance more generally, their clothes, their weight, their hair, and their partners, every element of their appearance and life is subject to comment. Equally, at no other time in their lives are ordinary healthy women given more sustained attention than when they are pregnant; they become celebrities for the period of their pregnancy, as the cases of the atypical pregnancies illustrated. Thus, they are all subject to sanction and intrusion into their private lives. For example, women report that people (often complete strangers) will touch them or their bump or ask questions that would at other times be off limits, or regarded as harassment. For celebrities, by contrast, this is routine and even deliberately sought. The risk for a celebrity of not participating in the surveillance is that they lose some aspect of their public identity. It could be argued that to some extent their private identity is actually already invisible; paradoxically, pregnancy provides a means of remaining under public, or at least media, surveillance but creating a shift in the gaze from the individual to their pregnancy, a disembodied event. Thus, what appears to be intrusive could almost be acceptable or even welcome. For women who are not celebrities, the public involvement may also be welcome, but it may be intrusive.

There are undoubtedly a number of other ways that the relationship between celebrity and pregnancy can be viewed which are well represented in the media images and articles. One of these is the way in which pregnancy may serve to normalise celebrity. Like everyone else, celebrities get pregnant and put on weight (at least temporarily) and they are subject to the same conflicting advice. But while such apparent frailties could at some times compromise celebrity status in the media, during pregnancy they may actually strengthen an individual's currency as a celebrity. A common comment about seeing celebrities in real life is how familiar they seem. The apparently shared experiences of pregnancy, with morning sickness and discomfort, may bring them closer to the viewer and thus further sustain public interest via the media.

Significantly, the impact of pregnancy may also be to extend the intrusion and surveillance that is part of the coverage of celebrities' lives more generally and further legitimate a critical framing of activity in the context of all women's public roles. When they are pregnant, celebrities' participation in the changed behaviours required of women who are taking their responsibilities seriously can also be commented on; the potential for increased criticism and identification of bad mothering is high.

Whether pregnancy serves celebrities well or ill in visibility terms, it is clear that the same tone of concern pervades the coverage of pregnancy as that applied to routine, normal pregnancies and those we identified earlier as atypical and the concept of good (and bad) mothers is invoked. By looking at celebrity pregnancy, albeit briefly, we hope to have demonstrated that the almost permanent visibility that keeps pregnancy in the public eye is in part the outcome of a complex web of surveillance that surrounds women as they go about their daily lives.

Note

1 The Magdalene Laundries were institutions sponsored and maintained by the Catholic Church in Ireland for the incarceration of young women thought to have transgressed public morals, including unmarried mothers. With the legal consent of their fathers, they were imprisoned and made to work for no pay in laundries, where they were exploited and often abused. The laundries existed until the 1970s and the last one closed in 1996.

8

EPILOGUE

Is pregnancy special?

In this book our thesis has been that the perceptions and beliefs held about pregnancy, including by women themselves, have determined both the research carried out on pregnancy, from a number of different perspectives, and the outcomes of that research in terms of its impact. On its own, this is hardly a novel thesis. However, we would argue that what we have been able to show, by looking at pregnancy in relation to the daily experiences of women's lives – cognition, employment, diet and exercise – is that it is crucial to see women's responses to their pregnancy as one dimension of an ongoing life of commitments, relationships, attitudes and expectations that goes beyond the pregnancy. Combining the different topics we have discussed, we have identified a number of common themes, including several familiar discourses of pregnancy. The very consistency of these themes across the domains highlights their potential impact on women's lives during pregnancy. Furthermore, it raises the question as to whether pregnancy can be said to be special or whether it can be regarded as simply another facet of the well-documented territory of people's lives, particularly women's lives, more generally.

Before considering what we mean by 'special' in relation to pregnancy and pregnancy research, we will summarise some of the main issues arising from each chapter, review the themes and discuss the various research perspectives.

The picture that has emerged from our review of a range of research on each of the topics, together with our own findings, is one of inconsistency; findings are frequently conflicting or contradictory. This means, as we have suggested in several chapters, that during pregnancy women have to work hard to assess what is relevant or helpful to their own circumstances. Advice or information that arises from a shifting flow of research evidence has to be weighed against their own experience and opportunities. However, the research is seldom explicit either in relation to how this might be achieved or in recognising that this is an inevitable concomitant of the mixed economy of information available through a variety of sources.

In Chapter 2 we raised various contrasting or paradoxical aspects of pregnancy and these have been integral to our discussion of each of the topics we have addressed. They have included the apparent invisibility of women, in favour of their unborn child, bound up in the discourses of containment and responsibility that we have discussed in relation to employment, diet and exercise in particular. Intertwined with this is the complex mapping of the natural process onto the dominant biomedical discourse, which focuses on the management of risk and the sanctioning of behaviours, inherent in the discussions of diet and exercise but also relevant to the work on cognition. These are further complicated by the persistent images and representations of pregnancy which refer to feminine stereotypes and call into question the suitability of women's role in the public domain during their pregnancy. This contrasts with the very visibility of pregnancy outside the routine; in the examination of celebrity and pregnancy 'out of place' we can see these various discourses operating to deliver uncertainty and making pregnancy outside very narrow boundaries open to the types of commentary and interference we have described. Finally, we would not want to represent women as complicit in these discourses and concerns, though it may be incumbent upon them to manage the uncertainty that has been created. It is important to represent women as proactive in their own surveillance; issues of agency and control are at the forefront of women's own experiences, as our own research findings on diet and exercise have indicated. Indeed, the individual responsibility for created risk is now the common experience of all, but not an entirely negative experience. As we and Bondas and Eriksson (2001) have suggested, women wish to take control, they no longer take their health for granted and try to change their behaviour. Whether this is regarded as the acceptance of the advice and information they receive will depend on women's own perceptions of their experience.

In the light of these parallel and competing concerns and in summary of the various topics we have covered in the book, we would like to highlight the following issues.

We dealt at some length in Chapter 4 with the topic of pregnancy and employment. The reason for this was that employment can be said to be a backdrop against which the various cultural beliefs about pregnancy are dramatically enacted. While it is by no means the case that all women encounter negative treatment, certainly the extent of such treatment serves to illustrate how much the stereotypes of femininity and women's roles remain endemic even in apparently enlightened societies. Women most likely to experience problems at work during pregnancy are those who would encounter them at other times: women with low-paid, low-status, low security jobs. The evidence that such attitudes hold sway across the spectrum of employment, however, confirms that pregnancy is constructed as problematic for all women, in keeping with the biomedical discourses.

While women's previous experience at work is sometimes referred to, their treatment in pregnancy is seen largely as exclusive to that state as a visible representation of the public beliefs and attitudes commonly held, but usually unspoken. Pregnancy in this context sanctions a set of comments and behaviour which are in many cases mostly actually illegal. In this case, therefore, pregnancy is the means by which other people can express their resentments or resistance to women's independence, choices and lifestyle, while women are held to account. Ironically, they are held to account in research, much of it outside the traditional sphere of psychology, which is concerned less with their own behaviour and more with pregnancy outcomes. Even within research which has taken a psychological approach, women have been marginalised in terms of their importance and women have been seen as pregnant first and individual women second.

In contrast to the other topics we have explored, research on diet is unusual in taking account of different cultural beliefs in relation to food choices and dietary behaviour. Therefore this work appears to avoid some of the traditional criticism that research adopts a largely monocultural approach. Despite this, the research and its findings are not necessarily helpful in contextualising dietary behaviour and do not tend to take account of the contexts of women's lives at other times, such as before they were pregnant. The research findings have again concentrated on the unusual rather than on the routine, at the same time reporting ambiguous or inconsistent information proposing the reduction or restriction of certain dietary items. This lends itself to uncertainty of response and makes the surveillance of women's behaviour more likely, which in turn leads to the sanctions on women's behaviour. Women are expected to behave responsibly in order to ensure a healthy outcome, with the emphasis on their role as provider and container.

As with research on employment and diet, the research on exercise and daily activity is generally undertaken from a perspective that attends primarily to the risks and dangers of such behaviour and leaves room for doubt and uncertainty. However, it does have a feature not present in some other areas, which is that it points to the potential physical and psychological benefits of such behaviour. Nevertheless, we would argue that this is very much from a position whereby women's behaviour is treated as problematic and sanctions are imposed. What is interesting is that women do not necessarily respond as might be expected to these sanctions, because of the need to balance the relative risks and dangers to their own health with those perceived as affecting their baby. Research in this instance has very often led directly to guidelines for practice, like research on dietary hazards and some on employment hazards, and thereby it has positioned women as responsible for pregnancy outcome and for their own health – the rhetoric of accountability. However, as with diet, lay beliefs remain clearly located within another discourse, that of moderation and even indulgence.

145

This, incidentally, could be seen as providing women either with an opportunity for agency, giving women a further role as educator of others, or as conforming to a stereotype of motherhood whereby family health and diet is a fundamental duty of care. If it is to be as a proactive agent of education, it should be the case that pregnant women who take up advice to sustain their exercise are also able to influence public attitudes and beliefs; put simply, if there are more pregnant women exercising in the gym, it becomes more normal or routine, and their own discomfort and that of others may be reduced. Whether this can be achieved is less clear, and the evidence on pregnancy discrimination at work suggests that it may not be, but clearly the opportunity could be said to exist. However, as with diet, the problem remains of how to change behaviour even when such changes are sought since research evidence is also interpretable in several inconsistent ways and women are able to adhere to advice and ignore it simultaneously.

By contrast with the preceding three topics, the study of cognition in pregnancy has been largely addressed from a psychological perspective. Before feeling too smug about this, the work is largely indistinguishable from that done from any other perspective and indeed it resonates very strongly with the biomedical tradition, taking as it does failure and incapacity as the starting point rather than development and skill: pregnancy as debilitation. Despite the absence of convincing evidence of incapacity, the research does women a significant disservice, affecting others' attitudes to women's abilities and performance, endorsing recourse by women and by others to the power of the physiology of the natural process. Research on cognition during pregnancy very rarely invites women to identify improvements or examines the strategies that they adopt to counter any perceived effects. Thus, the outcome of research on cognition is to confirm female stereotypes rather than to challenge them and this has a forward trajectory for women's lives as mothers and parents in the public domain; only rarely are the skills of multitasking and divided attention, which are frequently required in home life, regarded as valuable attributes in the job market for example.

The overarching theme arising from all the material we have explored, including that on celebrity pregnancy and atypical pregnancies, is that research has been accomplished to deliver sanctions on women's behaviour. Sanction carries a double meaning, that of a penalty for disobedience and of approval for obedience, both of which are applicable within the discourses of containment, responsibility and femininity that pervade public beliefs about pregnancy. In effect, the research evidence also countenances a status quo, with the additional expectation that women must be accountable through their vigilance.

Last, we turn to the concept of whether pregnancy is special. In the previous chapter, we concluded that pregnancy serves as a means by which women can be subjected to increasing surveillance. We discussed how pregnancy can be regarded as a form of celebrity and how the combination of visibility as represented by celebrity and the additional visibility accorded to special forms of pregnancy outside the narrowly defined boundaries of 'normal' can accentuate the culturally determined responses to pregnancy. Our conclusion to that chapter was not that pregnancy was special in that sense, rather that it provided an instantiation of a number of available discourses usually only referred to obliquely. However, when looking at all the issues raised by the chapters together, the answer to the question is perhaps not as clear. The word special means that something is in some way distinctive or exceptional, that is, that it is for a particular purpose or of a particular kind. Pregnancy cannot be defined as special without reference to the aspect that is being considered. This is not to say that the meaning or significance of pregnancy is relative, but rather that it is complex.

In a personal sense, for the women concerned and their families, pregnancy is special, it is something distinctive and exceptional. Furthermore, as we pointed out at the start, healthy women are accorded more attention during their pregnancies than at any other time in their lives thus far, and in this sense they feel special. From our point of view, however, the implication of such a designation of pregnancy as special engenders the discourses of containment that are implicit in such special treatment; as we have seen in the findings from research on employment and exercise, these discourses can dominate the way that women are treated during their special time. In a biological sense, too, pregnancy could be said to be special, something additional to the ordinary and, as a necessary activity for the reproduction of the species, pregnancy has a particular, unique purpose.

If we look, however, at the way research has dealt with pregnancy, we could perhaps say that pregnancy is not special. As we concluded in Chapter 7, the visibility of pregnancy is a manifestation of persistent and negative discourses which surround women and women's behaviour at all times. If we consider diet, for example, in pregnancy attention paid to diet and eating is surely only a version of the monitoring of behaviour that goes on all the time, through the commentary on women's appearance and clothing whether they are Princess Diana, Madonna or the US Secretary of State. The research and consequent guidelines developed for exercise and physical activity in pregnancy similarly reinforce the opportunity to assess whether women are working hard enough to maintain their own or their children's health, endorsing once again women's responsibilities and accountability, in this case frequently prioritising their infants' health over their own. The findings on cognition also point to the problematic nature of pregnancy and women's potential disadvantage, and the need for pregnant women to be treated with caution. In these senses therefore, we would suggest that pregnancy is not special. Neither is pregnancy research special in that it takes as its model one of failure and inappropriate behaviour rather than capacity and enhancement. But this may be more than a concern with surveillance of women's current or potential status. The focus on the risks and dangers of daily living is by no means exclusive to pregnancy. As Shulamit Reinharz (1999: 438) amusingly details, such warnings are everywhere: 'I would like to get through a day without being assaulted by warnings. I find this barrage of dire information intrusive, pervasive and depressing' (Reinharz, 1999 cited in Gray *et al.*, 2001: 438). If everyone is subjected to this high degree of contradictory and wide-ranging warnings then pregnancy could not be said to be special as such, but only to be a time when additional concerns are added to the mix. The negotiation of relative risks and benefits is managed by all of us in relation to the practicalities of our lives. On the other hand, precisely because of the foregrounding of the invisible – the baby or the foetus – perhaps pregnancy is special. The issues of choice appear more salient, the concept of the future more immediate and the visibility of the risk more critical. Thus, women are not just responding to prevailing beliefs and discourses but are being agents in their own destiny, in the course of which they may encounter setbacks or support, and thus pregnancy has the potential to provide women with an opportunity to develop the negotiation of their position with that expected of them.

As we suggested at the beginning of this book, pregnancy is a challenging topic for research. We were first attracted to this area because it appeared to be a nexus for many of the issues and concerns with which we as psychologists engage. While this may be satisfactory at an intellectual level, what seems to us to be regrettable is that only rarely are women accorded the opportunity in research to demonstrate the negotiation of the various different elements of their lives inherent in the experience of pregnancy. Rather, all that we have discussed above only serves to reinforce the research perspectives, which draw on the biomedical, the psychological and what could loosely be called the sociocultural. In the context of the research we have explored and discussed, the biomedical perspective is one where what is at issue is a set of processes out of the individual's control. Furthermore, a cultural or social perspective is one which also seems to us to disenfranchise women during pregnancy since it would appear that an individual is only able to exercise personal preferences and control when these are achievable in the face of publicly held beliefs and expectations. Perhaps surprisingly, one of the positive elements of the psychological perspective, even if it has not always been manifest in the work we have described here, is that the whole individual is the focus of study, and that research is seeking to explain normal behaviour in relation to underlying characteristics and a range of different experiences. This has also been considered one of the weaknesses of some traditional psychology with its emphasis on a psycho-biomedical approach by which means the focus of study has been on the minutiae of individual elements of a process or function, and within which the work on pregnancy and cognition could be said to be located. Nevertheless, a psychological perspective on pregnancy is one which acknowledges the very complex set of factors likely to impact on a person's behaviour or attitudes. While we have only been able to point to a limited set of findings using these kinds of approaches, including perhaps some of our own work, in the main we would argue that there is considerable potential for extension of the concept of the person into the research, as has been the case with qualitative approaches. So although pregnancy research has been open to the same problems of prevailing beliefs and expectations as other domains, there are areas which have provided significant illumination of the experience. In this sense, we would suggest that the viewpoint we have taken on pregnancy, as psychologists, is also special.

GLOSSARY

Antenatal Refers to events and experiences happening or existing during pregnancy before birth and pertaining to or concerned with the health and wellbeing of women during pregnancy, hence antenatal care.

Maternity leave Period of time allowed off from work to have a baby; length varies according to country, e.g. from 14 weeks minimum to 52 weeks maximum in Europe; may be paid at more than minimum benefit level.

Maternity pay Money paid to a woman while on maternity leave, comprising state-provided funds and for some employees money paid by their employer.

Multigravida A pregnant woman who has been pregnant before, but who has not necessarily given birth before.

Multiparous Having had more than one child; sometimes used to mean pregnant for a second or further time but having given birth to at least one child.

Perinatal Referring to the period around the very end of pregnancy, labour, delivery and childbirth, and including the period directly afterwards.

Postnatal and post partum Both terms refer to the period following birth.

Primagravida Term used for a woman pregnant for the first time.

Primiparous A term meaning bearing a child for the first time; sometimes used interchangeably with primagravida to mean pregnant for the first time.

Trimester Obstetrically, pregnancy is considered to last for 40 weeks and to have three stages, each of about 14 weeks in length, referred to as the first, second and third trimesters. Thus, the third trimester refers to the last three months of pregnancy. We have used the term to reflect the detail of research studies and elsewhere, as a form of shorthand for early, middle or late pregnancy.

REFERENCES

Abraham, S., King, W. and Llewellyn-Jones, D. (1994) 'Attitudes to body weight, weight gain and eating behaviour in pregnancy', *Journal of Psychosomatic Obstetrics and Gynecology*, 15: 189–95.

Abrams, B., Altman, S. and Pickett, K. (2000) 'Pregnancy weight gain: Still controversial', *American Journal of Clinical Nutrition*, 71: 1233–41.

Affonso, D., Mayberry, L. J., Lovett, S. M. and Paul, S. (1994) 'Cognitive adaptation to stressful events during pregnancy and postpartum: Development and testing of the CASE instrument', *Nursing Research*, 43: 338–43.

Affonso, D., Lovett, S., Paul, S., Arizmendi, T., Nussbaum, R., Newman, L. and Johnson, B. (1991) 'Predictors of depression symptoms during pregnancy and postpartum', *Journal of Psychosomatic Obstetrics and Gynecology*, 12: 255–71.

Al-Kanhal, M. A. and Bani, I. (1995) 'Food habits during pregnancy among Saudi women', *International Journal of Nutritional Research*, 65: 206–10.

Allen, T. (2005) 'Why do women choose to remain childless: A model of voluntary childlessness', Unpublished M.Phil thesis, Nottingham Trent University.

ACOG (American College of Obstetricians and Gynaecologists) (1994) *Exercise during Pregnancy and the Postpartum Period*, Washington, DC: ACOG Press.

Andersen, A. E. (1995) 'Eating disorders in males', in K. D. Brownell and C. G. Fairburn (eds) *Eating Disorders and Obesity: A Comprehensive Handbook*, New York: Guilford Press, pp. 177–87.

Anderson, V. N., Fleming, A. S. and Steiner, M. (1994) 'Mood and the transition to motherhood', *Journal of Reproductive and Infant Psychology*, 12: 69–77.

Artal, R. and Gardin, S. K. (1991) 'Physiological adaptations to pregnancy. Section 1: Historical perspectives', in R. Artal, R. A. Wiswell and B. A. Drinkwater (eds) *Exercise in Pregnancy*, Baltimore, MD: Williams and Wilkins.

Artal, R. and O'Toole, M. (2003) 'Guidelines of the American College of Obstetricians and Gynecologists for exercise during pregnancy and the postpartum period', *British Journal of Sports Medicine*, 37: 6–12.

Artal, R., Wiswell, R. A. and Drinkwater, B. A. (eds) (1991) *Exercise in Pregnancy* (2nd edition), Baltimore, MD: Williams and Wilkins.

Australian Bureau of Statistics (2004) *Births*, Doc. No. 3301.0, Canberra, Australia: Australian Bureau of Statistics.

Australian Bureau of Statistics (2005) *Births, Australia, 2005*, Doc. No. 3301, Canberra, Australia: Australian Bureau of Statistics. Online. Available HTTP:

<www.abs.gov.au/AUSSTATS/abs@.nsf/ProductsbyCatalogue/> (accessed 5 January 2007).

Baildam, E. (1991) 'Doctor as mum', *British Medical Journal*, 303: 424.

Baker, C. W., Carter, A. S., Cohen, L. R. and Brownkell, K. D. (1999) 'Eating attitudes and behaviours in pregnancy and postpartum: Global stability versus specific transitions', *Annals of Behavioural Medicine*, 21: 143–8.

Bandura, A. (1989) 'Human agency in social cognitive theory', *American Psychologist*, 44: 1175–84.

Barker, D. J. P. (1995) 'Fetal origins of coronary heart disease', *British Medical Journal*, 311: 171–4.

Barker, K. K. (1998) 'A ship upon a stormy sea: The medicalization of pregnancy', *Social Science and Medicine*, 47: 1067–76.

Bayley, T. M., Dye, L., Jones, S., DeBono, M. and Hill, A. J. (2002) 'Food cravings and aversions during pregnancy: Relationships with nausea and vomiting', *Appetite*, 38: 45–51.

Beard, J. L., Hendricks, M. K., Perez, E. M., Murray-Kolb, L. E., Berg, A., Vernon-Feagans, L., Irlam, J., Isaacs, W., Sive, A. and Tomlinson, M. (2005) 'Maternal iron deficiency anemia affects postpartum emotions and cognition', *Journal of Nutrition*, 135: 267–72.

Bech, B. H., Nohr, E. A., Vaeth, M., Henriksen, T. B. and Olsen, J. (2005) 'Coffee and fetal death: A cohort study with prospective data', *American Journal of Epidemiology*, 162: 983–90.

Beck, U. (1992) *The Risk Society: Towards a New Modernity*, London: Sage.

Bell, R. and O'Neill, M. (1994) 'Exercise and pregnancy: A review', *Birth*, 2: 85–95.

Berkowitz, G. S., Kelsey, J. L., Holford, T. R. and Berkowitz, R. L. (1983) 'Physical activity and the risk of spontaneous preterm delivery', *Journal of Reproductive Medicine*, 28: 581–8.

Berryman, J. C., Thorpe, K. and Windridge, K. (1995) *Older Mothers: Conception, Pregnancy and Birth after 35*, London: Pandora.

Bistline, S. (1985) 'Making room for baby', *Association Management*, 37: 96–8.

Blaxton, T. A. (1989) 'Investigating disassociations among memory measures: Support for transfer-appropriate processing framework', *Journal of Experimental Psychology: Learning Memory and Cognition*, 15: 657–68.

Bodnar, L. M. and Wisner, K. L. (2005) 'Nutrition and depression: Implications for improving mental health among childbearing-aged women', *Biological Psychiatry*, 58: 679–85.

Bondas, T. and Eriksson, K. (2001) 'Women's lived experiences of pregnancy: A tapestry of joy and suffering', *Qualitative Health Research*, 11: 824–40.

Boorstin, D. J. (1961) *The Image: A Guide to Pseudo Events in America*, New York: Harper and Row.

Bordo, S. (1993) *Unbearable Weight: Feminism, Western Culture and the Body*, Berkeley, CA: University of California Press.

Boscaglia, N., Skouteris, H. and Wertheim, E. H. (2003) 'Changes in body image satisfaction during pregnancy: A comparison of high exercising and low exercising women', *Australian and New Zealand Journal of Obstetrics and Gynaecology*, 43: 41–5.

Bosch, O. J., Meddle, S. L., Beiderbeck, D. I., Douglas, A. J. and Neumann, I. D.

(2005) 'Brain oxytocin correlates with maternal aggression: Link to anxiety', *Journal of Neuroscience*, 25: 6807–15.

Brady, C., Coveney, E., Davis, A. and Murphy Lawless, J. (1999) *New Mothers at Work: An Exploratory Study to Identify the Needs of New Mothers in the Workplace*, Dublin: Employment Equality Agency.

Bragger, J. D., Kutcher, E., Morgan, J. and Firth, P. (2002) 'The effects of structured interview on reducing biases against pregnant job applicants', *Sex Roles*, 46: 215–26.

Bramwell, R. (1997) 'Studying the impact of the psychosocial work environment on pregnancy outcome: A review of methodological issues', *Journal of Reproductive and Infant Psychology*, 15: 257–70.

Brannen, J. and Moss, P. (1988) *New Mothers at Work*, London: Unwin/Hyman.

Breen, D. (1975) *The Birth of a First Child*, London: Tavistock.

Brett, K. M., Strogatz, D. S. and Savitz, D. A. (1997) 'Employment, job strain and preterm delivery among women in North Carolina', *American Journal of Public Health*, 87: 199–204.

Brett, M. and Baxendale, S. (2001) 'Motherhood and memory: A review', *Psychoneuroendocrinology*, 26: 339–62.

Brindle, P. M., Brown, M. W., Brown, J., Griffith, H. B. and Turner, G. M. (1991) 'Objective and subjective memory impairment in pregnancy', *Psychological Medicine*, 21: 647–53.

Britney Spears' Pregnancy Binge. Online. Available HTTP: <www.femalefirst. co.uk/celebrity/60262004.htm> (accessed 23 November 2005).

Broadbent, D. E., Cooper, P. F., FitzGerald, P. and Parkes, K. R. (1982) 'The Cognitive Failure Questionnaire (CFQ) and its correlates', *British Journal of Clinical Psychology*, 21: 1–16.

Brockington, I. (1994) *Motherhood and Mental Health*, Oxford: Oxford University Press.

Brown, J. E., Khan, E. S. and Hartman, T. J. (1997) 'Profet, profits and proof: Do nausea and vomiting of early pregnancy protect women from "harmful" vegetables?', *American Journal of Obstetrics and Gynecology*, 176: 179–81.

Buckelow, S. P. and Hannay, H. J. (1986) 'Relationship among anxiety, defensiveness, sex, task difficulty and performance on various neuropsychological tasks', *Perceptual and Motor Skills*, 63: 711–18.

Buckwalter, J. G., Stanczyk, F. Z., McCleary, C. A., Bluestein, B. W., Buckwalter, D. K., Rankin, K. P., Chang, L. and Goodwin, T. M. (1999) 'Pregnancy, the postpartum, and steroid hormones: Effects on cognition and mood', *Psychoneuroendocrinology*, 24: 69–84.

BUPA (2005) *Preparing for Pregnancy*. Online. Available HTTP: <http:// hcd2.bupa.co.uk/fact_sheets/html/Planning_pregnancy.html> (accessed 4 December 2005).

Burchett, H. and Seeley, A. (2003) *Good Enough to Eat? The Diet of Pregnant Teenagers*, London: The Food Commission.

Burgoyne, T. (1994) 'The brain drain', *Nursing Standard*, 8: 44.

Butensky, M. C. (1984) 'Devaluation of the competence of pregnant women; does the spread phenomenon that operates with disabilities also occur with pregnancy?', Unpublished doctoral dissertation, State University of New York at Buffalo.

Butler, J. M. (1996) *Fit and Pregnant: The Pregnant Woman's Guide to Exercise*, Vermont: Vitesse Press.

Bynner, J., Elias, P., McKnight, A., Pan, H. and Pierre, G. (2002) *Changing Pathways to Employment and Independence*, York: Joseph Rowntree Foundation.

Callender, C., Millward, N., Lissenburgh, S. and Forth, J. (1997) *Maternity Rights and Benefits in Britain*, DSS Research Report 67, London: HMSO.

Campbell, S. (2004) *Watch Me Grow! A Unique, 3-Dimensional Week-by-Week Look at Your Baby's Behaviour and Development in the Womb*, London: Carroll and Brown.

Carruth, B. and Skinner, J. (1991) 'Regional differences in beliefs about nutrition during pregnancy', *Journal of the American Dietetics Association*, 91: 435–40.

Casey, P., Huntsdale, C., Angus, G. and Janes, C. (1999) 'Memory in pregnancy. II: Implicit, incidental, explicit, semantic, short-term working and prospective memory in primigravid, multigravid and postpartum women', *Journal of Psychosomatic Obstetrics and Gynecology*, 20: 158–64.

Cepeda-Benito, A. and Gleaves, D. H. (2001) 'A critique of food craving research: Theory, measurement and food intake', in M. M. Hetherington (ed.) *Food Cravings and Addiction*, Leatherhead: Leatherhead Food Research Association.

Chamberlain, G. (1984) *Pregnant Women at Work*, London: Royal Society/ Macmillan.

Chambers, R. A., Potenza, M. N., Hoffman, R. E. and Miranker, W. (2004) 'Simulated apoptosis/neurogenesis regulates learning and memory capabilities of adaptive neural networks', *Neuropsychopharmacology*, 29: 747–58.

Charles, N. and Kerr, M. (1986) 'Food for feminist thought', *Sociological Review*, 34: 537–72.

Cherry, N. (1987) 'Physical demands of work and health complaints among women working late in pregnancy', *Ergonomics*, 30: 689–701.

Choi, P. Y. L. (2000) 'Looking good and feeling good: Why do fewer women than men exercise?', in J. Ussher (ed.) *Women's Health: Contemporary International Perspectives*, Leicester: BPS Books.

Christensen, H., Poyser, P., Pollitt, P. and Cubis, J. (1999) 'Pregnancy may confer a selective cognitive advantage', *Journal of Reproductive and Infant Psychology*, 17: 7–26.

Clapp, J. F. (1980) 'Acute exercise stress in the pregnant ewe', *American Journal of Obstetrics and Gynecology*, 136: 489–94.

Clapp, J. F. (1990) 'The course of labour after endurance exercise', *American Journal of Obstetrics and Gynecology*, 163: 1799–805.

Clapp, J. F. (1998) *Exercising Through your Pregnancy*, Champaign, IL: Human Kinetics.

Clapp, J. F. and Capeless, E. L. (1990) 'Neonatal morphometrics after endurance exercise during pregnancy', *American Journal of Obstetrics and Gynecology*, 163: 1805–11.

Clapp, J. F. and Dickstein, S. (1984) 'Endurance exercise and pregnancy outcome', *Medicine and Science in Sports and Exercise*, 16: 556–62.

Clark, M. and Ogden, J. (1999) 'The impact of pregnancy on eating behaviour and aspects of weight concern', *International Journal of Obesity and Related Metabolic Disorders*, 23: 18–24.

Clarke, P. E. and Gross, H. (2004a) 'Women's behaviour, beliefs and information sources about physical exercise in pregnancy', *Midwifery*, 20: 133–41.

Clarke, P. E. and Gross, H. (2004b) 'Perceptions of effective advice in pregnancy: The case of activity', *Clinical Effectiveness in Nursing*, 8: 161–9.

Clarke, P. E., Rousham, E. K., Gross, H., Halligan, A. W. F. and Bosio, P. (2005) 'Activity patterns and time allocation during pregnancy: A longitudinal study of British women', *Annals of Human Biology*, 32: 247–58.

Cockburn, J. and Smith, P. T. (1994) 'Anxiety and errors of prospective memory among elderly people', *British Journal of Psychology*, 85: 273–82.

Cogswell, M. E., Scanlon, K. S., Fein, S. B. and Schieve, L. A. (1999) 'Medically advised, mother's personal target, and actual weight gain during pregnancy', *Obstetrics and Gynecology*, 94: 616–22.

Condon, J. T. (1987) 'Altered cognitive functioning in pregnant women: A shift towards primary process thinking', *British Journal of Medical Psychology*, 60: 329–34.

Condon, J. T. and Ball, S. B. (1989) 'Altered psychological functioning in pregnant women: An empirical investigation', *Journal of Psychosomatic Obstetrics and Gynecology*, 10: 211–20.

Conway, R., Reddy, S. and Davies, J. (1999) 'Dietary restraint and weight gain during pregnancy', *European Journal of Clinical Nutrition*, 53: 849–53.

Cooper, C., Cooper, D. R. and Eaker, L. H. (1988) *Living with Stress*, Harmondsworth: Penguin.

Corse, S. J. (1990) 'Pregnant managers and their subordinates: The effect of gender expectations on hierarchical relationships', *Journal of Applied Behavioural Science*, 26: 25–47.

Cram, C. and Stouffer Drenth, T. (2004) *Fit Pregnancy for Dummies*, New York: Wiley Publishing.

Crawley, R. (2002) 'Self-perception of cognitive changes during pregnancy and the early postpartum: Salience and attentional effects', *Applied Cognitive Psychology*, 16: 617–33.

Crawley, R. A., Dennison, K. and Carter, C. (2003) 'Cognition in pregnancy and the first year post-partum', *Psychology and Psychotherapy*, 76: 69–84.

Crystal, S. R., Bowen, D. J. and Bernstein, I. L. (1999) 'Morning sickness and salt intake, food cravings, and food aversions', *Physiology and Behavior*, 67: 181–7.

Curtis, M. (1986) 'The psycho-physiologic effects of bed rest on at-risk pregnant women: A pilot study', Unpublished PhD thesis, University of Wisconsin, Madison.

Da Costa, D., Larouche, J., Dritsa, M. and Brender, W. (1999) 'Variations in stress levels over the course of pregnancy: Factors associated with elevated hassles, state anxiety and pregnancy-specific stress', *Journal of Psychosomatics Research*, 47: 609–21.

Da Costa, D., Rippen, N., Dritsa, M. and Ring, A. (2003) 'Self-reported leisure-time physical activity during pregnancy and relationship to psychological well-being', *Journal of Psychosomatic Obstetrics and Gynecology*, 24: 111–19.

Dale, E., Mullinax, K. M. and Bryan, D. H. (1982) 'Exercise during pregnancy: Effects on the fetus', *Canadian Journal of Applied Sports Science*, 7: 98–103.

David-Floyd, R. E. (1994) 'Mind over body: The pregnant professional', *Pre and Perinatal Psychology Journal*, 8: 201–27.

Davies, K. and Wardle, J. (1994) 'Body image and diet during pregnancy', *Journal of Psychosomatic Research*, 38: 787–99.

de Groot, R. H. M., Adam, J. J. and Hornstra, G. (2003a) 'Selective attention deficits during human pregnancy', *Neuroscience Letters*, 340: 21–4.

de Groot, R. H. M., Hornstra, G., Roozendaal, N. and Jolles, J. (2003b) 'Memory performance, but not information processing speed, may be reduced during early pregnancy', *Journal of Clinical and Experimental Neuropsychology*, 25: 482–8.

De Joseph, J. F. (1992) 'Redefining women's work during pregnancy: Towards a more comprehensive approach', *Birth*, 20: 86–93.

Deary, I. J. and Tait, R. (1987) 'Effects of sleep disruption on cognitive performance and mood in medical house officers', *British Medical Journal*, 295: 1513–16.

Department of Health (2002) *Health Survey for England*, London: The Stationery Office.

Department of Health (2006) *The Pregnancy Book*, London: Department of Health.

Deutsch, H. (1947) *The Psychology of Women*, New York: Grune and Stratton.

Devine, C. M., Bove, C. F. and Olson, C. M. (2000) 'Continuity and change in women's weight orientations and lifestyle practices through pregnancy and the postpartum period: The influence of life course trajectories and transitional events', *Social Science and Medicine*, 50: 567–82.

Devlin, V. (1995) *Motherhood*, London: Polygon Press.

Dewe, P., Cox, T. and Ferguson, E. (1993) 'Individual strategies for coping with stress and work: A review', *Work and Stress*, 7: 5–15.

Dewey, K. G. and McCrory, M. A. (1994) 'Effects of dieting and physical activity on pregnancy and lactation', *American Journal of Clinical Nutrition*, 59(suppl): 446S-53S.

Dibblee, L. and Graham, T. E. (1983) 'A longitudinal study of changes in aerobic fitness, body composition and energy intake in primigravid patients', *American Journal of Obstetrics and Gynecology*, 147: 908–14.

DiPietro, J. A., Costigan, K. A. and Gurewitsch, E. D. (2005) 'Maternal psychophysiological change during the second half of gestation', *Biological Psychology*, 69: 23–38.

DiPietro, J. A., Millet, S., Costigan, K. A., Gurewitsch, E. and Caulfield, L. E. (2003) 'Psychosocial influences on weight gain attitudes and behaviors during pregnancy', *Journal of the American Dietetic Association*, 103: 1314–19.

Dooley, D. and Prause, J. (2005) 'Birth weight and mothers' adverse employment change', *Journal of Health and Social Behaviour*, 46: 141–55.

Douglas, A. J., Brunton, P. J., Bosch, O. J., Russell, J. A. and Neumann, I. D. (2003) 'Neuroendocrine responses to stress in mice: Hyporesponsiveness in pregnancy and parturition', *Endocrinology*, 144: 5268–76.

Downs, D. S. and Hausenblas, H. A. (2003) 'Exercising for two: Examining pregnant women's second trimester exercise intention and behaviour using the framework of the theory of planned behaviour', *Women's Health Issues*, 13: 222–8.

Downs, D. S. and Hausenblas, H. A. (2004) 'Women's exercise beliefs and behaviours during their pregnancy and postpartum', *Journal of Midwifery and Women's Health*, 49: 138–44.

Doyle, P., Roman, E., Beral, V. and Brookes, M. (1997) 'Spontaneous abortion in dry cleaning workers potentially exposed to perchloroethylene', *Occupational and Environmental Medicine*, 54: 848–53.

Drewett, R. F., Bowen-Jones, A. and Dogterom, J. (1982) 'Oxytocin levels during breastfeeding in established lactation', *Hormones and Behavior*, 16: 245–8.

Dunstan, R. (2002) *Birth Rights: A CAB Evidence Report on Maternity and Parental Rights at Work*, London: NACAB.

Dye, T. D., Knox, K. L., Artal, R. and Aubrey, R. H. (1997) 'Physical activity, obesity and diabetes in pregnancy', *American Journal of Epidemiology*, 146: 961–5.

Earle, S. (2003) 'Bumps and boobs: fatness and women's experiences of pregnancy', *Women's Studies International Forum*, 26: 245–52.

Ehlers, C. L., Frank, E. and Kupfer, D. J. (1988) 'Social zeitgebers and biological rhythms', *Archives of General Psychiatry*, 45: 948–52.

Elston, M. A. (1991) 'The politics of professional power: Medicine in a changing health service', in J. Gabe, M. Calnan and M. Bury (eds) *The Sociology of the Health Service*, London: Routledge.

EOC (Equal Opportunities Commission) (2004) *Tip of the Iceberg: Interim Report of the EOC's Investigation into Discrimination against New and Expectant Mothers in the Workplace*, Manchester: EOC.

EOC (2005) *Greater Expectations: Summary: Final Report – EOC's Investigation into Pregnancy Discrimination*, Manchester: EOC.

Erkkola, R. (1976) 'The physical work capacity of the expectant mother and its effect of pregnancy, labour and the newborn', *International Journal of Gynaecology and Obstetrics*, 14: 153–9.

Eurostat (2004) *Demographic Statistics: Fertility*. Online. Available HTTP: <http://epp.eurostat.cec.eu.int/portal> (accessed 4 December 2005).

Eurostat (2005) *Demographic Statistics: Fertility*. Online. Available HTTP: <http://epp.eurostat.cec.eu.int/portal> (accessed 5 January 2007).

Fairburn, C. G. and Beglin, S. J. (1990) 'Studies of the epidemiology of bulimia nervosa', *American Journal of Psychiatry*, 147: 401–8.

Fairburn, C. G. and Welch, S. L. (1990) 'The impact of pregnancy on eating habits and attitudes to shape and weight', *International Journal of Eating Disorders*, 9: 153–60.

Fallowfield, L. (1990) *The Quality of Life*, London: Souvenir Press.

Faludi, S. (1992) *Backlash*, London: Vintage.

Farrow, A., Shea, K. M. and Little, R. E. (1998) 'Birthweight of term infants and maternal occupation in a prospective cohort of pregnant women', *Occupational and Environmental Medicine*, 55: 18–23.

Fessler, D. M. T. (2002) 'Reproductive immunosuppression and diet: An evolutionary perspective on pregnancy sickness and meat consumption', *Current Anthropology*, 43: 19–61.

Figes, K. (1994) *Because of Her Sex*, London: Macmillan.

Fisher, S. and Hood, B. (1987) 'The stress of transition to university: a longitudinal study of psychological disturbance, absent mindedness and vulnerability to homesickness', *British Journal of Psychology*, 78: 425–41.

Fisher, S. and Hood, B. (1988) 'Vulnerability factors in the transition to university:

self reported mobility history and sex differences as factors in psychological disturbance', *British Journal of Psychology*, 79: 309–20.

Flaxman, S. M. and Sherman, P. W. (2000) 'Morning sickness: A mechanism for protecting mother and embryo', *Quarterly Review of Biology*, 75: 113–48.

Florack, E. I. M., Zielhuis, G. A., Pellegrino, J. E. M. C. and Rolland, R. (1993) Occupational physical activity and the occurrence of spontaneous abortion, *International Journal of Epidemoiology*, 22: 878–84.

Fowles, E. R. (2002) 'Comparing pregnant women's nutritional knowledge to their actual dietary intake', *American Journal of Maternal Child Nursing*, 27: 171–7.

Frazier, L. M., Ho, H. L. and Molgaard, C. A. (2001) 'Variability in physician management of employment during pregnancy', *Women and Health*, 34: 51–63.

Freeman, E. W., Purdy, R. H., Coutifaris, C., Rickels, K. and Paul, S. M. (1993) 'Anxiolytic metabolites of progesterone: correlation with mood and performance measures following oral progesterone administration to healthy female volunteers', *Neuroendocrinology*, 58: 478–84.

Freeman, E. W., Weinstock, L., Rickels, K., Sondheimer, S. J. and Coutifaris, C. (1992) 'A placebo-controlled study of effects of oral progesterone on performance and mood', *British Journal of Clinical Pharmacology*, 33: 293–8.

Gabbe, S. G. and Turner, L. P. (1997) 'Reproductive hazards of the American lifestyle', *American Journal of Obstetrics and Gynecology*, 176: 826–32.

Galea, L. A. M., Ormerod, B. K., Sampath, S., Kostaras, X., Wilkie, D. M. and Phelps, M. T. (2000) 'Spatial working memory and hippocampal size across pregnancy in rats', *Hormones and Behavior*, 37: 86–95.

Garcia, J., Kilpatrick, R. and Richards, M. P. M. (1990) *Politics of Maternity Care*, Oxford: Clarendon Press.

Geissler, P. W., Prince, R. J., Levene, M., Poda, C., Beckerleg, S. E., Mutemi, W. and Shulman, C. E. (1999) 'Perceptions of soil-eating and anaemia among pregnant women on the Kenyan coast', *Social Science and Medicine*, 48: 1069–79.

Giddens, A. (1991) *Modernity and Self-identity*, Cambridge: Polity Press.

Giles, D. (2000) *Illusions of Immortality: A Psychology of Fame and Celebrity*, London: Macmillan.

Godfrey, K. and Barker, D. (2000) 'Fetal nutrition and adult disease', *American Journal of Clinical Nutrition*, 71: 1344–52.

Goode, J. and Bagilhole, B. M. (1998) 'Gendering the management of change in higher education: A case study', *Gender, Work and Organization*, 5: 148–64.

Gray, B., Davey, A. and Seale, C. (eds) (2001) *Health and Disease: A Reader* (3rd edition), Buckingham: Open University Press, pp. 438–41.

Green, J. M. (1990) *Calming or Harming? A Critical Review of Psychological Effects of Fetal Diagnosis on Pregnant Women*, Occasional Papers, Second Series, No. 2, London: Galton Institute.

Green, J. M., Statham, H. and Snowdon, C. (1993) 'Women's knowledge of prenatal screening tests. 1: Relationships with hospital screening policy and demographic factors', *Journal of Reproductive and Infant Psychology*, 11: 11–20.

Grogan, S. (2000) 'Body image', in J. Ussher (ed.) *Women's Health: Contemporary International Perspectives*, Leicester: BPS Books.

Groner, J. A., Holtzman, N. A., Charney, E. and Mellits, E. D. (1986) 'A random-ised trial of oral iron on tests of short-term memory and attention span in young pregnant women', *Journal of Adolescent Health Care*, 7: 44–8.

Gross, H. and Pattison, H. M. (1995) 'Cognitive failure during pregnancy', *Journal of Reproductive and Infant Psychology*, 13: 17–32.

Gross, H. and Pattison, H. M. (2001) 'Being pregnant at work: A critical reading of advice and information on pregnancy and employment', *Feminism and Psychology*, 11: 511–25.

Grundy, E. and Tomassini, C. (2005) 'Fertility history and health in later life: a record linkage study in England and Wales', *Social Science and Medicine*, 61: 217–28.

Haas, J. S., Jackson, R. A., Fuentes-Afflick, E, Stewart, A. L., Dean, M. L., Brawarsky, P. and Escobar, G. J. (2005) 'Changes in the health status of women during and after pregnancy', *Journal of General Internal Medicine*, 20: 45–51.

Hagger, M. and Chatzisarantis, N. (2005) *The Social Psychology of Exercise and Sport*, Milton Keynes: Open University Press.

Hall, D. C. and Kaufmann, D. A. (1987) 'Effects of aerobic and strength con-ditioning on pregnancy outcomes', *American Journal of Obstetrics and Gynecology*, 157: 1199–203.

Halpert, J. A., Wilson, M. L. and Hickman, J. L. (1993) 'Pregnancy as a source of bias in performance appraisals', *Journal of Organisational Behaviour*, 14: 649–63.

Hanlon, J. (1995) 'The "sick" woman: Pregnancy discrimination in employment', *Journal of Gender Studies*, 4: 315–23.

Hanson, C. (2004) *A Cultural History of Pregnancy*, Basingstoke: Palgrave Macmillan.

Harris, K. and Campbell, E. (1999) 'The plans in unplanned pregnancy: Secondary gain and the partnership', *British Journal of Medical Psychology*, 72: 105–20.

Harris, N. D., Deary, I. J., Harris, M. B., Lees, M. M. and Wilson, J. A. (1996) 'Peripartal cognitive impairment: Secondary to depression?', *British Journal of Health Psychology*, 1: 127–36.

Harris, R. (1979) 'Cultural differences in body perception during pregnancy', *British Journal of Medical Psychology*, 52: 347–52.

Hatch, M., Ji, B. T., Shu, X. O. and Susser, M. (1997) 'Do standing, lifting, climbing, or long hours of work during pregnancy have an effect on fetal growth?', *Epidemiology*, 8: 530–6.

Hees Stauthamer, J. C. (1985) *The First Pregnancy: An Integrating Principle of Female Psychology*, Michigan: UMI Research Press.

Henderson, V. W., Watt, L. and Buckwalter, J. G. (1996) 'Cognitive skills associ-ated with estrogen replacement in women with Alzheimer's disease', *Psychoneuroendocrinology*, 21: 421–30.

Henriksen, T. B., Hedegaard, M. and Secher, N. J. (1995) 'Standing and walking at work and birthweight', *Acta Obstetrica et Gynecologica Scandinavica*, 74: 509–16.

Henriksen, T. B., Savitz, D. A., Hedegaard, M. and Secher, N. J. (1994) 'Employ-ment during pregnancy in relation to risk-factors and pregnancy outcome', *British Journal of Obstetrics and Gynaecology*, 101: 858–65.

159

Henry, J. and Kwong, A. M. (2003) 'Why is geophagy treated like dirt?', *Deviant Behavior*, 24: 353–71.

Herman, C. P. and Mack, D. (1975) 'Restrained and unrestrained eating', *Journal of Personality*, 43: 647–60.

Herman, C. P. and Polivy, J. (1983) 'The Boundary model for the regulation of eating', *Psychiatric Annals*, 13: 918.

Hewison, J., Hirst, J., Ahmed, S., Hucknall, C., Cuckle, H., Green, J. and Thornton, J. (2004) *Social and Ethnic Differences in Attitudes and Consent to Prenatal Testing*. Online. Available HTTP: <http://www.york.ac.uk/res/iht/researchfindings/HewisonFindings.pdf> (accessed 11 February 2006).

Hickey, C. A., Cliver, S. P., Mulvihill, F. X., McNeal, S. F., Hoffman, H. J. and Goldenberg, R. L. (1995) 'Employment related stress and preterm delivery – a contextual examination', *Public Health Reports*, 110: 410–18.

Higgins, J. R., Walshe, J. J., Conroy, R. M. and Darling, M. R. N. (2002) 'The relation between maternal work, ambulatory blood pressure and pregnancy hypertension', *Journal of Epidemiology and Community Health*, 56: 389–93.

Hill, A. J. and Heaton-Brown, L. (1994) 'The experience of food craving: A prospective investigation in healthy women', *Journal of Psychosomatic Research*, 38: 801–14.

Hofer, M. A. (1984) 'Relationships as regulators: A psychobiologic perspective on bereavement', *Psychosomatic Medicine*, 46: 183–97.

Holdcroft, A., Hall, L., Hamilton, G., Counsell, S. J., Bydder, G. M. and Bell, J. D. (2005) 'Phosphorus-31 brain MR spectroscopy in women during and after pregnancy compared with nonpregnant control subjects', *American Journal of Neuroradiology*, 26: 352–6.

Homer, C. J., James, S. A. and Siegel, E. (1990) 'Work-related psychosocial stress and risk of preterm, low birthweight delivery', *American Journal of Public Health*, 80: 173–7.

Hook, E. (1978) 'Dietary cravings and aversions during pregnancy', *American Journal of Clinical Nutrition*, 31: 1355–62.

Horne, J. A. and Pettit, A. N. (1985) 'High incentive effects on vigilance performance during 72 hours of total sleep deprivation', *Acta Psychologica*, 58: 123–39.

Horne, J. A., Anderson, N. R. and Wilkinson, R. T. (1983) 'Effects of sleep deprivation on signal detection measures of vigilance: Implications for sleep function', *Sleep*, 6: 347–58.

Horner, R. D., Lackey, C. J., Kolasa, K. and Warren, K. (1991) 'Pica practices of pregnant women', *Journal of the American Dietetic Association*, 91: 34–8.

Hulme Hunter, H. (2005) *Vitamins & Pre-eclampsia*. Online. Available HTTP: <http://www.babyworld.co.uk/information/pregnancy/health/eating/vitamins.asp> (accessed 4 December 2005).

Humphries, S. and Gordon, P. (1993) *Labour of Love*, London: Sidgwick and Jackson.

Hutchinson, P. L. (1981) 'Metabolic and circulatory responses to running during pregnancy', *Physician Sports Medicine*, 9: 55–61.

Ikeda, J. P. (1999) 'Culture, food and nutrition in increasingly culturally diverse societies', in J. Germov and L. Williams (eds) *A Sociology of Food and Nutrition*, Oxford: Oxford University Press.

Ineichen, B. (1986) 'Contraceptive experience and attitudes to motherhood of teenage mothers', *Journal of Biosocial Science*, 18: 387–94.

Ineichen, B., Pierce, M. and Lawrenson, R. (1997) 'Teenage mothers as breast-feeders: Attitudes and behaviour', *Journal of Adolescence*, 20: 505–9.

International Federation of Gynaecology and Obstetrics (1993) 'Nutrition during pregnancy: AGOC technical bulletin 179', *International Journal of Gynaecology and Obstetrics*, 43: 67–74.

International Labour Organisation (2000) *Convention Concerning the Revision of the Maternity Protection Convention (Revised), 1952*, Convention C183, Adopted 15 June 2000, Geneva: ILO.

Jackson, M. S., Schmierer, C. L. and Schneider, Z. (1996) 'Development, refinement and future usage of the scale: "Attitudes toward learning in pregnancy"', *International Journal of Nursing Studies*, 33: 37–46.

Jadva, V., Murray, C., Lycett, E., MacCallum, F. and Golombok, S. (2003) 'Surrogacy: The experiences of surrogate mothers', *Human Reproduction*, 18: 2196–204.

James, G. (2004) *Pregnancy Discrimination At Work: A Review*, Working Paper Series No 14, Manchester: EOC.

Janes, C., Casey, P., Huntsdale, C. and Angus, G. (1999) 'Memory in pregnancy. I: Subjective experiences and objective assessment of implicit, explicit and working memory in primigravid and primiparous women', *Journal of Psychosomatic Obstetrics and Gynecology*, 20: 80–7.

Jarrahi-Zahed, A., Kane, F. J., van de Castle, R. L., Lachenbruch, P. A. and Ewing, J. A. (1969) 'Emotional and cognitive changes in pregnancy and early puerperium', *British Journal of Psychiatry*, 115: 797–805.

Joffe, H. (2003) 'Risk: From perception to social representation', *British Journal of Social Psychology*, 42, 55–73.

Jones, G. (2002) *The Youth Divide*, York: Joseph Rowntree Foundation.

Jorm, A. F., Christensen, H., Henderson, A. S., Korten, A. E., Mackinnon, A. J. and Scott, R. (1994) 'Complaints of cognitive decline in the elderly: a comparison of reports by subjects and informants in a community survey', *Psychological Medicine*, 24 (2): 365–74.

Kabiru, W. and Raynor, B. D. (2004) 'Obstetric outcomes associated with increase in BMI category during pregnancy', *American Journal of Obstetrics and Gynecology*, 191: 928–32.

Kagan, K. O. and Kuhn, U. (2004) 'Exercise and pregnancy', *Herz*, 29: 426–34.

Kardel, K. R. (2005) 'Effects of intense training during and after pregnancy in top-level athletes', *Scandinavian Journal of Medicine and Science in Sports*, 15: 79–86.

Katz Rothman, B. (1993) *The Tentative Pregnancy: How Amniocentesis Changes the Experience of Motherhood*, New York: Viking.

Keenan, P. A., Yaldoo, D. T., Stress, M. E., Fuerst, D. R. and Ginsburg, K. A. (1998) 'Explicit memory in pregnant women', *American Journal of Obstetrics and Gynecology*, 179: 731–7.

Kelly, A. K. W. (2005) 'Practical exercise advice during pregnancy – guidelines for active and inactive women', *Physical and Sports Medicine*, 33: 24–30.

Keppel, K. and Taffel, S. (1993) 'Pregnancy-related weight gain and retention:

Implications of the 1990 Institute of Medicine Guidelines', *American Journal of Public Health*, 83: 1100–3.

Killien, M. G. (2005) 'The role of social support in facilitating postpartum women's return to employment', *Journal of Obstetric, Gynecological and Neonatal Nursing*, 34: 639–46.

Kinsley, C. H. and Lambert, K. G. (2006) 'The maternal brain', *Scientific American*, 294: 72–9.

Kinsley, C. H., Madonia, L., Gifford, G. W., Tureski, K., Griffin, G. R., Lowry, C., Williams, J., Collins, J., McLearie, H. and Lambert, K. G. (1999) 'Motherhood improves learning and memory', *Nature*, 404, 137–8.

Klebanoff, M. A., Shiono, P. H. and Carey, J. C. (1990) 'The effect of physical activity during pregnancy on preterm delivery and birthweight', *Obstetrics and Gynaecology*, 163: 1450–6.

Kleiverda, G., Steen, A. M., Anderson, I., Everaerd, W. and Treffers, P. E. (1990) 'Physical and psychological wellbeing in working nulliparous women during pregnancy', *Journal of Psychosomatic Obstetrics and Gynecology*, 11: 165–84.

Korcok, M. (1981) 'Pregnant jogger: What a record!', *Journal of American Medical Association*, 246: 201.

Kramer, M. (1993) 'Effect of energy and protein intakes on pregnancy outcome: An overview of the research evidence in controlled clinical trials', *American Journal of Clinical Nutrition*, 58: 627–35.

Kristeva, J. (1997) 'Stabat Mater', Reprinted in K. Oliver (ed.) *The Portable Kristeva*, New York: Columbia University Press.

Lankshear, G., Ettore, E. and Mason, D. (2005) 'Decision-making, uncertainty and risk: Exploring the complexity of work processes in NHS delivery suites', *Health, Risk & Society*, 7: 361–77.

Larsson, L. and Lindqvuist, P. G. (2005) 'Low-impact exercise during pregnancy – a study of safety', *Acta Obstetrica et Gynecologica Scandinavica*, 84: 34–8.

Launer, L. J., Villar, J., Kestler, E. and de Onis, M. (1990) 'The effect of maternal work in fetal growth and duration of pregnancy: A prospective study', *British Journal of Obstetrics and Gynaecology*, 97: 62–70.

Lee, E., Clements, S., Ingham, R. and Stone, N. (2006) *A Matter of Choice? Explaining National Variations in Teenage Abortion and Motherhood*, York: Joseph Rowntree Foundation.

Lee, J. I., Lee, J. A. and Lim, H. S. (2004) 'Morning sickness reduces dietary diversity, nutrient intakes, and infant outcome of pregnant women', *Nutrition Research*, 24: 531–40.

Lees, S. J. and Booth, F. W. (2004) 'Sedentary death syndrome', *Canadian Journal of Applied Physiology*, 29: 447–60.

Lemish, D. and Barzel, I. (2000) 'Four mothers: The womb in the public sphere', *European Journal of Communication*, 15: 147–69.

Lewallen, L. P. (2004) 'Healthy behaviors and sources of health information among low-income pregnant women', *Public Health Nursing*, 21: 200–6.

Lewando-Hundt, G., Sandall, J., Williams, C., Spencer, K. and Heyman, B. (2004) *Social and Organisational Implications of One Stop First Trimester Prenatal Screening*. Online. Available HTTP: <http://www.york.ac.uk/res/iht/researchfindings/HundtFindings.pdf> (accessed 11 February 2006).

Lewis, G. and Drife, J. (2004) *CEMACH: Why Mothers Die 2000–2002*, London: RCOG Press.

Linell, P. and Bredmar, M. (1996) 'Reconstructing topical sensitivity: Aspects of face-work in talks between midwives and expectant mothers', *Research on Language and Social Interaction*, 29: 347–79.

Long, B. C. and van Stavel, R. (1995) 'Effects of exercise training on anxiety: A meta-analysis', *Journal of Applied Sport Psychology*, 7: 167–89.

Longhurst, R. (2005) '(Ad)dressing pregnant bodies in New Zealand: Clothing, fashion, subjectivities and spatialities', *Gender, Place and Culture*, 12: 433–46.

Lopez, L. B., Soler, C. R. O. and de Portela, M. L. P. M. (2004) 'Pica during pregnancy: A frequently underestimated problem', *Archivos Latinoamericanos de Nutricion*, 54: 17–24.

Lotgering, F. K., Gilbert, R. D. and Longo, L. D. (1985) 'Maternal and fetal responses to exercise during pregnancy', *Physiology Review*, 65: 1–36.

Love, G., Torrey, N., McNamara, I., Morgan, M., Banks, M., Hester, N. W., Glasper, E. R., DeVries, A. C., Kinsley, C. H. and Lambert, K. G. (2005) 'Maternal experience produces long-lasting behavioral modifications in the rat', *Behavioural Neuroscience*, 119: 1084–96.

Lozoff, B., Brittenham, G. M., Viteri, F. E., Wolf, A. W. and Urrutia, J. J. (1982a) 'The effects of short-term oral iron therapy on developmental deficits in iron deficient anemic infants', *Journal of Pediatrics*, 100: 351–7.

Lozoff, B., Brittenham, G. M., Viteri, F. E., Wolf, A. W. and Urrutia, J. J. (1982b) 'Developmental deficits in iron-deficient infants', *Journal of Pediatrics*, 101: 948–51.

Lumbers, E. R. (2002) 'Exercise in pregnancy: Physiological basis of exercise prescription for the pregnant woman', *Journal of Science and Medicine in Sport*, 5: 20–31.

Lundgren, C. (2003) *Runners World Guide to Running and Pregnancy: How to Stay Fit, Keep Safe and Have a Healthy Baby*, Pennsylvania, PA: Rodale Press.

Luoba, A. I., Geissler, P. W., Estambale, B., Ouma, J. H., Magnussen, P., Alusala, D., Ayah, R., Mwaniki, D. and Friis, H. (2004) 'Geophagy among pregnant and lactating women in Bondo District, western Kenya', *Transactions of the Royal Society of Tropical Medicine and Hygiene*, 98: 734–41.

Lupton, D. (1997) 'Consumerism, reflexivity and medicine', *Social Science and Medicine*, 43: 373–81.

Lupton, D. (1999) *Risk*, London: Routledge.

Lupton, D. and Chapman, S. (1995) 'A healthy lifestyle may be the death of you', *Sociology of Health and Illness*, 17: 477–94.

Lurie, S., Gidron, Y., Piper, I., Ben-Aroya, Z., Sadan, O., Boaz, M. and Glezerman, M. (2005) 'Memory performance in late pregnancy and erythrocyte indices', *Journal of the Society for Gynecologic Investigation*, 12: 293–6.

Lyness, K. S., Thompson, C. A., Francesco, A. M. and Judiesch, M. K. (1999) 'Work and pregnancy: Individual and organizational factors influencing organizational commitment, timing of maternity leave and return to work', *Sex Roles*, 41: 485–508.

McAllister, F. and Clarke, L. (1998) *A study of Childlessness in Britain*, London: The Family Studies Centre.

McConnell, O. L. and Datson, P. G. (1961) 'Body image changes in pregnancy', *Journal of Projective Techniques*, 25: 451–6.

McDowall, J. and Moriarty, R. (2000) 'Implicit and explicit memory in pregnant women: An analysis of data-driven and conceptually driven processes', *Quarterly Journal of Experimental Psychology Section A – Human Experimental Psychology*, 53: 729–40.

McEwen, B. S., Alves, S. E., Bulloch, K. and Weiland, N. G. (1997) 'Ovarian steroids and the brain: Implications for cognition and aging', *Neurology*, 48, S8–S15.

McEwen, B. E., Gould, E., Orchinik, M., Weiland, N. G. and Woolley, C. S. (1995) 'Oestrogens and the structural and functional plasticity of neurons: Implications for memory, ageing and neurodegenerative processes', *Non Reproductive Effects of Sex Steroids*, Chichester: Wiley, pp. 52–73.

Macfarlane, A. J., Mugford, M., Henderson, J., Furtado, A., Stevens, J. and Dunn, A. (2000) *Birth Counts: Statistics of Pregnancy and Childbirth*, vol. 2, London: The Stationery Office.

McGlynn, C. (1996) 'Pregnancy dismissal and the Webb litigation', *Feminist Legal Studies*, 14: 229–42.

McKechnie, S. (1984) 'A trade union view of reproductive health', in G. Chamberlain (ed.) *Pregnant Women at Work*, London: Royal Society and Macmillan.

Mackey, M. C. and Coster-Schultz, M. A. (1992) 'Women's views of the preterm labour experience', *Clinical Nursing Research*, 1: 366–84.

McMurray, R. G., Mottola, M. F., Wolfe, L. A., Artal, R., Millar, L. and Pivarnik, J. M. (1993) 'Recent advances in understanding maternal and fetal responses to exercise', *Medicine and Science in Sports and Exercise*, 25: 1305–21.

McRae, S. (1991) *Maternity Rights in Britain*, London: PSI.

McRae, S. (1996) *Women's Employment during Family Formation*, London: PSI.

Magann, E. F., Evans, S. F. and Newnham, J. P. (1996) 'Employment, exertion and pregnancy outcome: Assessment by kilocalories expended each day', *American Journal of Obstetrics and Gynecology*, 175: 182–7.

Magann, E. F., Evans, S. F., Weitz, B. and Newnham, J. P. (2002) 'Antepartum, intrapartum and neonatal significance of exercise on healthy low risk pregnant working women', *Obstetrics and Gynecology*, 99: 466–72.

Maher, J. (2002) 'Visibly pregnant: Toward a placental body', *Feminist Review*, 72: 95–107.

Maloni, J. A. (1996) 'Bed rest and high-risk pregnancy', *Nursing Clinics of North America*, 31: 313–25.

Mamelle, N., Gerin, P., Maesson, A., Munoz, F. and Collet, P. (1987) 'Assessment of psychological modifications during pregnancy: Contribution of Derogatis Symptom Checklist (SCL90R)', *Journal of Psychosomatic Obstetrics and Gynecology*, 7: 39–50.

Marshall, P. D. (1997) *Celebrity and Power: Fame in Contemporary Culture*, Minneapolis, MN: University of Minnesota Press.

Marteau, T. M. (2002) 'Prenatal testing: Towards realistic expectations of patients, providers and policy makers', *Ultrasound Obstetrics and Gynecology*, 19: 5–6.

Martin, M. and Jones, G. V. (1983) 'Cognitive failures in everyday life', in J. E.

Harris and P. E. Morris (eds) *Everyday Memory, Action and Absent-mindedness*, London: Academic Press.

Mathews, F. and Neil, H. A. W. (1998) 'Nutrient intakes during pregnancy in a cohort of nulliparous women', *Journal of Human Nutrition and Dietetics*, 11: 151–61.

Mathews, F., Yudkin, P. and Neil, A. (1999) 'Influence of maternal nutrition on outcome of pregnancy', *British Medical Journal*, 319: 339–43.

Matthews, S. and Wexler, L. (2000) *Pregnant Pictures*, New York: Routledge.

Matthiassen, T. E. (2005) 'From hidden pregnancy to chic maternity fashion', Paper presented at the Interdisciplinary Conference of Fashion and Dress Cultures, Copenhagen, October. Online. Available HTTP: <http://www.dkds.dk.forskning/fashiondressconference21005/papers/Tove_E._Mathiassen.pdf> (accessed 21 November 2005).

Mauri, M., Sinforiani, E., Bono, G., Vignati, F., Berselli, M. E., Attanasio, R. and Nappi, G. (1993) 'Memory impairment in Cushing's disease', *Acta Neurologica Scandinavica*, 87: 52–5.

Maylor, E. A. (1990) 'Age and prospective memory', *Quarterly Journal of Experimental Psychology*, 42A: 471–93.

Mercer, R. T. (1986) *First time Motherhood Experiences from Teens to Forties*, New York: Springer.

Meredith, S. (2005) *Policing Pregnancy: The Law and Ethics of Obstetric Conflict*, Aldershot: Ashgate.

Messing, K. (1992) 'Research directed to improving women's occupational health', *Women and Health*, 18: 1–9.

Messing, K. (1999) 'One eyed science: Scientists, workplace reproductive hazards and the right to work', *International Journal of Health Services*, 29: 147–65.

Michener, W. and Rozin, P. (1994) 'Pharmacological versus sensory factors in the satiation of chocolate craving', *Physiology and Behaviour*, 56: 419–22.

Milligan, C., Gatrell, A. and Bingley, A. (2004) 'Cultivating health: Therapeutic landscapes and older people in northern England', *Social Science and Medicine*, 58: 1781–93.

Monaham, P. A. and De Joseph, J. F. (1991) 'The woman with preterm labour at home: A descriptive analysis', *Journal of Perinatal and Neonatal Nursing*, 4: 12–21.

Moore, P. (1997) 'Pregnant women get that shrinking feeling', *New Scientist*, 11 January, p. 5.

Morris, J. N. and Hardman, A. E. (1997) 'Walking to health', *Sports Medicine*, 23: 306–32.

Morris, N., Toms, M., Easthope, Y. and Biddulph, J. (1998) 'Mood and cognition in pregnant workers', *Applied Ergonomics*, 29: 377–81.

Morris, P. E. (1983) 'The validity of subjective reports on memory', in J. E. Harris and P. E. Morris (eds) *Everyday Memory, Action and Absent-mindedness*, London: Academic Press.

Morris, S. N. and Johnson, N. R. (2005) 'Exercise during pregnancy – a critical appraisal of the literature', *Journal of Reproductive Medicine*, 50: 181–8.

Moss, N. and Carver, K. (1993) 'Pregnant women at work: Sociodemographic perspectives', *American Journal of Industrial Medicine*, 23: 541–57.

Murdoch, G., Petts, J. and Horlick-Jones, T. (2003) 'After amplification:

Rethinking the role of the media in risk communication', in N. Pidgeon, R. E. Kasperson and P. Slovic (eds) *The Social Amplification of Risk*, Cambridge: Cambridge University Press, pp. 156–78.

Murphy Lawless, J. (1998) *Reading Birth and Death*, Cork: Cork University Press.

Myllinen, L. (1991) 'Work during pregnancy. a prospective study', *Acta Obstetrica et Gynecologica Scandinavica*, 70: 629–30.

NACAB (National Association of Citizens Advice Bureaux) (1992) *Not in Labour: CAB Evidence on Pregnancy Dismissal and Employment*, NACAB E/4/92, London: CAB.

Neumann, E. (1955) *The Great Mother*, Princeton, NJ: Princeton University Press.

Newell, S. (1993) 'The superwoman syndrome', *Work, Employment and Society*, 7: 275–89.

NICE/National Collaborating Centre for Women's and Children's Health (2003) *Antenatal Care: Routine Care for the Healthy Pregnant Woman*, London: RCOG Press.

Nicholls, J. A. and Grieve, D. (1992) 'Posture, performance, and discomfort in pregnancy', *Applied Ergonomics*, 23: 128–32.

Nicolson, P. (1998) *Postnatal Depression*, London: Routledge.

NIH (1998) *Clinical Guidelines on the Identification, Evaluation, and Treatment of Overweight and Obesity in Adults: The Evidence Report*, Bethesda, MD: US Dept Health and Human Services.

Nippert-Eng, C. E. (1996) *Home and Work: Negotiating Boundaries through Everyday Life*, Chicago, IL: University of Chicago Press.

Norman, E. D. and Adams, S. (1970) 'Survey of changes in food habits during pregnancy', *Public Health Reports*, 85: 1121.

North, T. C., McCullagh, P. and Tran, Z. V. (1990) 'Effect of exercise on depression', *Exercise and Sports Sciences Reviews*, 18: 379–415.

O'Grady, F. and Wakefield, H. (1989) *Women, Work and Maternity*, London: Maternity Alliance.

Oakley, A. (1980) *Women Confined*, Oxford: Martin Robertson.

Oakley, A. (1984) *The Captured Womb: A History of the Medical Care of Pregnant Women*, Oxford: Blackwell.

Ohlin, A. and Rossner, S. (1990) 'Maternal body weight development after pregnancy', *International Journal of Obesity Related Metabolic Disorders*, 14: 159–73.

ONS (Office for National Statistics) (2006) *Birth Statistics*, National Statistics Series FM1 No. 34, London: HMSO.

Orr, R. D. and Simmons, J. J. (1979) 'Nutritional care in pregnancy: The patient's view part 2', *Journal of the American Dietetic Association*, 75: 131–5.

Oski, F. A. (1975) 'The non-hematologic manifestations of iron deficiency', *American Journal of Disorders of Children*, 133: 315–27.

Oski, F. A. and Honig, A. S. (1978) 'The effects of iron therapy on the developmental scores of iron deficient infants', *Journal of Pediatrics*, 92: 21–5.

Ostgaard, H. C. and Anderson, G. B. J. (1992) 'Postpartum low back pain', *Spine*, 17: 53–5.

Oths, K. S., Dunn, L. L. and Palmer, N. S. (2001) 'A prospective study of psychosocial jobstrain and birth outcomes', *Epidemiology*, 12: 744–6.

Paauw, J. D., Bierling, S., Cook, C. R. and Davis, A. T. (2005) 'Hyperemesis gravidarum and fetal outcome', *Journal of Parenteral and Enteral Nutrition*, 29: 93–6.

Page, R. E. (2003) 'Cherie: Lawyer, wife, mum: Contradictory patterns of representation in media reports of Cherie Booth/Blair', *Discourse and Society*, 14: 555–79.

Parsons, C. D. F. and Redman, S. (1991) 'Self-reported cognitive change during pregnancy', *The Australian Journal of Advanced Nursing*, 9: 20–9.

Parsons, T. (1951) *The Social System*, London: Routledge & Kegan Paul.

Parsons, T. D., Thompson, E., Buckwalter, D. K., Bluestein, B. W., Stanczyk, F. Z. and Buckwalter, J. G. (2004) 'Pregnancy history and cognition during and after pregnancy', *International Journal of Neuroscience*, 114: 1099–110.

Pattison, H. and Bhagrath, J. (2003) 'Eating for one?', *Abstracts of 17th Annual Conference of the European Health Psychology Society*, September: 71.

Pattison, H. M. and Bhagrath, J. (2004) 'Dietary change during pregnancy', *Journal of Reproductive and Infant Psychology*, 22: 242.

Pattison, H. and Gross, H. (1996) 'Pregnancy, work and women's well-being: A review', *Work and Stress*, 10: 72–87.

Pattison, H., Gross, H. and Cast, C. (1997) 'Pregnancy and employment: The perceptions and beliefs of fellow workers', *Journal of Reproductive and Infant Psychology*, 15: 303–13.

Petridou, E., Salvanos, H., Skalkidou, A., Dessypris, N., Moustaki, M. and Trichopoulos, D. (2001) 'Are there common triggers of preterm deliveries?', *British Journal of Obstetrics and Gynaecology*, 108: 598–604.

Phillips, S. M. and Sherwin, B. B. (1992) 'Effects of estrogen on memory function in surgically menopausal women', *Psychoneuroendocrinology*, 17: 485–95.

Phoenix, A. (1991) 'Mothers under twenty: Outsider and insider views', in A. Phoenix, A. Woollett and E. Lloyd (eds) *Motherhood: Meanings, Practices and Ideologies*, London: Sage.

Pietrowsky, R., Braun, D., Fehm, H. L., Pauschinger, P. and Born, J. (1991) 'Vasopressin and Oxytocin do not influence early sensory processing but affect mood and activation in Man', *Peptides*, 12: 1385–91.

Pope, J., Skinner, J. and Carruth, B. (1992) 'Cravings and aversions of pregnant adolescents', *Journal of the American Dietetic Association*, 92: 484–9.

Pope, J., Skinner, J. and Carruth, B. (1997) 'Adolescents' self-reported motivations for dietary changes during pregnancy', *Journal of Nutrition Education*, 29: 137–44.

Poser, C. M., Kassirer, M. R. and Peyser, J. M. (1986) 'Benign encephalopathy of pregnancy: Preliminary clinical observations', *Acta Neurologica Scandinavica*, 73: 39–43.

Potter, J. E., Berquo, E., Perpetuo, I. H. O., Leal, O. F., Hopkins, K., Souza, M. R. and de Carvalho Formiga, M. C. (2001) 'Unwanted caesarean sections among public and private patients in Brazil: Prospective study', *British Medical Journal*, 323: 1155–8.

Purvin, V. A. and Dunn, D. W. (1987) 'Caffeine and the benign encephalopathy of pregnancy', *Acta Neurologica Scandinavica*, 75: 76.

Queneau, H. and Marmo, M. (2001) 'Tensions between employment and pregnancy', *Family Relations*, 50: 59–66.

Rabkin, C. S., Anderson, H. R., Bland, J. M., Brooke, O. G., Chamberlain, G. and

Peacock, J. L. (1990) 'Maternal activity and birthweight: A prospective population-based study', *American Journal of Epidemiology*, 131: 522–31.

Rainville, A. J. (1998) 'Pica practices of pregnant women are associated with lower maternal hemoglobin level at delivery', *Journal of the American Dietetic Association*, 98: 293–6.

Raphael-Leff, J. (1991) *Psychological Processes of Childbearing*, London: Chapman and Hall.

Rauramo, I. and Forss, M. (1988) 'Effect of exercise on maternal hemodynamics and placental blood flow in healthy women', *Acta Obstetrica et Gynecologica Scandinavica*, 67: 21–5.

Redelmeier, D., Rozin, P. and Kahneman, D. (1993) 'Understanding patients' decisions: Cognitive and emotional perspectives', *Journal of the American Medical Association*, 270: 72–6.

Reinharz, S. (1999) 'Enough already! The pervasiveness of warnings in everyday life', in B. Gray, A. Davey and C. Seale (eds) (2001) *Health and Disease: A Reader* (3rd edition), Buckingham: Open University Press, pp. 438–41.

Richardson, J. T. E. (ed.) (1992) *Cognition and the Menstrual Cycle*, London: Springer Verlag.

Robinson, S. M., Crozier, S. R., Borland, S. E., Hammond, J., Barker, D. J. and Inskip, H. M. (2004) 'Impact of educational attainment on the quality of young women's diets', *European Journal of Clinical Nutrition*, 58: 1174–80.

Rodin, J. (1976) 'Menstruation, reattribution and competence', *Journal of Personality and Social Psychology*, 33: 345.

Rodmell, S. and Smart, L. (1982) *Pregnant at Work: The Experiences of Women*, Milton Keynes: Open University Press.

Rodriguez, A., Bohlin, G. and Lindmark, G. (2000) 'Psychosocial predictors of smoking and exercise during pregnancy', *Journal of Reproductive and Infant Psychology*, 18: 203–23.

Rogers, P. J. and Smit, H. J. (2000) 'Food craving and food "addiction": A critical review of the evidence from a biopsychological perspective', *Pharamacology, Biochemistry and Behaviour*, 666: 3–14.

Romito, P. (1989) 'Women's paid and unpaid work and pregnancy outcome: a discussion of some open questions', *Health Promotion*, 4: 31–41.

Rose, N. (1990) *Governing the Soul: The Shaping of the Private Self*, London: Routledge.

Rose, N. C., Haddow, J. E., Palomake, G. E. and Knight, G. J. (1991) 'Self-rated physical activity level during the second trimester and pregnancy outcome', *Obstetrics and Gynaecology*, 78: 1078.

Rosen, B. and Jerdee, T. H. (1978) 'Effects of applicants' sex and difficulty of job on evaluations of candidates for managerial positions', *Journal of Applied Psychology*, 59: 511–12.

Rousham, E. K., Clarke, P. E. and Gross, H. (2006) 'Significant changes in physical activity among pregnant women in the UK as assessed by accelerometry and self reported activity', *European Journal of Clinical Nutrition*, 60: 393–400.

Rubenstein, M. (1992) 'Understanding pregnancy discrimination: A framework for analysis', *Equal Opportunities Review*, 42: 22–7.

Sady, S. P. and Carpenter, M. W. (1989) 'Aerobic exercise during pregnancy: Special considerations', *Sports Medicine*, 7: 357–75.

Saftlas, A. F., Logsden-Sackett, N., Wang, W., Woolson, B. and Bracken, M. B. (2004) 'Work, leisure-time physical activity, and risk of preeclampsia and gestational hypertension', *American Journal of Epidemiology*, 160: 758–65.

Saurel-Cubizolles, M. J. and Kaminski, M. (1987) 'Pregnant women's working conditions and their changes during pregnancy: A national study in France', *British Journal of Industrial Medicine*, 44: 236–43.

Saurel-Cubizolles, M. J., Subtil, D. and Kaminski, M. (1991) 'Is preterm delivery still related to physical working conditions in pregnancy?', *Journal of Epidemiology and Community Health*, 45: 29–34.

Saurel-Cubizolles, M. J., Zeitlin, J., Lelong, N., Papiernik, E., Di Renzo, G. C. and Breart, G. (2004) 'Employment, working conditions, and preterm birth: Results from the Europop case-control study', *Journal of Epidemiology and Community Health*, 58: 395–401.

Savitz, D. A., Brett, K. M., Dole, N. and Tse, C. K. J. (1997) 'Male and female occupation in relation to miscarriage and preterm delivery in central North Carolina', *Annals of Epidemiology*, 7: 509–16.

Schenker, M. B., Eaton, M., Green, R. and Samuels, S. (1997) 'Self reported stress and reproductive health of female lawyers', *Journal of Occupational and Environmental Medicine*, 39: 556–68.

Schneider, Z. (1989) 'Cognitive performance in pregnancy', *Australian Journal of Advanced Nursing*, 6: 40–7.

Schofield, G. (1994) *The Youngest Mothers*, Aldershot: Avebury.

Schramm, W. F., Stockbauer, J. W. and Hoffman, H. J. (1996) 'Exercise, employment, other daily activities and adverse pregnancy outcomes', *American Journal of Epidemiology*, 143: 211–18.

Sharp, K., Brindle, P. M., Brown, M. W. and Turner, G. M. (1993) 'Memory loss during pregnancy', *British Journal of Obstetrics and Gynaecology*, 100: 209–15.

Shephard, R. J. and Montelpare, W. (1988) 'Geriatric benefits of exercise as an adult', *Journal of Gerontology*, 43: M86–M90.

Sherr, L. (2000) *Women, Health and the Mind*, Chichester: Wiley.

Shetty, D. N. and Pathak, S. S. (2002) 'Correlation between plasma neurotransmitters and memory loss in pregnancy', *Journal of Reproductive Medicine*, 47: 494–6.

Sibley, L., Ruhling, R. O., Cameron-Foster, J., Christensen, C. and Bolen, T. (1981) 'Swimming and physical fitness during pregnancy', *Journal of Nurse-Midwifery*, 26: 3–12.

Silber, M., Almkvist, O., Larsson, B. and Uvnas-Moberg, K. (1990) 'Temporary peripartal impairment in memory and attention and its possible relation to oxytocin concentration', *Life Sciences*, 47: 57–65.

Simpson, E., Mull, J. D., Longley, E. and East, J. (2000) 'Pica during pregnancy in low-income women born in Mexico', *Western Journal of Medicine*, 173: 20–4.

Simpson, J. L. (1993) 'Are physical activity and employment related to preterm birth and low birth weight?', *American Journal of Obstetrics and Gynecology*, 168: 1231–8.

Skinner, J. D., Carruth, B. R., Ezell, J. M. and Shaw, A. (1996) 'How and what do pregnant adolescents want to learn about nutrition?', *Journal of Nutrition Education*, 28: 266–71.

Slade, P. (1977) 'Awareness of body dimensions during pregnancy: Analogue study', *Psychological Medicine*, 7: 245–52.

Smith, C. F., Williamson, D. A., Bray, G. A. and Ryan, D. H. (1999) 'Flexible vs. rigid dieting strategies: relationship with adverse behavioral outcomes', *Appetite*, 32: 295–305.

Smith, J. A. (1992) 'Pregnancy and transition to motherhood', in P. Nicolson and J. Ussher (eds) *The Psychology of Women's Health and Health Care*, Basingstoke: Macmillan.

Solomon, G. M. (1997) 'Reproductive toxins: A growing concern at work', *Journal of Occupational and Environmental Medicine*, 39: 105–7.

Sport England (2006) *Active People Survey*. Online. HTTP: <www.sportengland. org>.

Spink, K. S. (1992) 'Relation of anxiety about social physique to location of participation in physical activity', *Perceptual and Motor Skills*, 74: 1075–8.

Starkman, M. N., Gebarski, S. S., Berent, S. and Schteingart, D. E. (1992) 'Hippocampal formation volume, memory dysfunction, and cortisol levels in patients with Cushing's Syndrome', *Biological Psychiatry*, 32: 756–65.

Stein, Z. A., Susser, M. W. and Hatch, M. C. (1986) 'Working during pregnancy: physical and psychosocial strain', *Occupational Medicine: State of the Art Reviews*, 1: 405–9.

Steptoe, A. (1992) 'Physical activity and psychological wellbeing', in N. Norgan (ed.) *Physical Activity and Health*, Cambridge: Cambridge University Press.

Sternfeld, B. (1997) 'Physical activity and pregnancy outcome: Review and recommendations', *Sports Medicine*, 23: 33–47.

Sternfeld, B., Quesenberry, C. P. J. and Eskenazi, B. (1995) 'Exercise during pregnancy and pregnancy outcome', *Medicine and Science in Sports and Exercise*, 27: 634–40.

Stevens, C. and Tiggemann, M. (1998) 'Women's body figure preferences across the lifespan', *Journal of Genetic Psychology*, 159: 94–102.

Stim, E. M. (1976) 'Do-it-yourself pregnancy testing: The medical perspective', *American Journal of Public Health*, 66: 130–1.

Strand, K., Wergeland, E. and Bjerkedal, T. (1997) 'Workload, job control and risk of leaving work by sickness certification before delivery, Norway, 1989', *Scandinavian Journal of Social Medicine*, 25: 193–201.

Tavris, C. (1992) *The Mismeasure of Women*, New York: Simon and Schuster.

Taylor, S. E. and Langer, E. J. (1977) 'Pregnancy: A social stigma?', *Sex Roles*, 3: 27–35.

Taylor Myers, S. and Grasmick, H. G. (1990) 'The social rights and responsibilities of pregnant women: An application of Parson's Sick Role model', *Journal of Applied Behavioural Science*, 26: 157–72.

Tew, M. (1990) *Safer Childbirth: A Critical History of Maternity Care*, London: Chapman and Hall.

Thomas, J. and Paranjothy, S. (2001) *Royal College of Obstetricians & Gynaecologists Clinical Effectiveness Support Unit: National Sentinel Caesarean Section Audit Report*, London: RCOG Press.

Tomizawa, K., Iga, N., Lu, Y. F., Moriwaki, A., Matsushita, M., Li, S. T., Miyamoto, O., Itano, T. and Matsui, H. (2003) 'Oxytocin improves long-lasting spatial memory during motherhood through MAP kinase cascade', *Nature Neuroscience*, 6: 384–90.

Tulchinsky, D., Hobel, J. H., Yeager, E. and Marshall, J. R. (1972) 'Plasma estrone, estradiol, progesterone, and 17-hydroxyprogesterone in human pregnancy: 1. Normal pregnancy', *American Journal of Obstetrics and Gynecology*, 112: 1095–100.

Tversky, A. and Kahneman, D. (1981) 'The framing of decisions and the psychology of choice', *Science*, 211: 453–8.

Tyler, I. (2001) 'Celebrity, pregnancy and subjectivity', in S. Ahmed and J. Stacey (eds) *Thinking through the Skin*, London: Routledge, pp. 69–83.

Ukaonu, C., Hill, A. and Christensen, F. (2003) 'Hypokalemic myopathy in pregnancy caused by clay ingestion', *Obstetrics and Gynecology*, 102: 1169–71.

Unger, R. and Crawford, M. (1996) *Women and Gender: A Feminist Psychology* (2nd edition), New York: McGraw-Hill.

US Census Bureau (2005) *American Community Survey 2005*, Table S1301: Fertility. Online. Available HTTP: <www.factfinder.census.gov> (accessed 14 September 2006).

US Institute of Medicine (1990) *Nutrition During Pregnancy*, Washington DC: National Academy Press.

Ussher, J. (1992) 'Reproductive rhetoric and the blaming of the body', in P. Nicholson and J. Ussher (eds) *Psychology of Women's Health and Health Care*, Basingstoke: Macmillan.

Ussher, J. (2006) *Managing the Monstrous Feminine*, London: Routledge.

van den Akker, O. (2000) 'The importance of a genetic link in mothers commissioning a surrogate baby in the UK', *Human Reproduction*, 18: 1849–55.

Vanston, C. M. and Watson, N. V. (2005) 'Selective and persistent effect of foetal sex on cognition in pregnant women', *Neuroreport*, 16: 779–82.

Veiel, H. O. (1997) 'A preliminary profile of neuropsychological deficits associated with major depression', *Journal of Clinical and Experimental Neuropsychology*, 19: 587–603.

Vines, G. (1994) *Raging Hormones: Do They Rule Our Lives?*, London: Virago.

Walker, A. (1995) 'Theory and methodology in premenstrual syndrome research', *Social Science and Medicine*, 41: 793–800.

Walker, A. R. P., Walker, B. F., Sookaria, F. I. and Cannan, R. J. (1997) 'Pica', *Journal of the Royal Society of Health*, 117: 280–4.

Walker, A. R. P., Walker, B. F., Jones, J., Veraldi, M. and Walker, C. (1985) 'Nausea and vomiting and dietary cravings and aversions during pregnancy in South African women', *British Journal of Obstetrics and Gynaecology*, 92: 484–9.

Wallace, A. M., Boyer, D. B. and Dan, A. (1986) 'Aerobic exercise, maternal self esteem and physical discomforts during pregnancy', *Journal of Nurse-Midwifery*, 31: 255–62.

Wartella, J., Amory, E., Macbeth, A. H., McNamara, I., Stevens, L., Lambert, K. G. and Kinsley, C. H. (2003) 'Single or multiple reproductive experiences attenuate neurobehavioral stress and fear responses in the female rat', *Physiology and Behavior*, 79: 373–81.

Welch, J. (1991) 'Labouring brains', *British Medical Journal*, 303: 253.

Welford, H. (2005) *Diet and Health*. Online. Available HTTP: <http://

www.bbc.co.uk/parenting/having_a_baby/pregnancy_diet.shtm> (accessed 4 December 2005).

Westenhoefer, J. (1991) 'Dietary restraint and disinhibition', *Appetite*, 16: 45–55.

Westenhoefer, J., Broeckmann, P., Munch, A. K. and Pudel, V. (1994) 'Cognitive control of eating behaviour and the disinhibition effect', *Appetite*, 23: 27–41.

Wever, R. A. (1985) 'Man in temporal isolation: Basic principles of the circadian system', in S. Folkard and T. H. Monk (eds) *Hours of Work: Temporal Factors in Work Scheduling*, New York: John Wiley and Sons.

Whitaker, R. C. (2004) 'Predicting preschooler obesity at birth', *Pediatrics*, 114: E29–E36.

Wijwardene, K., Fonseka, P. and Gooaratne, C. (1994) 'Dietary cravings and aversions during pregnancy', *Indian Journal of Public Health*, 38: 95–8.

Wiles, R. (1994) 'I'm not fat, I'm pregnant', in S. Wilkinson and C. Kitzinger (eds) *Women and Health: Feminist Perspectives*, London: Taylor & Francis.

Willcox, D. L., Yovich, J. L., McColm, S. C. and Phillips, J. M. (1985) 'Progesterone, cortisol and oestradiol-17beta in the initiation of human parturition: Partitioning between free and bound hormone in plasma', *British Journal of Obstetrics and Gynaecology*, 92: 65–71.

Wilson, F. M. (1995) *Organizational Behaviour and Gender*, London: McGraw-Hill.

Wisborg, K., Kesmodel, L., Bech, B. H., Hedegaard, M. and Henriksen, T. B. (2003) 'Maternal consumption of coffee during pregnancy and stillbirth and infant death in first year of life: Prospective study', *British Medical Journal*, 326: 420–4.

Wise, R. A. (1988) 'The neurobiology of craving: Implications for the understanding and treatment of addiction', *Journal of Abnormal Psychology*, 97: 118–32.

Wong, S. C. and McKenzie, D. C. (1987) 'Cardiorespiratory fitness during pregnancy and its effect on outcome', *International Journal of Sports Medicine*, 8: 79–83.

Woo, G. M. (1997) 'Daily demands during pregnancy', *Annals of Behavioural Medicine*, 19: 385–98.

Wood Baker, C. W., Carter, A. S., Cohen, L. R. and Brownell, K. D. (1999) 'Eating attitudes and behaviours in pregnancy and postpartum: Global stability verses specific transitions', *Annals of Behavioral Medicine*, 21: 143–8.

Woodfield, R. L. (1984) 'Embedded Figures Test performance before and after childbirth', *British Journal of Psychology*, 75: 81–8.

Woollett, A. (1991) 'Having children: Accounts of childless women and women with reproductive problems', in A. Phoenix, A. Woollett and E. Lloyd (eds) *Motherhood: Meanings, Practices and Ideologies*, London: Sage.

Woollett, A. and Marshall, H. (1997) 'Discourses of pregnancy and childbirth', in L. Yardley (ed.) *Psychology of Women's Health: Material Discourses of Health and Illness*, London: Routledge.

Woolley, C. S. and McEwen, B. S. (1993) 'Roles of estradiol and progesterone in regulation of hippocampal dendritic spine density during the oestrous cycle in the rat', *Journal of Comparative Neurology*, 336: 293–306.

Wroe, A. L., Bhan, A., Salkovskis, P. and Bedford, H. (2005) 'Feeling bad about immunising our children', *Vaccine*, 23: 1428–33.

Yanovski, S. (2003) 'Sugar and fat: Cravings and aversions', *Journal of Nutrition*, 133: 835–7.

Young, I. M. (1990) 'Pregnancy embodiment: Subjectivity and alienation', in I. Young (ed.) *Throwing Like a Girl and Other Essays in Feminist Philosophy and Social Theory*, Bloomington, IN: Indiana University Press.

Zajicek, E. (1979) 'Self perceptions during pregnancy and early motherhood', in O. Harnett, G. Boden and H. Fuller (eds) *Woman Sex-role Stereotyping*, London: Tavistock Publications.

INDEX